The Elms
Orestan Lane
Effingham
Surrey KT24 5SL
Tel. 01372 458555

13 April 2007

A Historian and His World

The Library of Conservative Thought
Russell Kirk, Series Editor

A Historian and His World

A Life of Christopher Dawson

Christina Scott

With a Postscript by
Christopher Dawson
and a New Introduction by
Russell Kirk

Transaction Publishers
New Brunswick (U.S.A.) and London (U.K.)

Library of Congress Catalog Number: 91-19351
ISBN: 1-56000-013-9
Printed in the United States of America

Library of Congress Cataloging-in-Publication Data

Scott, Christina.
    A historian and his world: a life of Christopher Dawson, 1889-1970/Christina Scott; with a postscript by Christopher Dawson and a new introduction by Russell Kirk.
    p.   cm.
    Reprint. Originally published: London: Sheed & Ward, 1984.
    Includes bibliographical references and index.
    ISBN 1-56000-013-9
    1. Dawson, Christopher, 1889-1970. 2. Historians–Great Britain–Biography. I. Title.
CB18.D38S36   1991
907'.202–dc20   91-19351
[B]   CIP

Contents

This book is dedicated to my sons

Hugh, Julian, Antony,
Christopher
and Dominic

Introduction to the
Transaction Edition

A historian endowed with imagination, Christopher Dawson restored to historical writing both an understanding of religion as the basis of culture and a moving power of expression. This biography by his daughter, Christina Scott, admits the reader to the mind of a remarkable scholar.

"Unfortunately the boredom that is generated in people's minds by academic history leads to a positive anti-historicism which seems to be becoming characteristic of modern 'left wing' thought," Dawson wrote to G.K. Chesterton in 1932, when Dawson's book *The Making of Europe* was published. No critic ever has accused Dawson of being boring; neither has any critic called him unscholarly.

He was a historian so honest and temperate that he was spared most of the slings and arrows commonly directed at English Catholic writers by their Protestant adversaries. His being a convert to Catholicism, nevertheless, had a good deal to do with his not obtaining any full-time university post until, at an advanced age, he was invited to Harvard as the first Stillman Professor of Roman Catholic Studies.

Doubtless it was as well that Dawson was not enrolled in the roster of those "academic historians" who bored him. For Dawson's writing was done in his own study, among his thousands of books; he was perhaps the last of the great historians so to labor. Dawson's is the sort of history, marked by intellectual penetration and broad confident learning, that Francesco Guicciardini wrote in his splendid study in the Strozzi-Guicciardini palace. (Dawson's study, though, is not preserved: Dawson and his wife, Valery, shifted somewhat eccentrically from residence to residence.) Like Guicciardini, Dawson had the mind of a statesman; although unlike Guicciardini, he had no opportunity to practice statecraft. For besides being an eminent historian, Dawson was one of the principal English social thinkers of this century, much influenced by Troeltsch and Le Play; and Dawson's writings on the twentieth-century "Time of Troubles" in turn powerfully influenced T.S. Eliot.

The liveliest parts of *A Historian and His World* are the sketches of Dawson's family, early surroundings, and domestic life. Christina Scott shows us a Victorian and Edwardian England of which the vestiges now are being swept away. Dawson was born in 1889 at Hay Castle (today a huge bookshop) on the Welsh border; he inherited a landed property in Yorkshire, Hartlington Hall, but disliked the duties of a landed proprietor. He accumulated a noble library – part of which he transported to Harvard during his Stillman Professorship, preferring his own books to those of the Harvard stacks. One is reminded of the character Robert Parkinson, "Rotter", in Wyndham Lewis's novel *Self Condemned*. "Parkinson was the last of a species. Here he was in a large room, which was a private, functional library. Such a literary workshop belonged to the ages of individualism. Its three or four thousand volumes were all bookplated Parkinson. It was really a fragment of paradise where one of our species lived embedded in his books, decently fed, moderately taxed, snug and unmolested."

What was Dawson's principal achievement? It was to show that all civilizations arise out of religious belief: culture comes from the cult. This understanding, expressed somewhat differently by Arnold Toynbee and somewhat similarly by Eric Voegelin, now begins to dominate the history of ideas, and presently will be reflected in popular histories: Dawson's studies are winning the day.

And it is not upon historians only that Dawson's insights have worked. If one turns to Robert Graves's novel *Seven Days in New Crete*, published in 1948, one encounters an imaginary *Brief History* describing vividly the collapse of civilization in the 'post-Christian era' and the eventual renewal of a high culture through cultivation of religious belief. Graves's religion of the White Goddess is a far cry from Dawson's Christianity; but the historical analysis of the cause of social decay and the means of social renewal, in Graves's romance, is Dawsonian.

On Easter Day, 1909, young Christopher Dawson sat where Edward Gibbon had sat, on the great steps leading to the church of Santa Maria Aracoeli, in Rome; then and there Dawson determined to write a history of culture; indeed, he vowed it. "However unfit I may be," he wrote in his journal, "I believe it is God's will that I should attempt it."

In the corpus of his writings, Dawson succeeded in fulfilling his vow. Gibbon had cast his contemptuous glance upon the monuments of superstition; Dawson saw in those monuments the power and the truth of Christian culture.

It is altogether possible to look upon such monuments and to despair, as Henry Adams did at Chartres, leaving "the Virgin in her majesty, with her three great prophets on either hand, as calm and confident in their own strength and in God's providence as they were when Saint Louis was born, but looking down from a deserted heaven into an empty church, on a dead faith."

But also it is possible, with Christopher Dawson, to hope. As Dawson wrote near the end of his life, "We are living in a world that is far less stable than that of the early Roman Empire. There is no doubt that the world is on the move again as never before and that the pace is faster and more furious than anything that man has known before. But there is nothing in this situation which should cause Christians to despair. On the contrary, it is the kind of situation for which their faith has always prepared them and which provides the opportunity for he fulfillment of their mission."

The serious study of history virtually has been proscribed in American schools: it is supplanted by "social stew" or else survives for most young people only in the form of an alleged "world history" founded unconsciously upon Voltaire's *Universal History* (in which work there occurs a single mention of Christianity, in connection with Constantine's victory at the Milvian Bridge). Yet a vigorous and imaginative living historian, John Lukacs – much influenced by Dawson – argues that history will be the chief literary form of the dawning age, and that a renewed consciousness of the past may redeem mankind from many horrors of the present. If this renewal of the historical consciousness does come to pass, Christopher Dawson may yet be chief among its authors.

Russell Kirk

Preface

To write the biography of one's father is a daunting enough task and it becomes even more so when as it happens he was a scholar who lived almost entirely in the mind. I decided to tackle it using the same method that he had done in his fragment of autobiography *Tradition and Inheritance* and treat his life as part of the social and religious history of the age in which he lived. Writing of Newman, Keble and Hurrell Froude in his book on the Oxford Movement he said it was only possible 'to understand their characters by understanding the spiritual world in which they lived, the ideas that moved them and the faith that inspired their action.' The same is true of my father's life, and while this book is essentially a biography and not a study of his work, it is true also that the life explains the work. It has been my aim in writing this book to detach myself from the subject as far as I could and thus what seemed at first an almost impossible task became a fascinating one. In particular, I came to realise that even if his material world had ended the ideas which inspired his books continue to live on and have just as much meaning for us today as they had in his own time.

It has also been a pleasurable experience to re-read those books and in the course of my research on this biography to meet many of my father's friends and contemporaries who were my friends too.

In the study of my father's thought I am deeply indebted to Mr James Oliver who has assisted me by contributing summaries of his books and other writings. As an erudite scholar himself and a life-long admirer of my father's work he was ideally equipped to perform this task and I should like to express my warmest thanks to him.

My main sources of information for this book have been first my mother's recollections: after my father's death in 1970 and in the course of many conversations before she died in 1974, she gave me much information about their early married life and my father's struggles to establish himself as a writer, which

I would otherwise never have known. Added to this I have of course my own memories and those of my sister, Juliana, a nun of the Assumption order, and my brother Philip Dawson. To them I must record my gratitude for all their help and encouragement.

In the first chapter I have depended on my father's own autobiographical writing describing his early childhood. I have also had access to family archives such as my grandmother's unpublished family history, my grandfather's accounts of his foreign travels, and a memoir written by my father's sister, the late Gwendoline Dawson, describing their childhood in Yorkshire. I owe her much gratitude for this and the other recollections she gave me in conversations and letters.

I also owe an immeasurable debt of gratitude to my father's closest friend, the late E. I. Watkin, for all his help and encouragement. Although often they did not see each other for long periods at a time, their working association as well as their friendship lasted a life-time. They depended on each other for exchange of ideas and criticism of their books while E. I. Watkin also performed the laborious tasks of proof-reading and indexing for my father. Since his death in 1981, I have been greatly indebted to his daughter and Literary Executor, Mrs Magdalen Goffin, who has made available to me my father's correspondence with E. I. Watkin and also provided relevant extracts from his diaries. I also extend my thanks to Mrs Teresa Chapman (nee Watkin) who as my father's god-daughter gave me her recollections of him and their great friendship.

In America, I should like to extend my warmest thanks to the late Chauncey Stillman who endowed the Chair of Roman Catholic Studies at Harvard of which my father was the first occupant from 1958 to 1962. He was one of the first people who encouraged me to write this book and he has helped me with memories of his friendship with my parents when they were in America. Most of all I am grateful to him for inviting me to stay at Wethersfield, N.Y. in the Fall of 1979 where with my brother Philip and the late Frank Sheed as fellow guests, we indulged in many delightful and amusing reminiscences of the past.

I also owe much gratitude to Mr John J. Mulloy who over the years has worked untiringly to make my father's work better known in America and has provided me with copies of my father's correspondence with him and much information.

In connection with my father's term of office at Harvard University, I am deeply grateful to the Rev Francis Sweeney, SJ of Boston College not only for his own reminiscences but also for arranging for me to meet members of the faculty of the Divinity School; these included Prof George Williams and Prof Krister Stendhal. I also met Dr Daniel Callahan, my father's former assistant at Harvard, and Mrs Marietta Taylor, who had been his secretary there. I am grateful to her for her very efficient filing of my father's papers while he was at Harvard, and for entertaining us to lunch at her home in Amherst where we met two of my father's former pupils, Mr and Mrs John Ratté. I am grateful to them all for giving me their time and their recollections, and also to Miss Joan Lorenz who so kindly invited us to stay at her home in Cambridge, Mass.

I should also like to extend my warmest thanks to Prof Bruno Schlesinger of St Mary's College, Notre Dame University, who was closely associated with my father to promote a scheme for the study of Christian Culture. Although we have never met he has given me much valuable assistance and information in the course of correspondence. I am also grateful to him for allowing me to quote from his writings and letters.

Special thanks are due to my father's former publisher, the late Frank Sheed, for much information and many amusing anecdotes and for allowing me to use extracts from his own writings.

For information on my father's early career I should like to express my thanks to Mr Tom Burns (who was also his publisher in the early days at Sheed & Ward) for permission to use extracts from some of his letters; to Mr George Every for sending copies of my father's letters and other information; to the late Prof Wilkinson of Toronto University, who sent his reminiscences of the time when he was a colleague of my father's at Exeter University and likewise to Mr J. J. Saunders for his memories of that time.

I should also like to extend my warmest thanks to all those other friends and contemporaries of my father's who have helped me in various ways: the late Fr Martin D'Arcy, SJ; the late Canon V. A. Demant; Mrs Margaret Geidt; Dom Bede Griffiths, OSB (for permission to quote from his correspondence); the late René Hague (for sending copies of David

Jones's letters); the late David Jones; the late Dom David
Knowles, OSB; the late Fr Gervase Mathew, OP; Fr Clement
McNaspy, SJ (for sending copies of my father's letters to him
and for his reminiscences); the late Sir Charles Petrie (who lent
me his diaries describing the occasion of the *Convegno Volta* in
Rome); Mr Ralph Ricketts (for so kindly contributing a
memoir of his friendship with my father); the late Robert
Speaight (for information on my father's editorship of the
Dublin Review); the late Dr Arnold Toynbee (for his
memories of Winchester and Oxford in the early part of this
century and for permission to quote from his correspondence);
and the late Bernard Wall, who as editor of *Colosseum* was
closely associated with my father in the 1930s.

I should also like to thank Mrs Valerie Eliot, for giving me
copies of my father's letters to her late husband T. S. Eliot and
for permission to publish a letter from him.

Thanks are due to the Librarian of Georgetown University
for sending copies of correspondence between my father and
the late Douglas Woodruff and to Miss Dorothy Collins for a
copy of a letter from the Chesterton archive; also to Fr Ian
Boyd, Editor of *The Chesterton Review*, who first located that
letter.

I owe much gratitude to Dr Claude Locas for permission to
use part of his definitive bibliography of my father's works,
first published in the *Harvard Theological Review*. To him and
to the editors of the Review I extend my warmest thanks.

Finally, I should like to record my thanks to my own family:
above all to my husband for reading the manuscript at every
stage, for his advice and for his most valuable editorial comments; to my son, Julian, who also read the manuscript, and to
my youngest son, Dominic, who helped me with the Notes.

For the use of copyright material acknowledgement is made
to Messrs Chatto & Windus for extracts from *Kilvert's Diary*
edited by William Plomer and to Messrs Faber & Faber for
letters quoted from *Dai Greatcoat* edited by René Hague.

Finally on the text itself, I should explain that I have used the
term 'Anglo-Catholic' to denote the branch of the Anglican
Church which is closest to Rome and to which my father and
many of his friends once belonged. I refer to the Roman
Catholic Church throughout as the 'Catholic' Church in order
to avoid a clumsiness of style.

First Beginning

From quiet homes and first beginning,
Out to the undiscovered ends....
                    (Dedicatory Ode – *Hilaire Belloc*)

THE WELSH HAY

On 12th October 1889, 'Columbus Day', as it is called in America, Henry Christopher Dawson was born at Hay in the Wye Valley, known as 'the Welsh Hay', because it was just over the border from Herefordshire. He was the second child and only son of Henry Philip Dawson, then a major in the Royal Artillery, and Mary Louisa (née Bevan), the eldest daughter of Archdeacon Bevan of Hay Castle. He was christened in Hay Parish Church by his grandfather; the godparents were his great-uncle, the Rev William Dawson, the Hon Lionel Stanhope, and his aunt, Miss Frances Bevan. 'It was a lovely afternoon' his mother wrote of the christening to her mother-in-law:

> .... the sun shining in the church and the font was beautifully decorated. The dear little boy looked so nice in Henry's (his father) robe and cap. He was wide awake but did not cry till he felt the water on his forehead.
>
>   (18th November 1889)

Christopher was a fine healthy child and a photograph taken when he was about a year old, in 'short petticoats' in the Victorian fashion, shows a face of great character with dark intelligent eyes and a strong physique, very different from the pale and delicate looking boy he developed into later in his schooldays.

Hay Castle, the house where he was born, was a medieval castle, built in the 12th century by the Norman de Braose family, but redesigned in Tudor times. Celtic myth placed its origins earlier still associating it with a figure called Maude of St

Valery, mentioned by Giraldus Cambrensis in his Chronicles. Maude was reputed to have built the castle in a night, and a megalith in Clyro churchyard across the river was always pointed out as one of the stones which she dropped from her apron on her way to the castle.

Full of history and legend, it was a romantic house for a child in his early years; at one end was a ruined tower, reputed to be haunted, and there were secret passages to be explored, connecting the ancient castle and the later building – the ivy-clad walls increasing the general appearance of antiquity.

Today, Hay Castle is the centre of a second-hand book business, said to be the largest in the world, run by Richard Booth. Recently gutted by fire, it is somewhat changed since the days when Archdeacon Bevan lived there with his family, but the shell of the old castle still remains in its position looking down over the street of the little town below and across the river Wye to the Black Mountains.

Christopher, in later years, remembered how from an early age he was aware that Hay was at the centre where two worlds met:

> The rich Herefordshire countryside and the poor and wild Welsh hills of Radnor Forest to the North and the Black Mountain which rose immediately behind Hay to the South.[1]

English was the language generally spoken there but on market days when the farmers came down from the hills it became a Welsh-speaking town.

Since the time of which I am writing – more than eighty years ago – fame has come to Hay and the beautiful surrounding countryside through the pages of *Kilvert's Diary*[2] where this particular social scene is so faithfully described.

The Rev Francis Kilvert was curate to Mr Venables, the vicar of Clyro near Hay in the 1870s, and the people whom he knew and wrote about were Christopher's mother's family and friends. That seemingly archaic world which he described was almost exactly as Christopher remembered it in the 1890s, when he was a child. It was an 'Anglican theocracy' much as Trollope depicted in the Barchester novels, where the clergymen were landowners or younger brothers of landowners and there was a complete unification of religion, politics and social life.

The first six years of Christopher's life – years which are considered the most impressionable – were spent mainly at Hay Castle, for his father was still in the army and they had no settled home. It was the feeling of antiquity, he wrote, which impressed him most about the place, and there was also the sense of continuity with the past and present, for nothing had changed from one generation to the next, from the time when his mother had been a child in the same house.

Already history was shaping his life and setting the course for his future career, and it was the influence of his mother which first brought this about: 'No one' he wrote:

> .... could owe more to childhood impressions than I did. In fact it was then I acquired my love of history, my interest in the differences of cultures and my sense of the importance of religion in human life, as a massive, objective, unquestioned power that entered into everything and impressed its mark on the external as well as the internal world.[3]

He described his mother as 'thoroughly Welsh by nature, passionately devoted to the Welsh country and country people and the Welsh traditions, above all to the Welsh saints, a subject on which she was an expert.'[4] In fact, she was an unusually learned woman in the days when education for women was thought unnecessary and university education for them had scarcely begun.

From a very early age, he acquired his literary and historical tastes from her for, as he said, she had 'a simple and childlike gift of communication.' His earliest literary memory was of a poem she used to repeat – he never discovered the name of the author or the title of the poem – about 'Bran the Blessed, the mythical ancestor of the Holy Families of Wales – the story of the Lodestone river and the saying "He who will be chief, let him be a bridge." '[5]

His mother not only translated Celtic poetry but also composed poetry herself and once collaborated with Edward Lear in writing a poem; how this came about is told in Vivien Noakes's biography *Edward Lear*.[6] In the winter of 1879, when Edward Lear was wintering in San Remo, 'there was a new family there that winter to whom he took a liking. Their name was Bevan, and one day in April Miss (Mary) Bevan and Lear joined forces to write a new poem'. This was the one beginning, 'How pleasant to know Mr. Lear'. He sent her a copy illustrated with a drawing of himself.

Mary Bevan, however, was no blue-stocking. From her own account written in her diaries and letters before her marriage, she enjoyed the social life of Herefordshire and the company of the young officers stationed at Weymouth, a place the Bevan family also used to visit.

In *Kilvert's Diary* she is described as looking 'radiant with her beautiful eyes and brow'[7] and on another occasion seeing her waiting on the station platform, Kilvert wrote: 'Mary Bevan .... looked very pretty in her white-feathered hat and red and black check cloak.'[8] He was constantly calling at the Castle to see the four Miss Bevans, to play croquet with them or to practise archery, accompany them on picnics and to balls, or sing with them round the organ in the hall; of his last evening at Hay Castle Kilvert wrote: '.... a home to me for nearly 8 years, and its inmates like brothers and sisters.'[9]

The Bevans came from Glamorganshire and Carmarthenshire in South Wales and had one of those ancient Welsh pedigrees that go back into the mists of history, more colourful perhaps than credible. Through the old royal house of Gwynne which they represented they had inherited an heirloom in the form of a trinket given by Anne Boleyn to an ancestor, who was Captain of the Guard of the Tower when she was beheaded. The legend goes that she gave him the gold trinket which was fashioned like a snake saying as she did so: 'A snake it is, a snake it has proved to me.' It was Henry VIII's first gift to her and it is still handed down in the family.[10]

In spite of this Welsh ancestry, Archdeacon Bevan, Christopher Dawson's grandfather, seemed to him 'very un-Welsh in temperament – unemotional, cool, critical, dispassionate' (he had, too, some northern antecedents which may have contributed to these characteristics); he was in fact a hard-headed Victorian churchman, a doughty fighter for the cause of the established church in Wales, but much revered by his parishioners whom he served in a somewhat autocratic manner for fifty-six years. William Bevan had been educated at Rugby under the formidable Dr Arnold, whose son, Matthew Arnold, was one of his contemporaries. He subsequently went to Oxford where he was awarded the Lusby open scholarship in classics at Hertford College. After his ordination he obtained the living of Hay in his native Breconshire, which was in the gift of his relation, Sir Joseph Bailey (later Lord Glanusk). In the printed description of the appointment it was made quite clear that the financial rewards were even for those days ridiculously low but that it offered a way of life that was ideal for someone with scholarly interests, such as William Bevan. The description reads:

> There is no Parsonage house, but the Patron is ready to place at the disposal of the Vicar a spacious and most interesting residence of the Elizabethan period, built on the site of the old Castle at the nominal rent of £20. To a man of private means, this house will supply a strong inducement to accept the living.

And on the Archdeacon's retirement in 1901 a local paper stated:

> He found in that incumbency (of Hay) not a 'living' but a 'starving'; for we are well within the mark when we state that after making provision for the stipend of his Curate, the income which he received as Vicar did not exceed £25 or £30 a year – not sufficient to pay House-rent, for it is a benefice without a parsonage .... To hold such an incumbency without private means would, of course, be an impossibility. But it is not every clergyman with a competency who would be willing to work altogether without pecuniary reward.

As it happened the Bevans were far from starving, except in so far as the children were brought up by Victorian standards of frugality – half an egg was considered quite adequate for a child's breakfast for instance, while butter and jam were never allowed together – but this was in aid of a disciplined upbringing rather than for economic reasons. The Bevan fortune must have been considerable since on his death the Archdeacon left £100,000 among his six children in addition to numerous charitable bequests while during his lifetime he had spent a considerable sum from his personal fortune on restoring the parish church at Hay.

Archdeacon Bevan was a true Barsetshire figure, with side whiskers, tall hat, frock coat and buttoned gaiters, and except on formal occasions when he took the carriage, he drove round the countryside in a dog-cart visiting his parishioners in the outlying villages as well as the townspeople of Hay; often his eldest daughter, Mary, accompanied him on his parochial visits and organised social occasions. His wife was also a popular figure in local society (she belonged to the numerous Dew family from nearby Whitney Court) but she was something of an invalid and unable to participate much in active parish life.

One of Archdeacon Bevan's neighbours, who was also an adversary and a powerful personality, was Fr Ignatius (the Rev Leicester Lyne) who had founded an Anglo-Catholic Benedictine monastery over at Capel-y-Ffin, on the other side of the Black Mountain from Hay. It was, and to some extent still remains, a secret, mysterious place, shut in by the dark hills in the Honddhu valley near the ruins of Llanthony Abbey. Many years later in the 1920s Eric Gill and his 'Distributist' colony tried to build up Fr Ignatius's then deserted monastery and settle there, but even they found it too remote particularly when one winter the place was snowed up for six weeks and they were reduced to slaughtering their own sheep. The eccentric and emotional Fr Ignatius and the cool and dispassionate, intensely rational Archdeacon Bevan could hardly be expected to see eye to eye, for the latter as an Anglican of the old High Church tradition was strongly anti-Catholic and Fr Ignatius with his candles and incense was more Catholic than the Catholics themselves. 'The face is a very saintly one' wrote Kilvert, of Fr Ignatius:

.... and the eyes extremely beautiful, earnest and expressive, a dark soft brown. When excited they seem absolutely to flame .... (He) wore the black Benedictine habit with the two loose wings or pieces falling in front and behind, two violet tassels behind, the knotted scourge girdle, a silver cross on the breast, and a brazen or golden cross hanging from the rosary of black beads under the left arm.[11]

Fr Ignatius was known to cause embarrassing situations among the neighbouring clergy, as for instance on the occasion when he gave a mission in Hay without asking the permission of the Vicar. Archdeacon Bevan retaliated with a broadsheet issued to his parishioners in which he condemned such practices as 'collecting funds for Monastic purposes and the acceptance on the part of Father Ignatius of a kind of homage which is unusual if not objectionable.' (Letter addressed to the Parishioners of Hay, 1878.)

Archdeacon Bevan never neglected his parochial duties but a

great deal of his time was spent in the pursuit of learning which he continued to his dying day. He was, according to his daughter, Mary, Christopher's mother, a great linguist and was seldom without some foreign book or a dictionary. Besides Greek and Latin he knew French, German, Dutch, Norwegian and even studied Walloon!

Like his grandson, he was deeply read in German theology. He never preached in Welsh but he was thoroughly acquainted with that language and could strike terror into the hearts of the Welsh curates in Pembrokeshire by the questions which in his thirst for knowledge he used to put to them concerning the grammar and structure of the language. At the end of his life, when he was confined indoors, he took the opportunity to study Hebrew and his Hebrew books were brought up to him with his breakfast.

But geography was his favourite subject and for one who had seldomed travelled out of Wales his knowledge in this field was quite extraordinary. He wrote two text books of Ancient and Modern Geography which were used at Eton and many other public schools as well as being translated into Italian and Japanese.

The quiet rural life, free from stress and strain, seems to have produced an extraordinary longevity in the Bevan family; William Bevan lived for eighty-seven years and there is a marble tablet in Crickhowell Church (near Hay) on which is inscribed the names of eleven Bevan relatives and the ages at which they died, the sum total of which amounts to 893 years.

In 1886, Mary Bevan married Henry Philip Dawson, a soldier in the Royal Artillery, whom she had met some years previously when he was camping with his regiment at Hay – they were both nearly thirty-six years old when they married, he the elder by a few months. They had in common their many intellectual interests – 'they are both book-worms', a relation wrote at the time of their engagement – and a strong religious faith. While they were devoted to each other and were happily married for forty-six years, she was more dependent on social life than he and after they went to live in the Yorkshire Dales, Christopher felt that his mother was often 'homesick for Wales and the closely-integrated family society of Hay and the Welsh border.'[12]

A MILITARY TRADITION

> It is an exotic in England, unknown to the old constitution of the country . . . . disliked by the inhabitants, particularly by the higher orders, some of whom never allow their family to serve in it.

So wrote the Duke of Wellington, quoted by Christopher Dawson in his memoir *Tradition and Inheritance*; and he went on:

> Service in the army is an advantage to none. The officers and soldiers of the army are an object of dislike and suspicion to the inhabitants while serving with their regiments, and of jealousy afterwards, and they are always ill-treated.

These sentiments, expressed so characteristically by the Iron Duke, were probably true of an earlier military tradition, but they certainly did not apply to Christopher's father, Henry Philip Dawson, and his military career. Although he was a soldier for nearly twenty years, he never fought in a war, and the nearest he came to active service, which he was always anxious to experience, was when he went behind the French lines, in the Franco–Prussian war with his cousin, the future Lord Kitchener of Khartoum, and joined a field-ambulance unit. For this escapade they nearly lost their recently awarded commissions, and Kitchener nearly lost his life by catching pneumonia after they had been up in a captive balloon.

Before his marriage, Capt Dawson's army career led him far afield, from Jamaica to Cuba and Havana and to more wild and distant places such as the high passes of the Andes leading to Quito. By temperament, he was more of an explorer than a soldier: he loved rugged and lonely places, dangerous situations, strange fauna and flora and even stranger tribes. Throughout all his travels he kept a diary which shows a literary power of description far beyond an ordinary travelogue or a soldier's account of a military mission. After crossing the 'Arenal' pass in the Andes he wrote:

> It is a place utterly destitute of beauty and terrible in its desolation. Up the whole of the steep ascent, the skeletons of horses and other animals and human skulls covered the ground; to the right, the range shot up into rocky crags; high above to the left, appearing here and there through the clouds, were the snowfields of Chimborazo, while all around stretched the bare inhospitable *paramo*, all rock, sand and coarse grass, everlastingly swept by the icy wind

that has proved fatal to so many travellers. The white swirling mists that eddied up through the valleys behind us, shutting out all view of the inhabited world and winding shroudlike over the skeleton covered slope increased a hundred fold the wildness of a scene that would well have suited the approach to Hades.

Eventually, he and his companions reached an 'inn' at the summit of the pass, the only place of human habitation for miles around. 'A more wretched place cannot be imagined' he wrote. 'But no place is utterly bad, and the view from this pig-sty was magnificent.' He described his first sight of Chimborazo as 'one of those moments in one's life that is never forgotten. The whole thing looked as if it belonged to another world.'

By slow stages (they were travelling by mule) they came to Quito, the city of the Incas:

The most out of the way capital in the world and of immense antiquity .... I never saw a town so full of churches and convents .... the inside of the Jesuit church is a blaze of gold and gilding and the same with the Cathedral .... I never realised until I came here that Quito is quite a frontier town of civilisation, a day's journey from it the country is inhabited by wild Indians; three or four days journey and the country is inhabited by cannibals.

(*Diaries*, 1872–73)

Later, in 1882, Henry Dawson was sent on a circumpolar expedition, where for four months the party stayed at Fort Rae on Great Bear Lake, a place 'almost entirely surrounded by water'. Their role was to carry out magnetic observations, but the observations which Henry Dawson took extended beyond the scientific to almost a sociological survey of the Indians and Eskimos and a study of their religion and culture. This was his last foreign mission in the army and after his marriage in 1886 he only had two appointments, one at Woolwich and the other at Alverstoke near Portsmouth.

Alverstoke was, apart from Wales, Christopher's first memory (he must have been about three, and his sister Gwendoline five, when they were living there). 'I never liked Portsmouth and Alverstoke', he wrote:

.... not even the sea and the fascinating Victorian fortifications, which even a child could understand, compensated me for the raw ugliness of Gosport and Southsea and the loss of what I called 'the real country'.[13]

But there was a compensation not far away, at Easton, near Winchester, where his father's mother lived – 'the other place', he wrote 'which influenced my childhood most'.[14] He described Dymoke House, as it was called, situated at the end of a typical English village in the heart of Wessex. It looked down on a small Norman church and beyond it the water meadows of the river Itchen, which he thought was even more beautiful than the river Wye. He associated this place with a perennial springtime for the family always went there at Easter, year after year.

His grandmother Harriet Emma Dawson, had been a widow for forty years even when he first remembered her, for her husband, an officer in the Carabineers, had died early on in their marriage which took place in 1854. She returned to her parents after this at Titchfield, Hampshire, where she brought up her two sons in an almost pre-Victorian atmosphere.

She was the daughter of Gen Sir Philip Bainbrigge, who had served on the Duke of Wellington's staff in the Peninsular War. Fifty years later, in 1860, he received a knighthood from Queen Victoria for his services in that campaign. 'The honour has come too late' he wrote in a letter to his daughter. 'My title will be of use to put on my grave stone.'

Like the Dawsons, the Bainbrigges originated from Yorkshire, and contributed to the family characteristics a certain independence of spirit and determination of character. An ancestor, called Robert Bainbrigge, a member of Parliament, was imprisoned in the Tower of London for taking part in a debate in the House of Commons on liberty of speech in 1587. He left a carving of himself in the Beauchamp Tower – a kneeling figure with his name underneath and the inscription: *Vincet qui patitur* (He who suffers will conquer).[15]

Christopher's sister remembered their grandmother as 'a tall and commanding lady with independent and decided opinions, who might have been a soldier herself had she been a man.' Strongly Protestant in her religious beliefs, she had a certain biblical turn of phrase: on one occasion when she saw some village boys throwing stones at a building, she said tersely: 'There will come a chastening'. Sundays in her house were something of an ordeal and she herself kept a sermon book in which she wrote an account of every sermon she heard. Nevertheless and in spite of this rather awe-inspiring personality, her grandchildren were very fond of her and looked forward to their visits to Easton.

It may seem incongruous that Christopher, with his scholarly appearance and interests, should have belonged to a family with such a strong military tradition, but it has to be remembered that the British army in the 19th century did not consist entirely of Colonel Blimps or Guy Crouchbacks. The officers, whom Christopher remembered as a child, were, he said, on the whole better educated and with wider interests than the civilians but this may have been because his father's tastes were literary and scientific and he chose his friends accordingly: 'Although he had been a soldier all his life', wrote Christopher of his father many years later, 'he had little interest in the social side of regimental life. He cared nothing for sport and devoted himself mainly to the scientific side of his profession.'[16]

In 1896 Henry Dawson was informed by the War Office that he had been appointed to the Command in Singapore and was to report for duty within six weeks. Faced with the prospect of taking his wife and two young children to what was considered an unhealthy climate or of leaving them behind in England, he decided to retire from the army and go to live in Yorkshire where he had inherited a family property.

THE DAWSONS OF CRAVEN

Col Dawson, as he became on retirement, was forty-six when he left the army, and he had to start afresh and make a new life by moving to a different part of the country and even building a new house. This was Hartlington Hall, which stands on a hill above the River Wharfe, in that most beautiful part of the Yorkshire Dales known locally as Craven, between Burnsall and Bolton Abbey. The house was built, as Christopher described it, 'where two countries meet – on the one side, the dark fells, on the other the green hills'.

The property at Hartlington had been in the family for about 200 years – an ancestor, another Christopher Dawson, had bought the manor there in 1687 for about £1,000 – but the old house had been demolished in the 19th century and in fact no member of the family had lived there since the middle of the 18th century. The Dawsons, therefore, had not much Yorkshireness left by the time they returned in the 1890s and

Christopher thought that his father's choice 'was due to a conscious desire to recover contact with lost family traditions.'

The estate was kept intact by a family trust. It was for this
reason that when Christopher's father finally inherited the
estate unencumbered by debts or death duties, he had a large
enough capital to enable him to retire from the army with his
pension of £60 per annum and also to build a new house.

Originating from yeoman stock, like many of the landed
families in this part of Yorkshire, the Dawsons never became
typical country squires, who hunted and shot and fished, nor
did they ever distinguish themselves in county politics or
public affairs. Their interests always seem to have been more in
the fields of learning than in those of agriculture or sport. One,
William Dawson, of Langcliffe Hall, near Settle, was described
as 'a man of talent and literature'; a friend of Isaac Newton's at
Cambridge, he was said to have been one of the first people in
the north of England to tackle the *Principia* and was also a good
Latin scholar. A legend also survived that the famous apple
which prompted Newton's discovery of the law of gravity fell
in the garden at Langcliffe.[17]

It was this Dawson's youngest son, another William
(1723–1803), who inherited the property at Hartlington, and
then went south to seek his fortune. He did this most success-
fully, first as a linen merchant and then by marrying into a
Huguenot family, distinguished both for their intelligence and
their good-looks. Sarah Regis, his wife, was the daughter of a
Canon of Windsor, who was also chaplain to Kings George I
and II. William and Sarah had houses at Richmond and at
Windsor, where they lived in considerable grandeur: 'It was
like entering another world', a niece wrote who came to visit
them at their 'great mansion' at Richmond from a Northum-
brian parsonage. 'It's grandeur struck me with awe, the great
iron gates were thrown open when our humble gig entered the
sweep leading to the house, and the Butler introduced me to
my aunt and cousins ....' And from Windsor, where she went
in 1782, she wrote:

> They lived opposite the Queen's House and I had the opportunity
> of seeing all the Royal Family almost every hour of the day and in
> the evening on the terrace. The King (George III) always bowed to
> my aunt Dawson on the terrace, as there was something majestic
> in her looks; His Majesty had remembered her from the time she

was presented at Court, and the strong likeness she bore to her father.'

William Dawson's only surviving son, another William, married his second cousin, Sophia Aufrère, thus making the family doubly Huguenot. Beautiful and ambitious, as well as something of a snob, Sophia Dawson felt no attraction to the wilds of Yorkshire (she visited the place once and *recked* little of it); she was more at home entertaining the 'fashionables' of London society in her house in Manchester Square or calling at Windsor Castle, where she had the entrée.

Later on William and Sophia bought a 'country seat' in Windsor Forest, St Leonard's Hill, which was re-built for them by Wyatt in the neo-Gothic style and re-named Sophia Lodge. Sophia Dawson was often invited to play cards at Windsor Castle with King George III and Queen Charlotte, but she made it a rule never to play on a Sunday, even when invited by the King. Apparently he took no offence at this, but remarked to her: 'You are a good little woman, Mrs. Dawson.'

William and Sophia Dawson had eight children, three sons and five daughters. 'The ladies were all lovely,' a relative wrote of this family 'but the men only moderately handsome.' From all accounts, the daughters as well as being outstandingly beautiful were also fashionably romantic. The eldest, Sophia, who wrote poetry and eventually married an Irish baronet, Sir John Burke, was described by her younger sister, Charlotte, as:

> Sophy (who) mixed with the first society; she was sixteen nights consecutively at the Prince Regent's parties (at Brighton) and was present at the Grand Assembly given to the Allied Sovereigns after the Battle of Waterloo.

Charlotte was also romantically inclined, for 'though she had many suitors, she refused them all (including it was said, two Earls, Shrewsbury and Abingdon) and married Stanislaus, Count Gnorowski, a Polish nobleman, who had taken refuge in England.'[18]

But in the male line, the Yorkshire stolidity was the predominant trait so that in the Victorian age we find that the descendants of the Huguenots have deserted the drawing-rooms of Windsor and Brighton and the 'first society' for the quiet life of a country parsonage in Norfolk or Hampshire. William Dawson wrote of 'my son, Henry, who continually reminds me of my father from the placidity and extreme mildness of his disposition.'

Born in 1791, while the French Revolution was still raging, Henry took Orders in the Church of England, married into a Norfolk family, the Buxtons of Shadwell, and settled down at Hopton Rectory in that county for nearly fifty years. He died in the last years of Queen Victoria's reign, when he was nearly 100, two months after his great-grandson, Christopher Dawson, was born. The Rev Henry Dawson had no interest in the Yorkshire property (it was he who pulled down the old manor house at Hartlington).

A YORKSHIRE BOYHOOD

In building and planning Hartlington Hall, Col Dawson had the intention of building a small country house – 'a home' as he wrote to his son at a later date, 'that you could come to hereafter, which would be full of the associations and memories of childhood.' He himself had known such a house at Titchfield Priory, in Hampshire, which was his mother's home and where he had spent his early years. He visualised a place which would be inexpensive to keep up and fondly imagined that in the future a family could live there very cheaply and become self-supporting by running the farm as well. He continued:

> It would be a great mistake to try and make a great country house here; incomes in these days are more likely to diminish than to increase as the prosperity of the country wanes, and the probability is that taxation will be laid more and more on the shoulders of the well-to-do; and it is very probable that land will be taxed at a still higher rate than hitherto, landowners being in a minority and always regarded with jealousy by the landless majority.

These words have proved true, but what Col Dawson failed to realise, writing as he did before the First World War, was that Hartlington would never be an inexpensive place to run, with its large number of rooms by today's standards, its inconvenient planning and its ten acres of unmanageable grounds. Sadly, successive generations have never been able to live there for any length of time. It was indeed no great Victorian mansion, but a Yorkshire manor house, built in the traditional style of grey stone with gables and mullioned windows. It stood high on a hill looking south towards Burnsall Fell and the moors of the Bolton Abbey estate. A formal garden was laid out in terraces and beyond there were wooded slopes leading down to the stream in the valley below and to an old water-mill, which was in working order up till the Second World War.

For the young Christopher, this return to the north was as much an adventure as going to a new country. He wrote:

> Yorkshire was a new world and the whole aspect of the country with the stone walls climbing the hills and the naked rock thrusting itself out in great scars and promontories like sea cliffs, was entirely unlike anything I had seen before.[19]

He loved the sound of falling water which was always present 'as a gentle murmur in summer and rising to a thunderous roar in the winter floods when the hill seemed to vibrate like a taut string.'[20] For a child it was an earthly paradise, with unending scope for exploration and discovery: there was the 'beck', as it is called in Yorkshire, which ran back for miles into the hills through a wooded valley sometimes narrowing into a deep chasm in the rocks; there was also a deserted lead mine, where 'one could sit on a stone platform high up on the hillside looking down on the treetops two hundred feet below and see the whole extent of the solitary valley....'[21]

In these idyllic surroundings Christopher was brought up. It was, he wrote, 'a solitary and secluded boyhood in which I was extremely happy.'[22] Up to the age of ten, when he went away to school, he shared his sister's lessons with a governess, or when the family wintered at Brighton as they often did, he attended a small day school. A Victorian upbringing is usually thought as repressive but Christopher never found it so; he liked the freedom and absence of restraint that he felt in the wild moorland country and he also liked the freedom of the mind which he gained from books and the lack of regimented education. He discovered also at an early age the world of myth and legend – half history and half poetry:

> The old road which carries us back not merely for centuries but for thousands of years; the road by which every people has travelled and from which the beginnings of every literature have come.[23]

Religion also formed an important part in Christopher's early formation. His sister, Gwendoline, remembered how their day started with prayers in the hall taken by their father, and attended by the whole household. These were not the traditional Victorian family prayers, but something similar to the daily Office of the Catholic Church, said morning and evening. Every morning also they had religious teaching from their mother for half an hour. The Victorian Sunday held no fears for these children, since it was treated as a 'special' day, on which they had meals with their parents instead of in the nursery or schoolroom, and in the afternoon their father took them for a long walk or for an expedition further afield in the carriage. True, they had to learn the Collect for the day by heart and to render an account of the sermon in church. Once when questioned about the sermon, Christopher said it was about 'Miss Tickell forgiving sins' (this was the name of their governess). All were completely baffled until it transpired that the subject of the sermon was *the mystical forgiveness of sins!* After church, his sister recalled that 'Christopher would some-times run a race with little Annie down the hill from the church to the village; Annie was a farmer's daughter, the same age as Christopher, and a swift runner.'

Religion became associated in his mind with the elemental force of nature and particularly his love of the river which he found echoed in the words of the Old Testament. Such lines as 'Deep calleth to deep at the noise of Thy waterspouts', 'Let the floods clap their hands, let the hills be joyful together' and many more besides made him realise that the people in those days felt as he did. He found such things a compensation for 'the boredom of so much that seemed dull or incomprehensible in the long Anglican service' and he realised that:

> Religion was not simply concerned with the pious moralities which held such a prominent place in Victorian books for chil-dren, but stood close to that wonderful non-human world of the river and the mountain which I found around me.[24]

Even at this early age, he felt the link between history and religion in the ruins of the deserted monasteries in which Yorkshire abounds. As he was later to write:

> Bolton Priory which lies a few miles from Hartlington down the Wharfe, always seemed to me the perfect embodiment of this lost

element in the northern culture – a spiritual grace which had once been part of our social tradition and which still survived as a ghostly power brooding over the river and the hills.'[25]

Christopher's father was an Anglo-Catholic, a member of the Church Union party and a friend of Lord Halifax, a peer much involved with the Anglo-Catholic movement, but his mother was more conservatively Anglican and with a strong anti-Catholic prejudice which she had inherited from her Bevan relations. It was undoubtedly his father's early influence which inspired him with a love of the ancient Catholic religion, its ritual and art and literature, long before he knew anything of its theology and dogma. During the long winter evenings at Hartlington, he used to sit by the fire in his father's study, a room 'which was at once a workshop, an office and a library' poring over his books such as Botticelli's illustrations to Dante in three immense volumes which no bookcase could hold, and which to his childish imagination seemed the largest books in the world. His father's tastes were catholic in the widest sense; as well as his love of 'building and planning and planting, which occupied him to the end of his days' he was equally interested in modern science and ancient philosophy, medieval mysticism and modern history, Victorian novels and classical poetry: 'His admiration for Dante knew no limits, he rated him far above Shakespeare and Milton as the world's one perfect poet.'[26]

Christopher's early upbringing was secure but still adventurous, ordered but with an element of freedom which was totally lacking when he went away to school. He wrote:

> The country house in the Victorian age still stood for the old tradition of the family society, centred as it was on the institutions of the kitchen, the stables and the garden. The children felt that servants were important people because they held social office and authority in their own sphere. The world of the schoolroom was pale and uninteresting in comparison with the warmth and variety of the kitchen over which the cook ruled like a figure in a fairy story, or compared with the saddle room where everything was in its right place and yet the sense of discipline and order was stimulating and not repressive.[27]

Social life at Hartlington, particularly in the winter, was limited to the family circle and the neighbours who were few and far between. There were Christmas and birthday parties attended by the tenant farmers' children and those from the village school, and there was carol singing by local choirs and visiting brass bands in the hall at Christmas, but on the whole the children were left to invent their own games and amusements. Christopher and his sister invented a whole world of make-believe, peopled by historical characters usually fighting for a lost cause. In turn they identified themselves with the cause of Alfonso, the boy-king of Spain (after whom they named one of their pet mice) or with Bonnie Prince Charlie and the Jacobites. All their animals – the dog, the pony and the mice – were given Jacobite names and were part of the historical game. They also produced a newspaper, *The Hartlington Times* which carried items of local interest in addition to serials and stories. Christopher's first literary composition was written at the age of six and was an allegorical story about 'The Golden City and the Coal City' and described a battle between the Christians and the heathens.

All this took place in the last decade of the 19th century, the end of Queen Victoria's reign and for Christopher not only was it the end of a personal era – that of his happy carefree years before he entered the alien world of school – but also he felt on looking back that it was the end of 'a whole series of ages – a river of immemorial time which has suddenly dried up and become lost in the seismic cleft that has opened between the present and the past.'[28]

CHAPTER TWO

The Alien World

'A HORDE OF SAVAGES'

In 1899, when Christopher was ten, his parents decided to send him away to a preparatory school. Bilton Grange, near Rugby, survives to this day and is, as I have every reason to believe, an excellent establishment. Just as his happy childhood years at home had influenced his life for the good, so now the situation went into reverse and the sufferings of his schooldays – both physical and mental – could be said to have had a disastrous and permanent influence on his whole life.

Although this school was no more barbarous than any other at that time, he hated it from the day he arrived until the day he left. He never succeeded in acclimatising himself, he once wrote, to this new world and felt as though he had come among 'a horde of savages with no common interests or ideas or beliefs or traditions.' This experience prejudiced him for ever against 'England of the Diamond Jubilee, schoolboys, schools and even against the Midlands,'[1] which were indeed to him 'sodden and unkind' as Belloc described them in his poem, *The South Country*.

His happy and secluded childhood, the sheltered upbringing, the lack of friends of his own age, proved a great disadvantage when now he was confronted with the rough and tumble of a boys' boarding school. Not that he was a 'molly-coddle' but he preferred the more solitary activities of climbing trees, exploring caves or riding his pony to organised games at which he was never any good owing to poor sight. Now at school his health began to suffer, not only because he was unhappy but because of the complete change of environment; he put it down to the fact that having lived an isolated life in a very healthy climate, he had developed no immunity to common germs.

Christopher never reproached his parents for sending him to this school and they no doubt saw it as necessary preparation for the even worse hardships of a public school. His letters home were full of the usual schoolboy information which parents in every generation know so well – the place in class, the number of boys in the dormitory, the cricket results, requests for 'grub', stamps for his collection, and the equivalent 'comics' of those days, the *Boys Own Paper* and the *Captain*. There were no complaints of home-sickness or of bullying – it was only long after that he spoke of the terrible misery he had endured at school. As time went on, however, illnesses are mentioned more frequently in these letters and the impression is given that his health was steadily deteriorating. During the time he was at Bilton Grange, as well as going through the usual epidemics such as measles and chicken pox, he began to develop bronchitis which later became chronic. He wrote once of being isolated in the gardener's cottage, because he was in quarantine for mumps, and said that he was extremely lonely and besought his parents to come and visit him. Medical treatment seemed from all accounts on the primitive side: when he had a severe ear-ache after measles they attempted to cure it by placing a leach on the affected part. Deaths were not uncommon – he wrote in one of his letters: 'A boy died here yesterday. It was very sudden as he was only ill for about three days. The class is subscribing for a wreath.'

Owing to his frequent absences due to illness, his academic progress was not brilliant. He usually came top of his form in English and history, but was brought down by his low marks in mathematics. However, one of his school reports stated that 'his command of the English language made up for any amount of cramming for exams.'

Apart from the uncongenial society, and the organised games, what he really disliked at this school were the narrow limits set by the curriculum and the religion of the school chapel which he said he found 'strange and distasteful' in contrast to the Anglo-Catholic religion in which he had been brought up.

He left at the end of the Easter term in 1903 to go on to Winchester, glad to see the last of Bilton Grange and the hated Midlands.

WINCHESTER

Of all public schools, Winchester was perhaps the best for

Christopher: it was a school for traditionalists, intellectuals and even eccentrics and it seemed his father had been wise to choose it rather than his own school, which was Harrow. Although the school life was still uncongenial and the physical hardships, such as the cold baths in communal tubs and the spartan diet, even greater than those at Bilton Grange, he found it a great improvement on the latter in many respects. There was more freedom and less compulsory games and much more opportunity for reading and browsing in bookshops. Even the traditions, such as the Winchester language, which every new boy has to learn in the book of 'Notions' by a statutory time, were more interesting to him than irksome. Particularly, with his historical interests he liked the antiquity of the place, the old buildings such as the cloisters and William of Waynflete's Chantry chapel, the arch which had once held a statue of the Virgin Mary in pre-Reformation days, and to which a boy still had to raise his hat as he passed underneath.

Christopher never entered for the Winchester Scholarship examination and was therefore living in one of the more modern (that is, Victorian) school houses rather than the old part of the school. This was Culver House, known as 'Kenny's' after the house-master, Mr Kensington. (No house at Winchester to this day is known by its authentic name.) Had he been with the scholars, he would have met Arnold Toynbee, who as they both discovered later, was there at the same time. The only contemporaries he ever mentioned were Apsley Cherry-Garrard, the author of *The Worst Journey in the World*, an account of Scott's voyage to the Antarctic, and Charles Scott-Moncrieff, the future translator of Proust.

But it was Winchester Cathedral itself which left the greatest impression on his young mind and re-awakened his religious and historical sense. As he was to write later:

> I learnt more during my schooldays from my visits to the Cathedral at Winchester than I did from the hours of religious instruction in school. That great church with its tombs of the Saxon kings and the medieval statesmen-bishops, gave one a greater sense of the magnitude of the religious element in our culture and the depths of its roots in our national life than anything one could learn from books.[2]

Through the school archaeological society, which organised

expeditions to see old churches and buildings, he acquired another interest which remained with him through life. He also took up bicycling and explored the Hampshire countryside which he had always loved so well since his early childhood: his memories of it, he wrote later, were always those of spring in southern England 'the marigold meadows and the swift bright waters of the chalk streams, the spring air on the downs and the black yews and dark juniper bushes under the spring sun.'[3]

To a friend, Ralph Ricketts, a fellow-Wykehamist, who said that Winchester was 'a kill or cure school' Christopher replied, 'It maims'. He was also to write (around 1925):

> I got nothing from school, little from Oxford, and less than nothing from the new post-Victorian urban culture; all my 'culture' and my personal happiness came from that much-derided Victorian rural home life.[4]

Nevertheless it was at Winchester that he first started reading on a large scale and collecting books, and he also acquired an interest in the Italian painters of the Renaissance. At Wells' secondhand bookshop he bought most of the works of Walter Pater (*Marius the Epicurean* was his favourite book at this time), several Ruskin volumes (he wrote to his father in 1903, 'I am having rather a Ruskin rage at present'), *The Life of Tauler*, the German mystic, translated by Charles Kingsley, and William Morris's *Sigurd*. His range of reading in his early 'teens was amazing comprising Greek philosophy and Christian mysticism, art and history and poetry, as well as modern novels. In this interest he was encouraged by his great-uncle William Dawson, a retired clergyman who lived in Essex and whom Christopher often used to visit in his holidays from Winchester. During his years as a clergyman in the East End of London in the 1880's he had spent much of his time collecting antiquarian books in the days when even medieval manuscripts and *incunabula* could be bought for a few pounds, so that his house was a vast library with book-shelves to the ceiling in every room. Christopher was allowed to roam as he liked among these books; he found his uncle, in spite of his great age, or perhaps because of it, a very sympathetic character who shared his own interests. He described him as:

An immense reader, especially of history, a much more learned man than my father or my mother's father, and the only member of my family with a large library. He was a very remarkable character, a strong individualist, with a strong sense of humour, unconventional but very English, far more so than either of my parents.[5]

The Rev William Dawson was an Anglican of the old High Church tradition and a Christian Socialist extremely concerned with the Victorian urban population and with all the relative questions of housing and poverty. But in his young days he had been under Tractarian influences and according to Christopher was extremely anti-Ultramontane and influenced by Acton and Döllinger:

> He had rather an Actonian conception of the ethical judgment in history. We used to argue violently on this and every subject but for so old a man he was extremely broad-minded.

He was then about 70 and for Christopher he represented an interesting link with the past, for his great-uncle could recall in the days of his childhood meeting his grandmother, Sophia Dawson, the lady who had been painted by Romney and played cards with George III.

AN AGNOSTIC PHASE

Christopher was at Winchester for little more than a year: the austere life and the damp low-lying situation of the place brought on severe attacks of bronchitis. In 1904, his parents fearing consumption, the dreaded disease of that time, took him to see a specialist who advised that he should be immediately removed from school and sent to a private tutor.

He was barely fifteen when his formal education came to an end with his removal from Winchester, but he considered it nothing but a blessing in disguise. No one could have been less suited to the role of a successful public school boy: no one less likely to succeed in the field of a career in the Wykehamist tradition – that of the politician, the government servant or the church – and if his parents had such ambitions for him they must have been disappointed. But he realised that the fault was in himself and not in the school: in fact, as he was later to write, he thought that Winchester was 'the best of our English schools' and he admired the way it had been faithful to its founder and his original ideal 'of training scholars who would be good servants of the community through all the social and political changes of five and a half centuries.'[6]

He spent the autumn of 1904 at Montreux in Switzerland with his family recovering his health in the mountain air. It was his first visit to the Continent and he remembered particularly stopping at Rheims and being 'tremendously impressed by the Cathedral' and his first experience of Catholic worship.

The following summer, 1905, Christopher was sent to a private tutor at Bletsoe in Bedfordshire to continue his studies before going up to Oxford. Mr Moss was a country parson and a former public school master, who took about six pupils in his rectory. It seems to have been the reverse of a 'cramming' establishment, for the boys were left largely to their own devices. Christopher described it as one of the happiest periods of his life. He spent a lot of the time out of doors and recovered his health but he also read a great deal of his own choosing, for his tutor was no scholar and did not overload him with work. It was then, even more than at Winchester, that he started to educate himself and consequently found that he learnt and thought more there than either at school earlier or at Oxford later.

It was there also that he formed the first and greatest friendship of his life and it seems a remarkable coincidence that in this remote country rectory and among such a small group of boys, another new boy should arrive that term, of a brilliance and indeed eccentricity compatible with his own. This was Edward Watkin, who later as E. I. Watkin became well-known in Catholic intellectual circles for his books on philosophy and mysticism.

From a solitary childhood in Wales and an unconventional education with private tutors at home and abroad (which included a tour of Italy and Greece) he had come to Bletsoe at the age of sixteen before going on to St Pauls School; from there he took a classical scholarship to New College, Oxford. He was precocious for his age and a brilliant classical scholar although he always maintained that he was less well read than Christopher at that time. Christopher's future publisher, Frank Sheed (the co-founder of Sheed & Ward) once remarked that it must have been alarming to teach this pair of teenagers in a class.

In a memoir of his friend, written for the British Academy,[7] E. I. Watkin recalled their first meeting at Bletsoe and how it was 'hardly auspicious for a future friendship' for it was the occasion of a violent religious argument which provoked him to bring the back of the garden chair in which Christopher was sitting down upon his head! He was passing through a stage of religious scepticism at that time, and Edward Watkin, then an enthusiastic Anglo-Catholic, quite understandably did not enjoy having his views dismissed by a younger boy who called himself an agnostic.

As we have seen, Christopher too had from his early years been attracted to all that was 'Catholic' in the Anglican faith, under the influence of his father and his own reading from the writings of saints and mystics, but at school he found a different kind of religion which was arid and lifeless and the long hours of formal instruction which he described as 'more ethics than religion' only served to turn him away from 'Establishment religion' more than ever. Describing the situation later he wrote of:

> The haze of vagueness and uncertainty which hung around the more fundamental articles of Christian dogma .... [and how] the one standard of authority in the Protestant religious world, namely the Bible, was being swept away by the tide of the new Biblical criticism.

He looked for authority but he found none and still less did he find it in the Anglo-Catholic Church which was:

> .... weak in the very point where it claimed to be strongest. It was lacking in authority. It was not the teaching of the official church, but of an enterprising minority which provided its own standards of orthodoxy.[8]

It was due to this 'conflict of authorities' as he called it that he lost faith in religion altogether for a time. 'The intellectual current,' he wrote 'was, in fact, setting away from Christianity, and I felt the first influence of that wave of paganism which has since swept the country.'

The passages quoted above were written in retrospect in 1926. His thoughts in 1906, the time of which I write, were less calm and detached. He wrote in his journal 'There appears to me to be no certainty except my own existence, without which we can conceive nothing.' And again a year later he wrote: 'At present Christianity merely seems to me a possibility among other possibilities. I have not the slightest conviction.'

But it was a phase which did not last for long and by the time he went up to Oxford in 1908 he had resolved his doubts sufficiently to return to a belief in Christianity.

In spite of their first collision, Christopher and Edward Watkin soon established a bond of mutual interest which at that time was chiefly in books and writers. It was at Bletsoe, Edward Watkin remembered that Christopher introduced him to the works of Walter Pater, particularly *Marius the Epicurean* and to J. H. Shorthouse's *John Inglesant*, a historical novel of the time of Charles I. Pater's over-embellished and slow-moving prose is now unfashionable but for an earlier generation reared on the classics it was a different matter. In the memoir, quoted above, E. I. Watkin wrote:

> From Pater I learnt with Dawson to seek and seize passages of beauty, such as that of describing the poplar's distinctive music, 'a certain fresh way its leaves have of dealing with the wind, making its sound, in never so slight a stirring of the air, like running water.' I remember one day we visited a group of poplars by the riverside to enjoy their rich autumnal gold. That Dawson cherished the same memory appears from one of his early letters: 'I often think of our time at Bletsoe, of *Marius the Epicurean* and the Bedfordshire poplars.'

In the early chapters of *John Inglesant* there is a description of the 17th century Anglican community at Little Gidding and the church celebrated in T. S. Eliot's *Four Quartets* – 'the place where prayer has been valid'. During their last term at Bletsoe, Christopher and Edward made a cross-country journey to Little Gidding and they too were aware of 'a peculiar atmosphere of peace and prayer which invests the church.'[9]

Edward Watkin left Bletsoe in 1906 and Christopher soon after, for further coaching in Oxford and then in Germany, but the friendship first formed at Bletsoe was renewed at Oxford and was to continue over a span of sixty years. It was one of those rare friendships between two apparently opposite personalities who feel a close kinship of mind and spirit. With Edward Watkin, who was outgoing and talkative, Christopher's shyness and reserve departed and he found he could talk freely or remain silent if he chose: the affinity of their minds was such that speech could become unnecessary.

At Oxford, Christopher stayed with a tutor, Mr, later Sir, Henry Penson, who with his Swedish wife, kept a small tutorial establishment in Wellington Place, St. Giles'. Christopher wrote to his mother on arrival that he was delighted with the house and with his hosts, commenting that Mrs Penson was very nice 'though very foreign' and Mr Penson looked 'like a Russian anarchist'. There were other pupils there who came and went; someone he called 'Erse Fitz Erse', a girl who he could hear 'from his little den being instructed in feudalism' and a Swedish girl, Stina (Christina) Bildt, a relation of Mrs Penson's who was studying economics and who became a life-long friend. Life at Oxford seemed a social whirl, after his quiet years at Bletsoe Rectory; there were picnics on the river Cherwell, tea parties, visits to the Union where he once heard Hilaire Belloc speaking in the Eights Week Debate and Ronald Knox making 'a very brilliant speech in which he proved that the Stuarts were disinterested Socialists.' Some friends of his parents, the Camerons, whom they had met during a winter they spent at Montreux, also befriended him. Hardy Hay Cameron was one of the five sons of Mrs Julia Cameron, the formidable pioneer photographer and friend of Tennyson and the pre-Raphaelites. He had retired from the Colonial Service in Ceylon and had gone up to Oxford as an elderly undergraduate (he was past sixty), an ambition he had had since the days of his youth. When he called at the Pensons' house, Christopher wrote to his mother that Mr Cameron 'made love to Mrs Penson who was delighted with him' – he was well-known for his flirtatious nature!

To his father he wrote more seriously of his chances of winning the Brackenbury Scholarship at Balliol. His tutor thought he should enter for it, but Christopher thought the chances of his winning it were small, as it was the highest prize at Oxford and there was no age limit. (Belloc had been a former holder of the Brackenbury.) In this prediction he was right, for he failed to win the Balliol award but achieved one at Trinity instead, in December 1907.

During the summer of 1908 he travelled on the Continent with his father visiting Bruges, Cologne and Strasbourg. Their final destination was Baden-Baden in the Black Forest, where he was to spend some months learning German from a philologist called Herr Lenz, a friend of the great student of English dialect, Prof Wright. Col Dawson, always an inveterate sightseer, was an exhausting travelling companion, since he liked to see all the churches, monasteries and picture galleries as soon as he arrived in a place. From Bruges, that medieval city of pealing bells, Christopher wrote to his sister of its canals and the 'beautiful Lac d'Amour looking very melancholy in the rain'.

At the Villa Lenz in Baden-Baden he struggled unsuccessfully with German, and although he mastered it sufficiently so that he was able to read Goethe, Hegel, Troeltsch and later Spengler, he never learnt to speak it satisfactorily. No one could have been a greater admirer of German culture than he, of the philosophy, poetry and music of the Germans as well as the architecture of their beautiful baroque churches, but philology was never one of his interests and from the sociological and religious standpoints he found the country infinitely depressing.

He became disenchanted with Germany and the Germans; 'This country is most dreadful' he wrote to his sister from Baden 'it is really like the state of society in *Lord of the World*.' (This was Robert Hugh Benson's startling novel about the end of the world.) 'People get on so very well without religion. They do not seem bigoted like English "undenominationalists" but they examine Christianity as if it was a kind of beetle. It is all as different as if one was living among Chinese'. In another letter he added: 'This is a most soul-destroying place. The Lenzi are undenominational Zwinglians. Write again soon. Your letters are my one solace in this vale of tears. Another is that I have bought a gorgeous complete edition of Novalis – poems and all.' To his father he wrote: 'German is an awful language and I progress slowly with it. It's a pity they don't adopt Esperanto.'

CHAPTER THREE

Oxford in the Golden Age

THE PATH TO ROME

Christopher entered Trinity College, Oxford, in the Michaelmas term of 1908 at a time in Oxford's history which through literary and political memoirs has acquired a fame of its own. He once said that the Oxford he first knew was almost exactly as described in Compton Mackenzie's autobiographical novel, *Sinister Street*. There we see the hero, Michael Fane, fresh from a country parsonage, entering the ebullient world of Edwardian Oxford in that last golden age before the outbreak of the First World War: everyone except himself seems to be part of a group and he feels an intense loneliness – 'a loneliness more bitter even than when at Randell House he first encountered school.'[1]

There were the rich sporting aristocrats of 'the Bullingdon set', cracking their whips and view-hulloaing in the 'Quad'; the public school 'hearties' who ganged together and organised themselves for rugger and cricket or played callous practical jokes, such as burning an undergraduate's furniture to stoke their bonfires; and then there were the various cliques and coteries too numerous to mention which included the smart set of Balliol Etonians, such as Julian Grenfell, one of the poets of the First World War who died in the trenches, and Charles Lister. Christopher remembered the latter as the most handsome of all the god-like figures of that time and he also remembered Ronald Knox, whom he came to know better later on as a fellow Catholic writer. Knox too belonged to the smart Balliol group, although unlike the others he was not rich, handsome or dashing, but he was distinguished for his scholarship and the brilliance of his wit. He was also among the leaders of the fashionable Anglo-Catholic faction in the university and the founder of a group called 'The Spikes', so named on account of their extreme High Church views.

At nineteen, when he came to Trinity College, Christopher was still painfully shy and unsure of himself socially; having left Winchester early, he had no affiliation with any particular group, and found himself more or less an outsider. He wrote in his journal (which he kept intermittently during his first year at Oxford) of feeling nervous and unsettled and of the great disadvantage of having no friends in college. He must, in fact, have borne a certain resemblance to his great predecessor at Trinity, John Henry Newman, of whom he was to write: 'His seriousness together with his extreme shyness made him at first a lonely and silent member of his new college.'

In appearance he was dark-haired and of average height (5 ft 10 in) but below the average in weight. Indeed, for most of his adult life he seldom weighed more than eight stone and often even less, so that he looked, as Prof David Knowles once wrote, 'as if a gust of wind might sweep him out of sight.'[2] He was short-sighted and acutely conscious of a sense of physical inferiority with his contemporaries – in his journal he wrote of his nervousness which was 'for fear of inferiority' and of his 'shrinking from action and society.' His great-uncle, William Dawson, had already told him that he used his brain too much and his limbs too little and he advised him to get into the open air and ride and shoot and cycle; after a visit to Hartlington he wrote:

> You sat opposite to me all the way to London yesterday; I mean that I could not shut out your thin pale face which the fine bracing air that blows round your den in the tower ought surely to paint with roses and plump with a fatness such as the Psalmist attributes to the wicked!

But Christopher, like so many people, was a mixture of opposites: if he appeared physically frail, he made up for it in intellectual strength and he was determined to the point of obstinacy; there was also a virility in his character which was particularly evident in his writing. All his life he suffered from chronic insomnia – his active mind could take no rest – and from bouts of depression, which he referred to in his letters to Edward Watkin as 'Uncle Paul' (the character in Belloc's *Dedicatory Ode* who 'suffered from excessive gloom'). There was also a lady called 'Aunt Flabitha', imaginary sister to Paul, who stood for feelings of apathy and lack of energy. But conversely he had a strong sense of humour and an optimism in his view of life which was supported by his religious faith. His friends remembered him best for his dark expressive eyes, which betrayed his every mood and feeling, and his shy but attractive smile.

Had he won the Brackenbury scholarship and gone to Balliol he might have found the company of the other scholars just as daunting as that of the Philistines or 'hearties' of Trinity, and although Balliol prided itself on being the most liberal and broadminded of the Oxford colleges, so that theoretically the sons of miners were meant to be on equal terms with the sons of landowners, this was not so in practice. The public school men went round in their own gangs, particularly the Etonians who far outnumbered the rest, and disregarded the bright scholars from provincial grammar schools.

While Christopher belonged to the public school and landowning class, he never had any time for the snobbery and conventionalism which was typical of that particular *milieu* at Oxford, nor did he have the money to take part in much social activity had he so desired. During his time at Oxford his father allowed him £160 a year which was barely enough for his day-to-day needs even in those days. He had expected him to take up his Exhibition money at Trinity of £60 per annum but Christopher waived it for the privilege of a free glass of sherry before dinner. He also avoided the obligation of dining in hall on frequent occasions. Col Dawson was not rich, but he had the security of his land and the expectation of a further inheritance on his mother's death, and he could not therefore have really been hard pressed to keep his son at Oxford. It was more a question of withholding financial independence, for while he gladly settled all his son's bills, he liked to know what they were for. Nearly every letter Christopher wrote to his father from Oxford contained a request for money – for 'a new pair of boots', a dinner jacket or a new suit, for a railway ticket, for books, for College dues and so forth – everything down to the smallest item had to be asked for which must have been extremely irksome. His sister was likewise always in a state of penury, writing once for money to buy Christmas presents as she had only 2/6d left. She was then at least 20 years old.

On such a small allowance, social life therefore was necessarily limited; a rich undergraduate could hold breakfast and
luncheon parties in his rooms, waited on by his 'scout' but the
less well-off ordered 'commons' of bread and cheese from the
Buttery at mid-day and dined in Hall at night. During his first
two years, Christopher had rooms in college, which comprised
a small bedroom with a sitting-room adjoining, furnished with
the bare necessities, and able to be embellished according to its
occupant's means. His furnishings were mainly books, and a
few of his favourite pictures which he had brought from home
– Leonardo's *Head of Christ*, a drawing of Socrates, a Dürer
etching of some sheep and an engraving of Charles I.

His tutor was Ernest Barker, a strongly individualistic
character and 'a man of many sided interests', as Christopher
once said of him. Far from restricting him to the history
syllabus, Barker encouraged his pupil in his wide range of
reading and his interest in the philosophy of history, which he
was already developing. While Barker's own interest lay in the
field of Greek Political Theory – Plato and Aristotle – he was at
the same time a good medievalist and Christopher always
maintained that he owed him a great debt for initiating him into
medieval studies.

A former Balliol scholar, Ernest Barker had come from a
north country Noncomformist background and as Fr Martin
D'Arcy, who was also at Oxford at that time, recalled, had a
broad Manchester accent and a deep booming voice in which
he used to address the Oxford undergraduates as 'lads'. Oxford
was full of 'characters' in those days – the great Dr Spooner was
a legendary one – and Ernest Barker could also be described as
such. Christopher got on well with him and Barker on his side
appreciated his gifted if unconventional pupil. He once said
that he began to learn history the day that he became Dawson's
tutor.[3]

In later life, Christopher said that the greatest and perhaps
only benefit he derived from his Oxford education was the
knowledge and understanding he acquired of the ideas and
techniques of scholarship from his personal contact with
scholars such as Ernest Barker.

Edward Watkin, who was in his second year at New College
when Christopher went up, later remembered him as having
hardly more use for Oxford education than Gibbon, who

wrote in his autobiography of his time spent at Oxford as the most idle and unprofitable of his life. Christopher did not idle away his time but he had little interest in the set history syllabus – Stubbs on Constitutional History, Oman on the Normans and the like. He therefore devoted his time to following his own course of reading and studies which were mainly in the field of the philosophy of history and religion.

Christopher had come a long way from his earlier agnosticism, which had evoked Edward Watkin's wrath at Bletsoe, and by the time he went up to Oxford he had returned to his father's Anglo-Catholic faith. Ultimately, he said, 'he could not acquiesce altogether in a view of life which left no place for religion'. His early reading of the saints and mystics had made such a deep impression on his mind that he felt, even though he lacked intellectual grounds for faith, 'the spiritual side of life represented something real which could not be explained away as mere illusion.'[4]

It was above all in the mystical and transcendent elements of religion that he found the basis of his own personal faith, not only in these early days but throughout his long life. The spiritual writings of Baron von Hügel, the liberal Catholic philosopher, had a considerable influence on his thought in his Oxford days and were his first introduction to comparative religion which became one of his dominant interests later. From Hügel and other mystical writers he learnt the one truth which he thought essential to all religions:

> To know the unknowable, to grasp the incomprehensible, to receive the Infinite .... (this) has remained for thousands of years as the goal – whether attainable or unattainable – of the religious life, and no religion which ignores this aspiration can prove permanently satisfying to man's spiritual needs.[5]

The greatest influence of all on his thought at this time was St Augustine's *City of God*, which he said affected him most powerfully.

Like so many other converts to Catholicism of that era, such as Ronald Knox, C. C. Martindale, Vernon Johnson and E. I. Watkin, his path to Rome went by the middle way of Anglo-Catholicism which had a strong following in Oxford. It represented a reaction not only from the secularism and materialism of the age, but from the more worldly aspects of

'Establishment' religion or 'Mayor and Corporation religion', as Christopher used to call it. The beautiful Anglo-Catholic ritual was also a contrast to the severity of much of the Low Protestant tradition – the gloom of their Sundays, the long Bible readings and sermons, and the bare ugliness of their unadorned churches.

As an Anglo-Catholic at Oxford, Christopher admitted that his interest in the movement was half-hearted and without intellectual conviction. He had no affiliation with 'the Spikes' but he went to week-day Mass at Pusey House which was the centre of the movement in Oxford and came to know Dr Darwell Stone, its Head, whom he described as the 'most learned and wisest of Anglican theologians.' On Sundays he often went to the Church of the Cowley Fathers, where High Mass was celebrated with plainsong in the Solesmes chant. After he became a Catholic, he never lost his love for Anglican ritual, and deplored the fact that contemporary Catholicism had lost sight of much of its own heritage, its spiritual and intellectual treasures.

Roman Catholicism had hardly entered his life at this time, and apart from Edward Watkin, who had been converted during his first year at Oxford, he had no personal contacts with Catholics. As a religion it was not officially recognised in the university and it was only during the inter-war years, under the leadership of priests like Monsignor Ronald Knox at the Catholic Chaplaincy and the Jesuit fathers Martindale and D'Arcy at Campion Hall that Catholicism was seen to be a serious intellectual force as well as a spiritual one.

Before he went abroad, Christopher said he knew nothing of Catholicism as a 'living religion' and for some reason thought that Catholic civilisation had stopped with the Middle Ages. On his first visit to the Continent he remembered how in the magnificent Gothic cathedrals of Rheims and Strasbourg he had been struck by something in the atmosphere of the Catholic churches which was different to anything he had known in England. Writing to his sister from Strasbourg at that time, he described how he saw peasants with their families and livestock coming and going in the cathedral, children coming to light candles at the shrine of their favourite saint, fashionable ladies and ragged beggars all very much at home. It was all less orderly and respectable than an English cathedral but nonetheless it was more alive. Fr George Tyrrell described a similar circumstance at the time of his conversion when he found himself in the dark crypt of the London church of St Ethelreda's, Ely Place:

> Amidst the smell of a dirty Irish crowd .... here was continuity, that took one back to the catacombs; here was no need of, and therefore no suspicion of, pose or theatrical parade; its aesthetic blemishes were its very beauties for me in that mood.[6]

Above all, a visit to Rome during the Easter vacation of 1909, when he was 19, came 'as a revelation' to him and opened his eyes 'to a whole new world of religion and culture', for he discovered that contemporary with English Protestant development the Counter-Reformation had produced 'the wonderful flowering of the Baroque culture.'[7] He realised that Italian Catholicism could be as much of a hindrance as a help in attracting English converts: Newman, himself, on his Mediterranean journey was:

> At once attracted and repelled by the spectacle of a Christianity so unlike that which he had known. In comparison with the sobriety of Anglican worship the highly coloured piety of the Catholic south struck him as half pagan and half Methodist.[8]

Ronald Knox had also visited Rome in his Anglican days and according to his biographer, Evelyn Waugh, was 'unimpressed by the Baroque or Papal magnificence, and complained in his letters home of the difficulty of procuring *Punch*';[9] later, as a Catholic priest, he liked it even less and made the often-quoted remark: 'If you are a bad sailor stay away from the engine room.'

Not only was there this foreign and un-English quality about the Roman Catholic Church but Italy itself was viewed with deep suspicion by travellers from Northern Europe: the ornate churches, the bejewelled statues, the processions which seemed more like carnivals, the papal magnificence, all spoke of the corruption which they believed to be in the heart of the Church of Rome – 'her corruption so manifest',[10] as Newman had written before his conversion – while the dirt and squalor of the Roman streets and the poverty of the inhabitants seemed only another aspect of the same thing.

Christopher had been invited by Edward Watkin to join a party organised by his mother to visit Rome during Holy

Week and Easter. The other member of the party was a cousin, a clergyman's widow of strong Protestant allegiance who showed her disgust at the grim pictures of tortured martyrs in San Stefano Rotondo. In Rome they were joined by a priest friend of Edward Watkin's, one Fr Carter, who was useful as a guide and in organising a Papal audience at the Vatican. He was deeply shocked when he heard that the two undergraduates had spent the eve of their departure in London at the theatre seeing Oscar Wilde's *The Importance of Being Earnest*. Apparently theatre-going in Lent was frowned on by Catholics and Protestants alike.

Rome was full of pilgrims from all over Europe who had come for the Holy Week ceremonies. At this time, during the Pontificate of Pope Pius X, it was altogether a quieter and more orderly place than it had been in the 19th century, when pilgrims often became violent and unruly, fighting their way into the Sistine Chapel and sometimes being trampled underfoot and even crushed to death at the ceremony of the Washing of the Feet on Maundy Thursday.

From the Hotel Royale, near the station and the Baths of Diocletian, Christopher wrote home enthusiastically that Rome had quite fulfilled all his expectations and that it was much less spoilt by modernisation than he had expected. He described the baroque churches – 'all gilt and coloured marble' – and in a later account of his conversion he wrote of this experience:

> To me the art of the Counter Reformation was a pure joy and I loved the churches of Bernini and Borromini no less than the ancient basilicas. And this in turn led me to the literature of the Counter Reformation, and I came to know St. Theresa and St. John of the Cross, compared to whom even the greatest of non-Catholic religious writers seem pale and unreal.[11]

He attended the Holy Week services in the great Basilicas and an audience with Pope Pius X, when even the clergyman's widow overcame her anti-Catholic prejudices and joined the rest of the party for the occasion. He also wrote of expeditions into the *Campagna* – to the monastery at Grotta Ferrata, to Rocca di Papa in the Alban Hills and to the little baroque church of Domine Quo Vadis on the Appian Way. Rome before the First World War was remarkably unspoilt, and it is hard now to imagine that a traveller could enter the city from the wild and bleak *Campagna* without the endless vista of blocks of flats and factories that we know today.

'Religion is the key of history' Lord Acton had written; and this favourite Actonian dictum was very much in Christopher's mind in Rome at this time. He became aware then of the continuity of history and of how religion was the dynamic power which transformed the dying civilization of Imperial Rome into a new world of Christianity. He remembered particularly visiting the church of the *Ara Coeli*, built on the summit of the Capitol on the site of a former temple of Jupiter, and one of the oldest churches in Rome. It was here, according to an ancient legend, that Augustus, after hearing a Delphic prophecy foretelling the coming of the Saviour, built an altar to the Son of God (the *Ara Primogeniti Dei*), while later, in the time of Gregory the Great, the church was dedicated to the Mother of God. Even the architecture of the interior shows the same link between the two worlds, the one of pagan classical antiquity and the other of Christianity. Classical columns, mosaic pavements and the marble tombs of Roman dignitaries are reminders of that earlier pagan civilization while medieval and Renaissance Rome is represented by the baroque high altar, the great gilded ceiling commemorating the victory of Lepanto and Pinturicchio's frescoes depicting the life of St Bernadino of Siena.

Looking back on that Easter day in 1909 Christopher remembered that he went to visit this church and sat on the steps of the Capitol in the same place where Gibbon had been inspired to write *The Decline and Fall* and it was there that he first conceived the idea of writing a history of culture. An entry in his journal later that year refers to 'a vow made at Easter in the Ara Coeli' and stated that he had since 'had great light on the way it may be carried out. However unfit I may be (he wrote) I believe it is God's will I should attempt it.' Gibbon himself would probably have thought it strange that a future Catholic historian should have drawn such inspiration from his work, nor could he have realised the immense influence *The Decline and Fall* would have on historical writing long after his death. At that time Christopher's admiration for Gibbon was only matched by his enthusiasm for St Augustine and his *City of God*. On the subject of the inspiration of historians one can compare Arnold Toynbee's own description in his *History of*

Civilization of how the synoptic view of history first unfolded itself to him physically before his eyes as he contemplated the plain of Sparta from the summit of Mistra on 23 May 1912.[12]

Rome had given Christopher a goal to work for but it had not yet changed his religion. He wrote that even after his first visit to Rome he was 'still far from conversion' and claimed that he 'lived on the outside of Catholicism' subsisting on its ideals in a half-hearted way with no intellectual conviction.

As I have said earlier, Edward Watkin was his first Catholic friend, and undoubtedly the most influential, and through him he came to know other Catholics and a few priests. Chief of these was Fr Francis Burdett, then a Jesuit scholastic (or student), who combined intellectual brilliance with great personal holiness. He was a mystic who in his youth looked like an Edwardian aesthete while later in life he resembled an 18th century French abbé, with a flowing mane of white hair. He had in common with Christopher his learning, the originality of his mind, and his fastidiousness. Fr D'Arcy, who was a contemporary in the Jesuit order, remembered with what horror Burdett spoke of the novitiate he had been at in Ireland, where the food he said was unspeakable and the fleas were even worse!

At the Newman Society (the Oxford Catholic society for undergraduates) Christopher heard Wilfrid Ward (Newman's biographer) speak on the circumstances in which Newman wrote the *Apologia Pro Vita Sua* – it was about this time that he first became interested in the Oxford Movement and the *Apologia* particularly had a considerable influence on his own conversion.

Finally, there was the influence of his future wife, who was also a Catholic. In the summer of 1909, he had met Valery Mills, then eighteen, at a party given by the Camerons in their house on Folly Bridge (which overlooked the college barges and the fatal towpath, where Beerbohm's heroine Zuleika Dobson threw herself into the Isis). It was no accident of fate that they had met, for Mr Cameron had noticed Christopher gazing with admiration at a photograph of the daughter of a friend dressed as Joan of Arc for a pageant, and being an inveterate matchmaker, he was determined to arrange a meeting. When Christopher saw Valery and discovered that she was more beautiful in real life than in the photograph, he fell immediately and hopelessly in love.

Four years later, when they became engaged to be married, he wrote to her 'I loved you before I knew you ....' and this was true, because first he loved her photograph (of which he somehow obtained a copy) and then he loved her from the fleeting glimpse, the chance encounter or the short and formal conversation at an 'At Home' or tea party. This may sound unenterprising but it has to be remembered that given the social customs of the time and the fact that Oxford was almost entirely a male enclave, it was extremely difficult to meet a girl, except at formal occasions when a chaperone was always present. Before a young man could present himself as a suitor, he had to be in a position to propose marriage, and Christopher, being only nineteen, and with no financial independence, had no immediate prospects of doing this.

Valery (spelt as in the French, St Valery) was the youngest daughter of Mrs Walter Mills, then living in Oxford and recently bereaved. On the death of her husband, an architect, she had been left with three daughters to provide for on only £500 per annum, and therefore Valery had little or no money of her own. On the occasion of their first meeting, Mr Cameron was heard to say 'poor Christopher' when he saw the effect of his introduction, for knowing Christopher's mother and her ecclesiastical background, he could foresee trouble ahead if he were to marry a Catholic. And indeed this was so, for both his engagement and his conversion to the Catholic faith took place in the same year (1913) and caused a considerable family upheaval. But this was still some way off. Until he left Oxford, Christopher kept his love for Valery a secret from everyone except Edward Watkin, to whom he showed the Joan of Arc photograph when dining at Buol's restaurant one evening. It was a romantic attachment but love and courtship were never so romanticised and idealised since the ages of chivalry than they were in the years before the First World War before the arrival of the Bloomsbury cult, the Jazz age and the sexual revolution.

A GREAT FRIENDSHIP

In his last year at Oxford, Christopher shared lodgings with Edward Watkin who was then in his fourth and final year. It

was then that they came to know each other well and through
Edward Watkin's diary, which has survived, the scene comes
to life in a record of their conversations which often went on far
into the night, as undergraduate conversations are wont to do.
It shows their intense shared feeling for the beauty of nature,
whether it was in the Oxfordshire countryside or the wild hills
of Yorkshire, and that sympathy of ideas which was the true
foundation of a friendship which lasted a lifetime. Not that
they always agreed. Just as at Bletsoe, discussion often ended
in argument and tempers rose high, but as Edward Watkin
wrote on one such occasion:

> However, good came out of evil .... as I discovered that Chris-
> topher's mild language and outward impassivity about such
> matters is but a reserve hiding very deep feelings. I wish I could
> understand reserved people but I never can.[13]

This was true and it is the key to Christopher's lonely
personality: his solitary but happy childhood and his unhappy
schooldays, when he could not feel himself one of the herd,
produced this appearance of reserve and introversion. But at
the same time he evidently felt an intense need for friendship
and communication which on the whole he found difficult to
achieve.

Another entry in Edward's diary, for 25th January 1911,
reads:

> I had a long talk after dinner with Christopher on religion in its
> relation to natural beauty, art etc. He believed in the reconciliation
> of the religious life with secular ideals and beauty by clinging to
> both. I really got to know him better than ever before.

This humanism, so different in meaning from the word in
the atheistic and materialist sense, became a very important
factor in Christopher's ideas and writings and is nowhere more
evident than in his book *The Making of Europe*.

Both young men, even at this early stage, were seekers of
beauty, truth and knowledge with little or no interest in
worldly achievements and possessions. Their conversations
ranged round discussions on the nature of love, aesthetics,
books and religion, but this is not to say that being youthful
and human they could not descend from the sublime to the
ridiculous. After a long discussion they had about love which

took place during a visit to Christopher's home in 1911, Edward Watkin wrote:

> We agreed that it (mutual attraction) had been a matter very much neglected by thinkers. Plato and Schopenhauer alone seem to have dealt with it. We were reluctantly obliged, I at least was most reluctant to admit that the basis of love was always physical.

Then the discussion ended very lightly:

> When at dawn, I mean at 2.45 a.m., we went up to bed we were joking, talking nonsense and roaring with laughter. Christopher cleverly imitated an Italian bravo. If anyone else had heard our inane laughter and conversation at that hour of the night or rather day, he must have thought we were a pair of maniacs. I got to bed when the clocks were striking 3 and the cocks and birds beginning their concert.

At Oxford, on 1st May, they were up at dawn (4.45 a.m.) to hear the traditional madrigals sung from Magdalen Tower, but this did not deter them from talking until past midnight. Edward Watkin wrote:

> After dinner instead of working I talked for hours to Christopher. He thought our age was one of earnest scepticism and great change, that from 1870 to the Boer War one of frivolity and unreality, that before 1870 one of puritanical earnestness. We discussed the morality of the cultivation of aesthetic sensibility. I think it is excellent if disciplined by moral purpose in life. After all beauty is a great and eternal reality. We talked about our old Bletsoe days and recalled the craze for aesthetic impressions which followed the reading of Pater's *Marius*.

But life at Oxford was not all high seriousness and earnest conversation. Christopher in his own journal mentions visits to the theatre, a weekly dinner at Buol's restaurant with Edward Watkin and other friends, and expeditions to the surrounding countryside. Oxford in the early years of this century was still an academic city and anyone who knew it before it had been commercialised and ringed round by a complex of arterial roads and industrialised suburbs, as it is today, was fortunate. Although, as I have already said, Oxford like Winchester meant little to Christopher educationally, as a place it meant a great deal to him and he kept these memories all his life – not only of the ancient college buildings, the gardens, the meadows and the rivers but of the country which Matthew

Arnold described in *The Scholar Gipsy* and *Thyrsis*, and the Binsey Poplars celebrated in Gerard Manley Hopkins's poem of that name. He also recalled expeditions with Edward Watkin further afield to the White Horse at Uffington on the Berkshire downs and the ruined abbey of Minster Lovell, in the Windrush valley, with historical associations of Richard III's reign. Years later on my first visit to Oxford when I was fourteen or so, my father introduced me to his well-loved haunts and I too became enamoured of the place and made it my ambition from that time on to go to Oxford University, which I eventually did.

At the end of the summer term in 1911, Christopher and Edward left Oxford having taken their final examinations, and Edward Watkin spent some weeks in August staying with Christopher at Hartlington while waiting to hear the results. It was one of many visits there and he wrote in his diary: 'It was delightful to see the green hills of Yorkshire again. This scenery which originally I thought too bleak I delight in more and more.' He described his oak-panelled and tapestried room (which was later converted into a chapel):

> I love that room. It has an outlook across the wooded valley and stream to the grass clad hill beyond studded with a few trees. Above the fireplace is a plaque of the Madonna and Child and below this is a little crucifix. The general sense of the room is utter calmness and not untouched with a religious solemnity .... the more I see of the Dawsons and their house, the more delightful they are. The house is full of books of all sorts of kinds, including a collection of mystical and other theological books worthy of a monastery. The whole family love books and are definitely Christian to a degree rare today. Oh that they were also Catholics.

The two friends spent their days walking and rock-climbing in the hills – a favourite place was 'the earthly paradise', so christened by Edward Watkin. It was a grassy plateau above a wood, covered with rocks and wild roses and on the hill above was the site of an ancient British village.

In the evenings they often went out on to the terrace outside the house to look at the night sky, for astrology was one of Col Dawson's interests. On a certain night in August 1911 two bright planets appeared close together. He said that this conjunction of Mars (war) and Saturn (pestilence) in Aries signified war followed by pestilence for Britain, France,

Germany and Russia, and this prediction in broad terms of course came true.

Edward Watkin liked to talk with Christopher's father who enjoyed recounting his adventures in South America. He had said that Ecuador took one back to the Middle Ages in its isolation from the world. Emeralds and other precious stones abounded and he remembered an Archbishop who went about with huge emeralds in his hat! Col Dawson, however, had no truck with the anti-clericals of his day.

Eventually the moment arrived when they expected to hear the results of their Finals and, perhaps to relieve the strain, they took their lunch up the river valley to a deserted lead mine. High on the hills in this lonely place they discussed the modern age and Christopher 'was eager for some practical scheme for reform, for some new society or colony to be a nucleus of the better life.'

When they returned they found telegrams with the news of their examination results. Edward Watkin had got a First Class Honours degree, one of the highest in his year as he later heard, while Christopher had got a Second in history. That he failed to achieve a First was not particularly surprising, least of all to himself, for he used his time at Oxford in pursuing knowledge for its own sake and not for the purpose of an academic career.

For himself he had never aspired to the life of an Oxford don and certainly the social and administrative side of university life held no attractions for him. From one aspect the career of a Fellow of an Oxford college might seem to have its allurements – a life of academic peace away from the dusty arena – and to converts such as Newman and Ronald Knox the necessity of giving up their Fellowships was a terrible sacrifice. But from another point of view such a career could seem more like a life-sentence. It had been part of the old Oxford tradition that a young man who was elected to a Fellowship after taking his degree was there for life, in some ways as if he had taken monastic vows, although the former rule of celibacy had now been discontinued. There was also the monotony of High Table conversation in Hall and Senior Common Room politics. Arnold Toynbee, who was contemporary with Christopher at Oxford, said that he had similar feelings, particularly when in Balliol Hall, he looked at the High Table and saw the monolithic figure of the Master, at that time Strachan-

Davidson, who had spent a life-time in the college, and he mentally rejected the prospect of a similar fate.

A SENSE OF VOCATION

Christopher had always had literary ambitions, but it was at Oxford that he started writing systematically. In his 'teens he had written poetry – a hymn to St John of the Cross at the age of fifteen, an epitaph on the death of a child, and several others in following years. He had started his journal with the object of learning to express himself but at first this did not come easily as he admitted: 'As regards writing I find the greatest difficulty in expressing my simplest thoughts and feelings' and he came to the conclusion that it was better to stick to facts.

His earliest prose writing was an essay on that most neglected of all literary subjects – *Early Welsh Literature* – written in 1909. It was partly a work of collaboration with his mother, who first gave him the interest in the subject and translated the poems quoted from the original Welsh. It was not written for publication (as far as I know) but there is a foreshadowing of the ideas he later expressed in his book *The Making of Europe*. He described how this strange and barbaric poetry produced a new spirit which replaced the Hellenism of the past:

> In the mountain refuges of a defeated people, in the cells and hermitages that covered the coast of the Atlantic and the Irish channel, medieval civilization had its first spiritual birth.

An essay on mysticism, also unpublished, written about the same time, was his first attempt in the field of spirituality and it demonstrates already his great interest in and wide grasp of this subject. Here he made the point that mysticism was at the heart of all *natural* religion and it was common to all ages and faiths. He saw it as a power to perceive through the barrier of the material world to the spiritual reality which lay beyond. He wrote:

> There is no essential difference between the mysticism of the medieval Germans, of the early Christians of Syria and Egypt, of the Sufis of Persia and of the ascetics of India and the Far East.

And again:

> Mysticism is simply Natural Theology translated from the bare knowledge of the Reason, to the living experience of the Spirit and the Emotions.

During his time at Oxford, Christopher developed a clear idea of becoming a historian and from the time of his visit to Rome his ambition was to write a history of culture: nothing was going to deflect him from this aim but without money and the encouragement of his parents it was hard to make a start.

For his parents had very different ambitions for him and would have liked to have seen him follow a profession such as the Church or politics. All his mother's family were Anglican churchmen, and she therefore would have liked to have seen her son follow in the same path, but this was impossible because of his uncertain allegiances, although he could not explain this to his parents. A political career was a completely misguided idea for Christopher with his shy and unassuming manner and lack of physical stamina. However, out of filial duty and against all his own instincts, he agreed to give politics a try.

But first, on leaving Oxford, he spent a few months in Sweden in the autumn of 1911, staying with the economist, Prof Gustav Cassell, who was a friend of his former tutor, Sir Henry Penson. As he explained later in a letter to an American correspondent, he did not go there to study economics as was supposed. He was only there for a short time and not even long enough to learn Swedish properly.

In the spring of 1912 he was offered and accepted the post of unpaid private secretary to Mr Steel-Maitland, a Conservative Member of Parliament who was interested in agricultural policy. The post had been found for him by his great-uncle William Dawson who took a keen interest in Christopher's career. The work was in the Research Department of the Conservative Central Office and consisted in looking up political cases to give a basis for questions in the House, as Christopher described it. He found neither the work nor London life congenial and he must have led a lonely existence living in lodgings in Robert Adam Street off Manchester Square and eating in an Italian restaurant in Baker Street. Edward Watkin recalled seeing Christopher at this time. They went together to Loughton in Essex to visit the aforementioned uncle, the great collector of books. They talked and walked in Epping Forest. Edward Watkin wrote:

> I found Christopher's tendencies of thought more pronounceably orthodox than ever. I hope he may yet be a Catholic. He is full of mysticism and history. He is also eager for apologetic work. He is

now busy with an essay on the religious significance of history. He finds in revelation the necessary key to the interpretation of history. He ought to do splendid work on these lines.

They also discussed mysticism and the vocation of Francis Burdett with the Carthusians at Parkminster. Ernest Barker had written to Christopher about this step: 'It is somewhat terrible to think of Burdett entering an eternal silence today, but each man to his last!' Christopher, as Edward Watkin remembered 'thought that those called to mystical love will never feel a pure human love to tempt them from it.' He added 'Query. I mean is this so or no? I'm not sure.'

Christopher had written in a letter to his friend that he loathed London and found his only consolation in country walks and in the study of Huysmans's mysticism. In July he summoned the courage to tell his father that he had decided to end his work at the close of the parliamentary session. 'It is an experiment which I have been glad to make,' he wrote, 'but I think it would be a mistake to prolong it after I have found I am not suited to it.' His father responded by suggesting that he should take a post-graduate course in Agricultural Economics at the school of Rural Economy in Oxford; he had already given him a tenanted farm, Woodhouse Manor, near Hartlington, when he came of age, and he thought he should know something about the management side of farming. Christopher also agreed to this plan and followed the course half-heartedly while giving all his spare time to the study of religion and history.

CHAPTER FOUR

Love and Conversion

ENGAGEMENT

While Christopher had been in Sweden and in London, Valery Mills had been spending the time in Italy with her mother and elder sister. Mrs Mills found that on her small income they could live far more comfortably and pleasantly abroad than in genteel poverty in North Oxford. During the winter of 1912 they were living in a pension in Florence enjoying the life of English expatriates that E. M. Forster described so well in his novel *A Room with a View*. They acquired a circle of friends and were never without company to share the many social activities that Florence provided. Valery had singing lessons there; she had a fine soprano voice and was often asked to sing at private concerts and sometimes in churches. Her teacher would have liked her to train as an opera singer, but that was considered quite out of the question for a young lady. She also finished her education by studying Italian art and architecture, and she spent many hours in the Florentine galleries which she came to know intimately. Tall, slim and dark, Valery was unquestionably beautiful and while she was neither intellectual nor learned she shared Christopher's interests in history and antiquities.

From the outset, although she had several other admirers, Valery was fascinated by the shy young man she had first met at the Cameron's party; she called him the 'walking encyclopaedia' for he seemed to have every subject at his finger-tips. But she had no idea in these early days that she would ultimately marry him. She admitted that she was caught up in the whirl of Oxford society, and thought only of dances, parties and flirtations. But she knew he was in love with her and later when she was separated from him in Italy, she began to think more seriously about him.

It was on a visit to Rome, as she said later, that she

experienced a change of heart, what might be described as a spiritual experience when she had an audience with Pope St Pius X. The occasion was described by her mother in detail in a diary she kept at the time; the drive to the Vatican in a carriage and pair, the great audience chamber with a crimson carpet and silk walls to match and white silk curtains. She wrote:

> When the Holy Father entered the room we felt to be in the presence of a saint, his expression is wonderful, never to be forgotten. He looked earnestly at each one when he gave his hand to be kissed and his eyes seemed to search one's heart. I was able to ask in French for his special blessing on my family and he seemed to speak and gently inclined his head; he looked twice at Valery, the second time when he stood at the end of the room and gave his blessing to all of us and to our families.

Valery never forgot how the Pope looked at her and it was then she knew that there was something she must do to change her life.

When she returned to Oxford in the summer of 1913 Christopher proposed to her and she no longer had any hesitation about accepting him, although both sides of the family were against the match, Valery's mother on the grounds of health, because she thought that Christopher looked too delicate to survive for long and the Dawsons on the grounds of Valery's Catholic faith. Col Dawson had no objection since he was close to the Catholic Church himself, but his wife and all her relations were strongly anti-Catholic and felt that to marry outside the Anglican church was an act of desertion. His grandmother Dawson, herself an arch-Protestant, could not even be told of the engagement (she was then of a great age) in case she should change her will, and even Christopher's sister, although an Anglo-Catholic, was full of 'anti-Roman' prejudices. Mrs Mills knew no such bigotry, for while she was a 'born Catholic' as the expression goes, she herself had married a Protestant and run the full gamut of her family's disfavour. She remembered the time when her relations sent their sons to be educated abroad at Douai, when the Catholic priest was stoned in the streets of Banbury, and when her grandfather travelled every year to Rome by carriage to spend the season of Lent and Easter there. But even these Catholics could not understand the fuss that was being made by Christopher's family over the prospect of a 'mixed marriage'. One elderly cousin remarked: 'It is not as if he was going to marry a chorus girl!'

Valery, too, at the beginning, had some reservations about marrying a non-Catholic for Christopher had not yet decided to take the final step and change his allegiance – that was a blow yet to come for his family. But he managed to calm her misgivings in a letter written a few days before they became engaged: he said it was not as though he was in any real sense of the word a Protestant. He had been brought up in Catholic doctrine, though not in the Roman Catholic Church. All his greatest friends had been Catholics and for his spiritual reading he had relied entirely on Catholic books. He wrote:

> Surely, if you believe the Catholic Church to be the one true church you cannot think that God's grace would bring us so far and no further. The way of the intellect is always difficult even for men within the Church but it is always safe to trust that God will do his part.

Finally, on 11th July 1913, they became engaged and Christopher marked the occasion by giving his fiancée a copy of *Aucassin and Nicolette*, a tale of courtly love in the time of the troubadours. Everything was still very formal and correct; up till now they had not even been on Christian name terms, nor had they ever corresponded. But now Christopher wrote to his 'dearest Valery' every day he was separated from her during their long engagement (as it turned out to be) and she wrote back to him. (There are upwards of 200 letters in existence over a period of three years). All during his life, on the rare occasions when they were separated from one another, he wrote to his wife every day. Of necessity it seemed that their engagement would be long for Christopher was still not settled in a career, and then the completely unforeseen outbreak of war in 1914 dashed all his hopes of starting to write. It seemed also as if their respective families were almost counting on a long engagement in the hope that it might come to nothing. His uncle, the Rev William Dawson had much to say both about his career and his engagement:

> I believe hard strenuous work would benefit you immensely. But then it must be work to your taste and that you really love. Fyfe of Merton, whom I think you know, might advise you as to literary

work which I think would be more suitable for you than any other though I suppose it is not too late for you to take up professional work such as e.g. a barrister or in some branch of the Civil Service.

You have in Miss Mills and your attachment to her a spur to exertion which I trust will enable you to leap over all difficulties in the way of earning what may be needful. May I say that I was *charmed* with her? Of course I regret deeply that she is not of our faith not so much for your sake as because of the abominable requirements of the Roman Curia that the children of mixed marriages must be brought up R.C.s. This will be a blow to the cause of the Church in Burnsall and Settle and indeed in the West Riding generally. But no doubt you thought over all this before you made your choice and are alive to any inconvenience it may bring you and which your true affection for one who seems to me to be quite worthy of your deepest love will smooth over. I trust it may be so and that you will soon find congenial work which will enable you, not perhaps at once but after a few years, to make her your wife. Jacob waited seven years for Rachel – I am sure Miss Mills is worth the same patient waiting.

(1913)

CONVERSION

About the autumn of 1913, Christopher made his decision to 'go over to Rome' in the current phrase of the day. Personal reasons, even the influence of his future wife, counted for little in his conversion in comparison with intellectual and historical ones.

In one of his last Harvard Lectures, Christopher Dawson described the circumstances of Newman's conversion, and one is struck by the similarity to his own spiritual struggle and the same historical approach.

When Newman was brought face to face with the necessity for a decision he found this 'exceedingly hard to make and it took him four years of agonizing intellectual and moral examination to sever the links that bound him so closely to the Church of England and the University of Oxford.' Christopher had much the same problem: he felt strongly bound to his family affiliations and his Anglican past and he took at least two years to make up his mind to take this irrevocable step.

Again of Newman, Christopher wrote: 'No convert has ever made a more careful and conscientious approach to Catholicism, testing every step, weighing every alternative and con-

sidering every objection.' During the two years since he had
left Oxford, and indeed before that, Christopher had made an
intensive study of the Bible, the Fathers of the Church –
Athanasius, Irenaeus, Cyprian and Augustine – as well as
Newman's *Apologia* and the Oxford Movement. Like Newman his approach to Catholicism was through history. 'The
Fathers made me a Catholic' Newman once wrote in a letter to
Pusey; and on another occasion he wrote: 'To be deep in
history is to cease to be a Protestant.' By this he meant, as
Christopher explained from Newman's *Essay on Development*, that the cumulative evidence of the Christian past led
him to a full acceptance of the Catholic present:

> There were but two paths – the way of faith and the way of
> unbelief, and as the latter led through the halfway house of Liber-
> alism to Atheism, the former led through the half way house of
> Anglicanism to Catholicism.[1]

Ironically, in Christopher's case, it was the writings of a
Protestant 19th century German theologian, Adolf Harnack,
which finally convinced him that it was the Church of Rome
which alone held the true faith in an unbroken tradition from
the Apostles. He once said:

> Harnack, a liberal Protestant, never knew how much he con-
> tributed to the process of my conversion to the Catholic Church!
> He had never heard of me, of course, but I wonder if it ever
> occurred to him that he might have helped anyone along that
> particular road.[2]

In volume VII of his *History of Dogma*, Harnack dealt with
Luther's criticism of dogma, and he made it clear at the outset
that Luther attacked the whole Catholic (not only the
medieval) ideal of Christian perfection and so made the breach
with the Christian past which was finally sealed with the
Reformation. From the Oxford Movement onwards, men like
Hurrell Froude and the Tractarians and Anglo-Catholics who
were basically anti-Roman in sympathy, were all violently
opposed to the Protestant reformation: Froude, in a letter to
Newman wrote:

> I never mean if I can help it to use any phrases even, which can
> connect me with such a set (i.e. the reformers). I shall never call the
> Holy Eucharist 'the Lord's supper', nor God's priests 'Ministers
> of the Word,' nor the Altar 'the Lord's Table,' etc., etc.[3]

Christopher Dawson never changed his views on Luther's reformation even though he lived to see his fellow Catholics take a completely new line on the subject. This is not to say that he did not think that there should have been a reformation. As a historian, fully aware of the corruption of the Church in the later Middle Ages, he could not have thought otherwise. He explained his views at length in his last Harvard Lectures in the most broad-minded way before an audience of mainly Baptist ministers and showed that there were two movements in the Reformation, the first was one of religious reform represented by Erasmus and More and Pole and the other was one of religious revolution, anti-Humanist in character, represented by Luther and Calvin and Munzer, who broke with the whole Catholic tradition and did their best to destroy the Church and the sacraments. As he described the Protestant Reformation in an earlier writing:

> It was a classic example of emptying out the baby with the bath. The reformers revolted against the externalism of medieval religion, and so they abolished the Mass. They protested against the lack of personal holiness, and so they abolished the saints. They attacked the wealth and self-indulgence of the monks and they abolished monasticism and the life of voluntary poverty and asceticism. They had no intention of abandoning the ideal of Christian perfection, but they sought to realise it in Puritanism instead of Monasticism and in pietism instead of mysticism.[4]

But historical and intellectual reasons apart, it was the enlightenment he received through the Bible that finally convinced him of the truth of the Catholic Church. This he explained in an article on his religious development written in 1926:

> It was by the study of St Paul and St John that I first came to understand the fundamental unity of Catholic theology and the Catholic life. I realised that the Incarnation, the sacraments, the external order of the Church and the internal work of sanctifying grace, were all parts of one organic unity, a living tree whose roots are in the Divine nature and whose fruit is the perfection of the saints .... This fundamental doctrine of sanctifying grace, as revealed in the New Testament and explained by St Augustine and St Thomas in all of its connotations, removed all my difficulties and uncertainties and carried complete conviction to my mind.[5]

But it was still not easy for him to leave the Anglican Church. There were ties of sentiment and friendship. Above all he knew that his mother would be deeply affected by his change of religion and she was in fact never reconciled to it. His father had no such feelings, but he had a strange and inconsistent reaction when he told Christopher on hearing of his decision that 'no man has the right to leave the church to which his fathers belonged.' In this, as Christopher observed, 'he was more Roman than Catholic' and had a kind of hereditary 'political' loyalty to the Church of England.[6] Nevertheless, he had strong personal leanings towards the Catholic Church – when he was abroad he always attended Catholic churches and he habitually read Catholic books on mysticism and the lives of the saints. This was partly, Christopher said, a reaction against his mother's extreme Protestantism in which he had been brought up. Christopher knew that his sister, who was a devout Anglo-Catholic, would find it hard to understand or accept his reasons for joining the Roman Church, and indeed this caused a rift between them so that the close relationship of their early years was never quite restored.

It was then a rule in the Roman Catholic Church that a prospective convert should have a lengthy and thorough series of instructions before his reception. The priest, to whom Christopher went for instruction, Fr Considine, a well-known Jesuit of that time, found that he had never had so learned a convert and settled for two instructions only. Christopher was received at St Aloysius Church in Oxford, by Fr O'Hare, SJ, on the eve of the Feast of the Epiphany, 5th January 1914, Edward Watkin standing as sponsor.

OUTBREAK OF WAR

Later in January 1914, Christopher joined his fiancée and her mother at Florence where they were spending the winter. He had been in a state of mental conflict over his change of religion, and that combined with the effect of family disapproval had brought him to the brink of a nervous breakdown. Valery's mother, too, had not yet reconciled herself to their engagement; she referred to him as 'that poor young man' and thought that her daughter would be throwing herself away on an invalid with no apparent future.

It was the worst winter that Florence had known since 1876

and the icy *tramontana* from the Appenines brought snow and later floods to the surrounding countryside. In Florence they were in a cold hotel, with marble floors, and workmen adding to the general discomfort, but after a move to the Hotel Aurora, at Fiesole, which lies on a sunny hillside overlooking Florence spread out like a map below, the situation became brighter. Christopher spent three happy months with Valery, enjoying the Tuscan landscape, getting to know the art and architecture of Florence and studying the history of medieval and Renaissance Italy. He re-read Dante in its authentic setting, and for the first time read Berenson's books on the Italian painters.

All too soon this idyllic time came to an end and for Christopher, though he could not be aware of this fact, it was the last time he would go abroad for many years. At Oxford that summer everything was going on as usual with all the gaiety of Eights' Week and the Commemoration Balls and few people had the slightest inkling that this pre-war golden age was soon to pass away for ever. But Arnold Toynbee remembered when he was travelling in the Balkan peninsular in the summer of 1914 how all the peasants were talking about the war that was about to break out in Europe, though in England there was no mention of it. Even when war was declared, it was generally thought that it would be over before the end of the year.

Christopher with his short-sight, weak chest and generally poor physique was unfit for military service, and when he presented himself at Cowley Barracks for the army medical examination he was classed as Grade III. According to Valery, what he had dreaded most was not being sent to the trenches but being allocated to administrative office work in the army. He was never a pacifist like his friend Edward Watkin, who became a conscientious objector, but while he was intensely patriotic (in both world wars) he would nevertheless have found life in the services extremely uncongenial.

The outbreak of war not only brought his hopes of starting to write to an end, but postponed any hopes he had of an early marriage. For the time being he took a teaching post in the Franciscan school at Cowley, which was classed as war-work, and went into what Fr D'Arcy described as 'an eremitical existence somewhere in the Cowley Road'. He rented a workman's cottage there and as it happened at the bottom of the garden there was a bicycle shop owned by a Mr Morris. This was none other than the future Lord Nuffield who was later to build his motor car empire at Cowley.

It was a lonely time for him, in those first years of the war. Valery was living at Chipping Campden in Gloucestershire, where her mother had rented a house, and they were therefore separated for long intervals. Edward Watkin was already married and was living at Sheringham in Norfolk, and his other friends had already enlisted for active service. From now on and for many years to come Christopher devoted all his free time to intensive study – which he later described as 'fourteen years of isolated study' before he began to write his books; they were years in the wilderness, perhaps, but the time was spent in storing away knowledge that was to bear fruit in due time.

CHAPTER FIVE

Early Married Life

A WAR-TIME WEDDING

In 1916, the year of the battles of Verdun and the Somme, when the war was at its fiercest, Christopher and Valery decided to postpone their wedding no longer, even though he had no settled occupation and they did not have a house to live in. Sir William Osler, a famous physician of that time, had declared that Christopher would never be fit for a full-time occupation or a professional career and his father agreed to give him a modest income which would enable him to get married. Early in life, he seemed to have accepted the role of an invalid, 'a providential ill-health', as Gibbon wrote of himself, which, fortunately for Christopher, created the situation in which he was able to write his books.

Looking back one can see how destiny shaped his life and career. Had he not been content to live the quiet and seques-tered life of a scholar, 'ploughing a lonely furrow', as he once put it, he would never have been able to achieve his great work, that unique study of history and religion to which he devoted a lifetime.

His marriage too was linked with that destiny, for only with the love and devotion of a wife such as Valery could he have supported the lonely life of a freelance scholar and writer. In fact, it was a harder life for her than for him. For while she was completely devoted to him and his work, she was not mentally equipped to share the intellectual side of it with him. For most of her married life she was deprived also of the social life to which she was naturally inclined and it was only when they were in America late in life that she was able to share the social side of his academic life at Harvard and their travels together when he lectured in different parts of the United States. Then people commented on her exuberance and evident enjoyment of social occasions, not realising of how much of this she had been deprived during forty years of married life.

Christopher and Valery were married at the Catholic Church in Chipping Campden, Gloucestershire, on 9th August 1916, the feast-day of the Curé d'Ars. Apart from the fact that Christopher had a particular devotion to this saintly French priest, the next day, 10th August, happened to be the feast of St Lawrence, and Valery remembered that her maternal grandfather had once said: 'I was married on the feast of St Lawrence and I have been on the grid-iron ever since!' It was therefore a day to be avoided.

A report of the wedding in the *Craven Herald* described it as:

> A very quiet one, only nearest relatives and a few friends being present.... The bride's dress was of pale grey crêpe de chine with transparent sleeves of ninon and a bunch of silver roses at the waist, with a hat of grey georgette to match, trimmed with white ospreys.

The celebrant was Valery's uncle, Fr James Perry, then chaplain to Lord Camoys at Stonor Park, where he lived a life of extreme solitude. Immensely learned and an amusing conversationalist, he was completely wasted in such a place but was reputed to have fallen out with the bishop of his diocese (who happened to be the son of Fr Perry's uncle's footman!) Christopher's mother was in tears throughout the wedding service – it must have been the only time she ever set foot inside a Catholic church – but Fr Perry succeeded in making her laugh at the reception which followed. This was at Woolstapler's Hall in Chipping Campden, a medieval building (now a museum) which was then Valery's home. The honeymoon was spent at Kemerton in Worcestershire at a house lent by some friends.

Christopher and Valery's first house was at Boars Hill, near Oxford, but they were not there for long before they moved to London. For the last year of the war, Christopher worked for the Admiralty Intelligence Department at Hertford House (which now houses the Wallace Collection) in a section dealing with history and ethnology. Valery did voluntary work for the Catholic Women's League (then run by Mrs Virginia Crawford, Cardinal Manning's famous convert) consisting of send-

ing parcels to the front or writing letters to the bereaved
relations of soldiers killed in action.

At night, in their room in lodgings in Manchester Square,
they listened to the Zeppelins groaning overhead, and Valery
remembered how she shook with fear. Just as poison gas
attacks in the trenches were a complete innovation in wartime
tactics, so aerial warfare and bombing was a new and horrible
development not hitherto imaginable.

After the armistice in 1918 Christopher and Valery left
London and returned to Chipping Campden for a short time
while house-hunting. During this time Christopher caught the
dreaded Spanish 'Flu which was sweeping the country. They
were staying at the local inn at the time and the macabre
situation was intensified by the noise of coffins being ham-
mered in the yard outside.

In 1919 they went to live at Tisbury in Wiltshire, not far
from Salisbury, where they rented an old cottage called the
Chantry, which had neither running water nor electricity.
Here their first child, a daughter named Juliana, was born.

They had chosen to live at Tisbury because Christopher's
friend, Fr Burdett, having left the Carthusians, had become
parish priest, a post which was combined with being chaplain
to Lady Arundell of Wardour, a not altogether enviable
position. The dowager Lady Arundell was a dragon built on
the lines of Jane Austen's Lady Catherine de Burgh, but Fr
Burdett was no Mr Collins. Once a week he was summoned to
dinner at Wardour Castle where for years the bill of fare had
been one sardine followed by rice pudding. According to Fr
D'Arcy, Burdett was the only chaplain who dared to confront
Lady Arundell on this score: every time the butler hovered
near his chair, he asked for another helping until he had a
plateful of sardines, and for this the old lady came to respect
him. When, later on, private benefices and lay interference in
church affairs was finally brought to an end, Lady Arundell
refused to comply or even surrender the key of the chapel and
the bishop was forced to excommunicate her.

STARTING TO WRITE

In the Catholic Church, Christopher went his own solitary
way and was not affiliated to any particular group, neither that
of Fr Martindale nor of Chesterton and Belloc, who represented

the two dominant trends in the 1920s. Christopher admired Chesterton's work and also came to know him later. Belloc he preferred as a poet than as a historian, for he considered his views one-sided and unreliable, nor did he feel at home with Belloc's particular brand of triumphant Catholicism.

The immediate post-war years were difficult ones for Christopher. He was still making an intensive study of the civilizations of the world for a five-volume history of culture, which was then his goal, but at the same time he realised the importance of starting to get his work published.

His first publication was a thirty-page essay, written in 1920 and called 'The Nature and Destiny of Man', which he contributed to a symposium entitled *God and the Supernatural* edited by Fr Cuthbert, OFM. The contributors represented almost all the new generation of Catholic writers – Ronald Knox, Fr C. C. Martindale, Fr Martin D'Arcy, E. I. Watkin and Christopher himself – nearly all of them converts. In this essay, as he wrote later, he expressed almost exactly his own approach to the Catholic faith.

He discussed the whole concept of man as a bridge between the spiritual and the material worlds. Spiritualists from Gnostics to Theosophists saw matter as evil, while from Rabelais to Darwin came an emphasis on man as an animal. Even the most primitive societies accepted the conflict of spirit with instinct. Indian thought and Buddhism asserted spirit by a radical rejection of sense and matter. But Christianity was a dynamic force which denied the pantheism and nihilism of the East as much as it rejected the humanism and materialism of the West.

The great dynamic force of the Christian life, said Christopher, was faith, manifested in the mind, and charity or spiritual love, which was man's participation in God's Will. This was the conclusion of the essay:

> In nothing less than this does the destiny of humanity consist, according to the teaching of the Catholic faith. Without losing his own nature, man is brought into an inconceivably close relation with God, so that he lives by the Divine Life, sees God with God's Knowledge, loves God with God's Love, and knows and loves everything else in and through God .... In the Sacraments, in the life of faith, in every act of spiritual will and aspiration of spiritual desire, the work of divine restoration goes ceaselessly forward. In that work is the whole hope of humanity.

The Nature and Destiny of Man was republished later in *Enquiries into Religion and Culture* (Sheed & Ward, 1933). Fr Cuthbert apparently had the habit, common to editors but maddening to aspiring writers, of sitting on manuscripts indefinitely; some years later, when Christopher had offered him another article, subsequently rejected, he wrote to Edward Watkin:

> I hope Paul (i.e. uncle 'Paul' of Belloc's poem) has fled now before the glorious sun we have been having. I think I am going to re-christen that venerable person Uncle Cuthbert, as Fr C. has been such an ally of his lately. After writing I don't know how many letters I eventually got the second copy of my essay back, but still got no letter from Cuthbert himself and no return of the original copy. I don't know what code of moral theology authorises holy friars to stick to mss. that they have not paid for! Perhaps he has lost it but at any rate he might say so.

In another letter of the same era touching on the problems of writers, Christopher advised Edward Watkin to impress on his son, also called Christopher, and now Dom Aelred Watkin, OSB, titular Abbot of Glastonbury and a former headmaster of Downside School, that 'if he wishes to be a man of letters, he must above all things cultivate the sensitiveness of a rhinoceros and the modesty of a gorilla.'

He had better fortune contributing articles to *The Sociological Review*, whose editor was Alexander Farquarson, the founder with Sir Patrick Geddes and Victor Branford of the group known as Le Play House. When asked who were the most important influences on his sociological ideas, Christopher invariably replied, 'Troeltsch and Le Play', one a German sociologist and the other a member of the French school which included Comte, the founder of positivism and inventor of the term sociology.

Troeltsch, who died prematurely in 1923, regarded the religious beliefs of a particular age as relative, but all related to the absolute: 'We cannot live without a religion', he wrote, 'yet the only religion we can endure is Christianity, for Christianity has grown up with us and has become a part of our being.'[1] He had a strong belief in the future of European culture – though secularised, he argued, it remained Christian underneath, as modern ideas were Christian in a modified form.

If Augustine was his chief influence in religion, Le Play had more effect on Christopher's social studies. Le Play, who died in 1882, was an engineer and professor in the School of Mines who made in his great work, *Les Ouvriers Européens*, the first detailed social study of workers from the Russian steppes to the north of England. He analysed social structures in terms of work, place and people. This formula was applied and amplified by the group in charge of *The Sociological Review*. Christopher Dawson was closest to Geddes, a distinguished biologist, and he largely adopted work, place and people as the chief factor in social life. Indeed, he added a fourth, with marked originality, for society was 'also, and above all, a community of thought, and it is seen and known best in its higher spiritual activities to which alone the name of Culture was first applied.'[2] All errors in social studies, Christopher argued, arose from attempts to explain society by one of these factors and to exclude all the others.

The classical example of this was Marxism, centred on Work, as Hegel on Thought, Nazism on People, Materialism on Place.

Against such theories he constantly insisted that the study of real societies, that of Islam or China, the Hellenic cities or medieval Christendom, offered more hope than 'all the Utopias that philosophers and poets have ever dreamed.'

Probably his most important writing of this period was a paper he read to the Sociological Society in 1922 on *The Life of Civilizations*, written before he had read Spengler in which he outlined his own theory of the cycles of civilizations. What he most criticised in Spengler later was his unhistorical treatment of every culture as a closed system, which ignored more frequent contacts and influences. His own plan, shown on a chart published with this essay to cover the course of civilization from 4000 BC to this century, was based on parent-cultures which in their third phase produced younger cultures, and these in turn passed through similar stages of growth, progress and maturity when they in turn gave birth to a new culture:

> The ultimate barriers are not the racial and geographical ones, but those of cultural tradition which are expressed in the contrast of Hellene and Barbarian, of Moslem and unbeliever, and which were seen in their full intensity in China during the European penetration of the last century.[3]

Later when he was writing *The Age of the Gods* he slightly modified his views on the cycles of civilization but in essence the theory was the same. In a letter to Edward Watkin during 1928, Christopher wrote of our own civilization: 'All the events of the last years have convinced me what a fragile thing civilization is, and how near we are to losing the whole inheritance, which our age might have acquired.'

While he criticised *The Decline of the West* for its fatalism, its special pleading and forcing of the facts, he later defended Spengler and Toynbee from general attacks on 'metahistory', because he believed that vision, 'partaking more of the nature of religious contemplation than of scientific generalisation, was a mainspring of creative power in them as it had been in Tocqueville and Ranke.'

CHAPTER SIX

Exeter

UNIVERSITY LECTURER

Christopher's own financial situation needed more to support it than his father's allowance and his literary earnings from articles and reviews, so with one child already born and another on the way, he began to think seriously of finding some regular employment to supplement his inadequate income.

It was through his work for *The Sociological Review* and the influence of its editor, that he found a post as part-time lecturer in the History of Culture at Exeter University, then University College of the South West. Farquarson wrote to the principal, Mr H. J. Hetherington, introducing Christopher as 'one of my most valued colleagues among the group interested in *The Sociological Review* and also a great friend.' He went on to describe him as 'a life-long specialist in historical studies', adding:

> Working closely with him, as I have done, I have had convincing proof of his sound scholarship and remarkable range of knowledge; indeed I do not know anyone who has quite the same clear and broad view of civilization in its historical development.

On the strength of this introduction a post was created for him as lecturer in the History of Culture which entailed giving one lecture a week and a small number of tutorials to specialist pupils. One of these was Mr J. J. Saunders, now Reader in History at the University of Canterbury in New Zealand. He remembers that Norman Sykes, then Professor of History at Exeter, arranged for him and another student to have special tuition from Christopher at Dawlish, where he was living, near Exeter. Mr Saunders writes:

> I still recall the awe with which I gazed at the great shelves of books reaching to the ceiling of a very high room: a tall ladder

reached to the top shelves. On one occasion he broke off with apologies in the middle of his discourse, and asked us to excuse him for a short while as he particularly wished to listen to something on the radio, I think some Beethoven quartets.

Another friend and colleague was Prof Wilkinson, later of the University of Toronto: he and his wife remembered that among all their friends in the college:

> He stood alone in his scholarship, and the depth and breadth of this was obvious; though Christopher was the last man to make any display of it. He was one of the least assuming scholars I have ever met. .... He was the only one, incidentally, who had books three deep on his shelves, and knew where every one was.

He added that he and his colleagues thought Christopher was rather wasted in that 'frontier post of learning' (as it was then) but this never seemed to occur to him.'

For his own part, Christopher took the view expressed in a letter to Edward Watkin that although his lecture audiences had been very poor both in quantity and quality he hoped to make something printable out of the course. He felt that as long as he was really interested in the work himself he could put up with an absence of interest in others. Another time he wrote that his lectures on comparative religion had been attended by half a dozen spinsters and a retired sea-captain and his daughter, but even this did not worry him unduly. The fact was that all the work he was putting into these lectures, and they absorbed the whole of his time, became the nucleus of his three major books, *The Age of the Gods, Progress and Religion* and *The Making of Europe*.

The Dawsons now settled at Dawlish, a seaside town in Torbay sheltered by red sandstone cliffs. The railway from Paddington to Penzance ran along the coast past Dawlish, the station overlooking the beach, and the memory remains of the pungent smell of steam engines and salt sea spray, the sound of the waves crashing on the shingle and the seagulls mewing and wheeling overhead.

The house, called 'Ashley', was on a hill above the town in a private park of Victorian villas built about 1850. The rooms were high and spacious and, before the days of central heating, often cold and draughty with large rattling windows but with ample and necessary book-space. At about the time when the family first moved to Dawlish, Christopher had inherited his uncle's enormous library, which he had to house in addition to the large number of books he had collected himself. Everywhere there were books, upstairs and downstairs – I can remember them all and where they were even to this day. One enormous and remarkable book was displayed open on a large oak chest: this was one of the earliest printed books, *The Decretals of Gratian*, printed at Basle in 1474.

In the winter, Christopher worked in an armchair by the fire, never at a desk – he said he liked to keep his feet warm and his head cool – but more often than not, in that mild Devonshire climate, he worked in a summer house or in a deck chair in a secluded corner of the garden, well away from the interruptions of children. In the 1930s he grew a beard before beards were fashionable except among Bloomsbury intellectuals, and it has often been commented that he bore a marked resemblance to D. H. Lawrence, although he resembled him in nothing else. His writing hours were limited to five hours a day, three in the morning and two in the evening, seldom more nor less but it was intensive work and when he wrote it was fast and furiously as if he was possessed with ideas he could not commit to the page quickly enough.

His methods of work can be seen more exactly from his copious notebooks, which Mr James Oliver, who has studied them in detail, describes as 'simply his finished work in miniature, for they show the same breadth and precision of mind, the same calm and judicious learning.' He started by assembling a list of books usually in four of five languages, then by examining a work by a leading thinker in more detail:

The notes for *Progress and Religion* for instance open with an analysis of Lessing's *Education of the Human Race*. His theory of the Three Ages is set out and some striking quotations are selected. Then Fichte, Schelling, Goerres, and Krause are similarly treated. Sometimes quotes, as from writers on science, Needham or Whitehead, appear more striking from their juxtaposition. Then a few pages of original writing, some unaltered in the final version, show the play of mind over the field of ideas explored, and at moments, as is natural with an historian of ideas, his work rises with a life of its own from the ground of these other works nourished with their substance. Notes have the same style as finished work: clearly phrases have formed in immediate reaction to ideas confronted. If he studied as a thinker, he reacted as a writer in lucidity and elegance of style, just as Gibbon put some of his most polished epigrams into his footnotes.

Where he worked, in study or summer-house, the floor was covered with books open at the relevant page. He said that from twenty books he might produce a page of his own, as Johnson alleged that a man might turn over a library to produce one book. Nor was he so far from Johnson as the contrast in their figures and tempers might suggest: the same firmness of principle, the same awe before mystery, the same authority and even the same alternation of despondency and hope that marked that great man.

His relaxations were listening to classical music on a newly acquired radio (Beethoven and Mozart were his favourite composers – music, he said, helped him to collect his thoughts); talking to his friends, chiefly from Exeter University; and going for long walks along the cliffs or on the sands at low tide. One of his ex-pupils, a scholar in Byzantine studies, George Every, remembers coming over from Exeter in the afternoons to have a short tutorial over tea and a long walk on the cliffs and on one such occasion, he says, Christopher 'expounded the anthropological history of the 5th of November, in defence of his childrens' delight in fireworks.' George Every, who later joined the Anglican community at Kelham, and then in more recent years became a Catholic, was one of his most brilliant pupils, who gained a First in History; he remembers what a painstaking tutor he had in Christopher and he illustrated this by sending me a four-page tutorial letter on Byzantine history which he had received from him when he was ill and unable to come to Exeter.

Another friend was Enid Starkie, at that time a young lecturer at Exeter, who even then had a startlingly eccentric appearance with her bright blue beret which matched her even brighter blue eyes. For an intellectual, she was surprisingly good with children, and Juliana, Christopher's eldest daughter, remembers being left in her charge when her parents were in Exeter and having a wonderful time rampaging all over the house. Once, to amuse the children, she dressed up in the academic regalia she wore when she received her degree at the Sorbonne in Paris.

FAMILY LIFE

Christopher and Valery eventually had three children: two daughters, Juliana and Christina, and a son, Christopher Philip, born soon after they arrived at Dawlish. Valery was seriously ill with phlebitis after his birth which left her with a swollen and painful leg for the rest of her life. I think this illness was a major crisis in their lives and, after that, active life became difficult for her. Fortunately they had a mainstay, a kind of pillar of the family, in the children's nurse, Elizabeth Bates, always known as Beth. She came in an emergency for a fortnight but stayed for twenty years – no matter who came and went in the way of cooks or housemaids, Beth remained, only leaving eventually to look after her father in his old age; even after her retirement she often returned to the family to 'help out' in time of need or crisis. Such faithful retainers, who were just as much family friends, are now a race almost extinct, but they gave a sense of stability and continuity to family life which future generations will never know.

Every year for about two months in the summer the whole family migrated to Yorkshire to stay with Christopher's parents; it was a long day's journey by train from Dawlish to Leeds and thence by branch line to Bolton Abbey where they were met by a Buick of the 1920s vintage and a lorry to take the vast paraphernalia of luggage, which included a large selection of books which Christopher would never be without – he said they were the tools of his trade.

When they arrived, they found the house '*en fête*' to welcome them, the hall festooned with flags like a Victorian railway station decorated for an important arrival. The children came to love Hartlington as a second home and were thoroughly spoilt by their grandparents. While Christopher always seemed terrified of his father, never daring, for instance, to be late for a meal, for Col Dawson had an alarming way of standing in the hall with his watch in his hand, the children had no such fear and enjoyed accompanying their grandfather on walks and picnics, when he would pitch a tent he had bought for them and light a camp fire, as he would have done in his army days on his expeditions. Their grandmother would entertain them with stories of her youth in Wales, let them dress up from a fancy dress box she kept for church fêtes

and such junketings, and on Sundays she taught them to sing
hymns like 'Onward Christian Soldiers' at the organ she
played in the hall, which added an ecumenical slant to their
religious upbringing.

With his own children, Christopher was always approach-
able, except during working hours, but as they grew up he
seemed less at ease with them. But in those early days at
Dawlish he was with his children a great deal – only in infancy
were they segregated to the nursery. When they were old
enough, he took them on his afternoon walks; he walked fast
with long springing strides and climbed rocks like a mountain
goat so that it was hard work keeping pace. There was no
family car in those days, so all expeditions were made by train:
to Exeter, to Torquay, where Col and Mrs Dawson always
spent the winter, and sometimes further afield to Dartmoor.
One expedition, which must have been made later when they
had acquired a car, was to visit Hurrell Froude's house near
Dartington, which Christopher described later in his book *The
Spirit of The Oxford Movement*:

> .... On the other bank of the Dart, in the woods of Little Hemp-
> ston, there still stands the little 14th century manor house, which
> Hurrell regarded as the most beautiful place in the world, with its
> effaced fresco of the mystery of the Resurrection, a memorial at
> once of Froude himself and of the old Catholic England to which
> he had pledged his faith.

Those early years at Dawlish were a time of great happiness
and harmony in family life, and the children were brought up in
much the same atmosphere of educational freedom that Christopher had experienced himself in his pre-school years. Today
educational psychologists might say they led a 'deprived life',
for they saw few other children, but they had the freedom of
living in the country and, as soon as they could read, the
freedom to browse through any of the books in the house.

Before they went away to school, Juliana and Christina were
taught at home by a friend of their parents and Philip went to a
small nursery school. Margaret Houghton (now Mrs Margaret
Geidt) was hardly one's idea of the conventional governess, for
she was young and pretty and had a great sense of humour. She
recalls that the children were high-spirited and sometimes
difficult to control. At lunch, for instance, which they had in
the dining-room with their parents, whenever the telephone

Hay Castle, Hay-on-Wye, where Christopher Dawson was born.

Harlington Hall, near Skipton, Yorkshire. Christopher Dawson's home.

Mary Louisa Bevan,
Christopher Dawson's
mother, at the time of her
engagement.

Col Henry Philip Dawson,
Christopher Dawson's father,
with his grandson Philip
(the author's brother).

Christopher Dawson and his sister Gwendoline.

At Bletsoe Rectory: on the ground in the front row are Christopher Dawson (left) and E. I. Watkin (right).

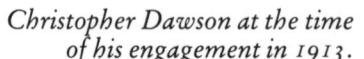

Christopher Dawson at the time of his engagement in 1913.

Valery Mills, also at the time of her engagement to Christopher.

rang Philip would get down from his chair and run round and round the table until he was caught; they were also rather noisy which must have interrupted their father's writing considerably. In a letter to Edward Watkin he once wrote: 'Juliana has been given a concertina for Christmas and marches round the house all day singing a doleful song: "The cat is dead!"' She had also apparently asked him a theological question: 'Is the cat's God a cat and does he have wings?'

It was not altogether surprising that when Margaret Houghton eventually left, Christopher and Valery decided to send the two eldest children away to a boarding school, the Convent of the Assumption in nearby Sidmouth. Christopher never had anything to do with the choosing of schools for his children. It seemed almost as if after his own unhappy experience of school even the thought of it made him shy away with alarm and repulsion. So it was Valery, who had never been to school herself, who did the round of visiting schools and interviewing headmasters and Reverend Mothers.

There was the occasion when they both set out with a friend to prospect a public school for their son, Philip. When they drew near the place – The Oratory, near Reading – Christopher suddenly said, 'I can't face it', got out of the car and sat in a wood reading a book while Valery and the friend went on to see the headmaster!

Valery was more than a wife to Christopher and a mother to the children; she provided the buttress for him from the world outside and the calming influence in a household which otherwise might have been chaotic as all writers' households tend to be. She had to be practical and businesslike, because Christopher was essentially unpractical and lacked organisation and method. She it was who did all the accounts, paid the rates and taxes as well as the household bills so that he was left entirely free for his lecturing and writing. In those days, he could never afford a secretary (his books were all written in microscopic longhand) so very often his wife became his amanuensis as well, copying out his articles and reviews in her own clearer hand. As far as was humanly possible she tackled the 'filing' but this was virtually a hopeless task. There were no filing cabinets, only the drawers of a bureau, where necessary documents such as publishing contracts might be stowed away; otherwise, there was a large table in the library where

papers were stacked high. It was fatal to attempt to tidy them as
Christopher maintained that he knew where he had put everything – and rather as in the game of pelmanism, he actually did.
In every subsequent house where they lived, there was always
such a table with its piles of papers which in some mysterious
way always seemed to remain static; the frequent house
removals must have accounted for the fact that the mountains
were periodically reduced before they were added to again.

Strangely enough, it was not an overpoweringly religious or
intellectual atmosphere in which to be brought up. History,
religion and literature, it was true, were all around one – in the
books and pictures in the house as well as in the conversations
overheard when learned visitors arrived from time to time. But
it is the visual images that imprint themselves most clearly on
the mind of the child. Two pictures particularly stand out in
my own mind: one was a reproduction of Benozzo Gozzoli's
great fresco of the *Journey of the Magi* from the Medici chapel
in Florence with its wonderful Tuscan landscape in the background of castles and hills and flora and fauna; the other, by the
same artist, was of a vision of St Augustine. The saint, it
seemed, was walking by the sea-shore and saw a child trying to
fill a hole with water from the sea. As the legend goes, when he
pointed out that this was an impossible thing to achieve, the
child replied that it would be easier to put the whole sea into
that hole than for the human mind to grasp the meaning of the
mystery of the Trinity.

'THE AGE OF THE GODS'

Christopher's first book, *The Age of the Gods*, published
when he was approaching forty, was the fruit of fourteen years
of writing and research; it was intended to be the first volume
of his projected history of culture, which was to be entitled
The Life of Civilizations. It was at once the most scholarly and
erudite of all his books and the longest. Why he published this
book first, when his second work, *Progress and Religion*, was
in fact the introductory volume to the whole work is not
known, but he may have been advised that this more factual
and less philosophical work would be more easily publishable
as an unknown author's first book. *The Life of Civilizations*
was never completed as a five volume work, but Mr George
Every, his former pupil, with whom he often discussed the

project, has thrown some light on the order in which the volumes were intended to appear.

Progress and Religion (1929) which has been described as his most brilliant work of synthesis, was conceived as a summary of the whole design. The first volume was *The Age of the Gods* (1928) and *The Making of Europe* (1932) was to be the third. The second volume, partly written but never completed, was to have as its title *The Rise of the World Religions* and was to cover the period from 1200 to 300 BC. The fourth volume was intended to cover the later Middle Ages and part of it was evidently in *Medieval Religion* (1934). A final volume covering the period from the Enlightenment to the Modern Age remained unfinished. The chapters dealing with the French Revolution appeared in a posthumous publication, *The Gods of Revolution* (1974).

Christopher's first publisher was John Murray, to whom he had been recommended by his former tutor, Ernest Barker, then Principal of Kings College, London. Barker described the book as no ordinary 'Outline of History'. Based on genuine archaeological and sociological study, it was original in its treatment and its suggestions, and as a sustained argument, presenting a considered point of view, Barker thought it deserved the most serious consideration by scholars.

The book was accepted by Sir John Murray on 9th May 1927; he said in his comments that it naturally challenged comparison with Professor Breasted's recently published book *A Conquest of Civilization* but he considered it a more scholarly book than this and more up to date. He held out no great hopes for a spectacular sale but thought 'its merit' would help it to success.

The Agreement he enclosed was described as a 'Statement of Mr Murray's practice in making up the accounts to authors for works on which a royalty is paid to the author.' This was before the days of large royalty advances, particularly for first-time authors: the rate was 10 per cent to 500 copies sold, 12½ per cent to 1,500, and 15 per cent thereafter. By the following year, 935 copies had been sold, priced at 18 shillings a copy, which was considered quite satisfactory progress for a scholarly work of this nature.

The Age of the Gods, which was subtitled 'A Study in the Origins of Culture in Prehistoric Europe and the Ancient

East', covered the whole of the formative period of the European civilization from the birth of communal life in the old Stone Age to the end of the Age of Bronze when the Age of the Gods (in Vico's phrase) became the Age of the Heroes.

The originality of the book lay in the fact that it was the first attempt to bring together in one narrative the results of digs and research, in particular to relate European prehistoric culture to the archaic culture of Asia. For the first time Christopher Dawson defined 'culture as a common way of life' more than a racial circumstance. The book was also more than an outline of archaeological discoveries but a study of the social and religious life of ancient society, discovering in this primitive world a key to the origin of ideas and institutions which have been active forces in the life of mankind ever since. He pointed out, for instance, the somewhat extraordinary fact that by the year 3000 BC:

> All the great achievements on which the life of civilization rests had already been reached, and there was no important addition to its material equipment until the rise of the great scientific and industrial movement in Western Europe in modern times.

The long years that had gone to the making of the book showed not only in the wide range of authorities consulted and the detailed tables of Egyptian dynasties or maps of Baltic sites, but in the judgement which weighed different hypotheses on such problems as the origin of the Indo-European peoples or the relation of the Terranova culture to the Etruscans.

What later so much distinguished Christopher's judgement on issues such as the Reformation or Revolution, when he appreciated Erasmus no less than Ignatius, or Marat no less than Jacques Roux, is here evident in sympathy with scholars of conflicting views. Often this serenity enabled him to see a little further, to admit and combine one view on the Asian origin of the Etruscans with another on the time of their arrival in Italy. Such solutions, then tentatively advanced, have been confirmed by later research.

That the book has not lost its value is proved by its reissue in 1970, for the greatest discoveries, whether in Crete or Mycenae, at Boghaz Keui or in Egypt, had already been made when he wrote, and much later work has gone to evaluation of them, some of which the book anticipated.

The book was well received by the reviewers, particularly by Prof Gordon Childe, one of the first authorities, who noticed the book in *Antiquity* (December 1928). He wrote:

> I have always hoped that someone with more ample leisure and a wider vision would reassemble the dry bones served up by myself and others, and, with the aid of kindred sciences, reanimate the frame of prehistoric humanity. The book before us is the most successful effort in that direction that I have come across.

Later that year Christopher was writing to Edward Watkin that Padraic Collum had written a most satisfactory article on the book in the *Dial* (New York) and added that 'a good American sale would be the salvation of it.'

But on the whole, he was in a depressed state of mind at this time, not only about his personal affairs but with the general political situation. At Christmas (1929) he was writing again to Edward Watkin:

> Altogether I find the world rather depressing. We seem to have reached the time prophecied by the inspired poet,
>
> *When none can speak for fear*
> *   And Liberty in every land lies dead*
> *And the Two Tyrannies unchallenged reign.*
>
> The most loathsome phenomenon is Mussolini's puff of St Francis. He ought to present a picture to the convent at Assisi showing the saint forcibly administering a dose of castor oil to Brother Ghibelline!

In the same letter he suggested the idea of going to live abroad to escape the English climate: 'I really think we must all move camp to some more wholesome clime,' he wrote. 'Certainly I don't think I can stay another winter here. I kept wassail yesterday on a poached egg in bed!' He thought of Fribourg or Grenoble, the latter having the benefit of the library of the Grande Chartreuse. But this was no more than wishful thinking; his job at Exeter, although it often depressed him because his lectures were so poorly attended, was his life-line.

That year was the time of the depression, or the great 'slump' and the falling pound, and Christopher was writing again to his friend:

> Dividends are falling like leaves in Vallombrosa. Heaven knows

what will become of us all when the pound begins to go. I am sorry now that I didn't follow your example and live on capital – at any rate we would have got something out of it while it lasted. O happy Victorians who put their money in railway stock and lived happily ever afterwards. .... If the world is not coming to an end, *a* world is, and as it is our world it doesn't make much odds for us which it is.

In 1931 when the worst had happened and the pound had fallen he wrote a parody of Belloc's poem, *The Moon's Funeral*. It was called *The Pound's Funeral* – with apologies to Hilaire Belloc. Here is *Stanza II*:

And will it never rise again
  The Sterling Pound? Oh never more.
Perhaps on some Lethean shore
  With shadows dark
Of the Gold Rouble and the pre-war Mark
The Krone, the Lira and the Franc –
To us who loved it never more
  The pound will never rise again.
Oh never more the Bank Clerk bold
  Will ask his question as of old
'How will you take it – notes or gold?'
  For why?
The pound is dead. I saw it die.

SHEED & WARD

While Christopher was working on the second volume in his proposed history of culture, *The Rise of the World Religions*, a new Catholic publishing firm had come into being under the imprint of Sheed & Ward. Frank Sheed, a dynamic young barrister from Australia, had come over to England in 1926 and the same year married Maisie Ward, the daughter of Wilfrid Ward, Newman's biographer, and grand-daughter of W. G. Ward of the Oxford Movement, and with her founded the firm. As Frank Sheed explained in his book *The Church and I*,[1] the 'Ward' of the firm was originally intended to be his brother-in-law, Leo, but when he became a priest his place was taken by his sister, Maisie. Together they began what was to be the most remarkable enterprise in religious publishing between the wars. Hitherto, Catholic publishing had been in the doldrums; the best-known firm, Burns, Oates & Washbourne, carried a heavy weight of officialdom and the majority of their books bore the *Imprimatur* of the ecclesiastical censor. Sheed & Ward's books, unless they were written by priests, hardly ever did and if any bishop demanded that the firm alter statements in their published works, Sheed asked him to put his queries in writing, with the result that no more was heard.

There were other firms, such as Longmans Green, with departments specialising in Catholic books, but Sheed & Ward was something new – a firm which deliberately set out to raise the level of English Catholic culture and make it an intellectual force as well as a spiritual one. It was true that this aim, as Christopher once put it in a letter to a friend, 'was not always successful, or far-seeing or adequately financed'. But the attempt was genuine and it played an important part in the Catholic revival of the 1920s and 1930s both in England and on the Continent.

Leo Ward, whom Christopher had known at Oxford, persuaded him to make the difficult decision to leave John Murray, with which firm he would probably have continued to write books of a more strictly academic nature rather than writing for the educated public generally, and join the group which formed the nucleus of Sheed & Ward's first authors, amongst whom were Belloc, Chesterton, Maritain, Ronald Knox, D'Arcy and E. I. Watkin.

Although the firm was run on a shoe-string, for neither Sheed nor Ward had much capital, the terms of Christopher's first contract made with them in 1928 for *Progress and Religion* were a slight improvement on John Murray's for his first book. These rates were as good as any publisher at that time would have paid for a scholarly work and indeed, with the exception of best-selling novelists, few writers expected to earn much from the life they had chosen and which they enjoyed.

Apart from Frank Sheed himself, Christopher's closest contact in the firm was with Tom Burns (afterwards editor of *The Tablet* for many years), who in a remarkable way ran the editorial, publicity and production departments simultaneously and almost single-handed. Sheed & Ward also had its full quota of eccentric authors including Fr Vincent McNabb, the famous Dominican, who wrote on the insides of old envelopes, and Edward Watkin who once submitted a manuscript which he had typed on a machine without a ribbon saying that if the printer held it up to the light he would be able to read it. Author-publisher relationships were also fostered by Tom Burns who, before the days of expense account lunches, would take despondent authors to the pub round the corner rather than offer them Sheed & Ward's tea.

Tom Burns's particular gift was his eye for colour and typography, which enabled him to lift the pall from the almost universally dreary format of religious publishing of those days. Not for nothing was he the friend of David Jones, Eric Gill and Stanley Morison and they influenced his own ideas considerably in producing books for Sheed & Ward.

Christopher seldom visited his publisher's office; more often Frank Sheed caught the Cornish Riviera Express to Dawlish and somehow he managed to cram these journeys to distant outposts into his exceedingly busy life. A friend of his once remarked: 'Frank always thinks he can be in two places at once provided there is a night train.' Once he caught the 'milk train' arriving at 4 a.m. and slept on the cliffs above the sea for a few hours in the dawn, arriving at the Dawsons' house in time for breakfast.

Frank Sheed found his visits to Christopher a strain because, as he said, 'one's mind was continually on the stretch', but at the same time he found his learning a constant source of wonderment. There was, however, the one solitary fact of Church history known to Sheed and not to Christopher, which the former recalled:

> I had remarked that Hormisdas was the only Pope whose son became Pope: He seemed surprised, asked was I sure, checked and found that it was so: he asked me how I happened to know: I said, 'You told me.' That slip apart, his memory was close to infallible – I imagine because each new thing learned found its place in a mental structure he had spent his whole life building.[2]

To Sheed, Christopher's originality lay in his amazing knowledge of the Scriptures, the Fathers of the Church, and what modern historians were saying, but he was also an enigma to him. Frank could not understand how, living as he did so completely in the mind, Christopher was also abreast of all that was happening in the world around him: he knew of the latest events in some remote corner of the globe as accurately as he knew some equally remote fact of history. It was a mystery that he was never to solve.

CHAPTER SEVEN

Achievement

'PROGRESS AND RELIGION' (1929)

In 1925 Christopher had written an article in *The Quarterly Review* under the title *Religion and the Life of Civilization*. It was a development of his earlier theme expounded in the paper he read to the Sociological Society in 1922 (*The Life of Civilizations*) and in it he worked out the theory which was the mainspring of his thought throughout his life as an author but particularly in *Progress and Religion*, namely that 'the vitality of a society is bound up with its religion':

> The great civilizations of the world do not produce the great religions as a kind of cultural by-product; in a very real sense, the great religions are the foundations on which the great civilizations rest. A society which has lost its religion becomes sooner or later a society which has lost its culture.[1]

The question remained to be answered as to what would happen to our own great modern civilization which had 'gained a wealth of power and knowledge which the world has never known before?' Would it perish for 'lack of vision' and 'waste its forces in the pursuit of selfish and mutually destructive aims' or would society 'once again become animated by a common faith and hope, which will have the power to order our material and intellectual achievements in an enduring spiritual unity?'

He wrote to Edward Watkin that he wanted to write a book on the same subject, working in his theory of civilization cycles and it was on religion that he had his essential things to say. 'Pray for me', he added, 'that it may get published (and written) and that it may not land me in the dungeons of the Inquisition.'

The book that emerged was *Progress and Religion* published in 1929 by Sheed & Ward, the first of his many books to appear under their imprint. It was at once the most original and influential of all his books, and while it is not as well known as his subsequent work, *The Making of Europe*, it made the greatest impression on its first appearance and was regarded as an important contribution to the history of ideas. Even Dean Inge (known as the 'gloomy Dean'), who once said that Christopher Dawson was the only Roman Catholic who didn't annoy him, referred to this book as 'a great work, one of the best that we have had in recent years.'

What then were the qualities which made this book so original as well as influential on the younger generation of that time as it would seem? Harman Grisewood, in his autobiography, *One Thing at a Time*, records that it was the discussion around *Progress and Religion* that sent him to the British Museum to achieve an education omitted at Oxford, and so eventually to direct the Third Programme of the BBC. Writing on this subject, James Oliver, whose first contact with Christopher Dawson's work was with *Progress and Religion*, says:

> This influence on the young was all the more remarkable, and possibly deeper and more lasting, because Christopher Dawson had none of the violence and exaggeration which often divert the student from the dullness of his studies. But his wit was undamped by his scholarship: before the outbreak of war, he had become a master of the generation that went into it.

In effect, this book set out to debunk the doctrine of Progress: the belief, popularly held since the early 18th century, that 'every day and in every way the world grows better and better.' Christopher Dawson took the argument one stage further by pointing out that material progress was not necessarily progress at all; in the idiom of the 1920s, progress meant 'more cinemas, motor-cars for all, wireless installations, more elaborate methods of killing people, purchase on the hire system, preserved food and picture papers.' He went on to point out that material factors do not explain a civilization:

> It may be questioned, as indeed it has been questioned by many, whether the modern advance of material civilization is progressive in the true sense of the word; whether men are happier or wiser or better than they were in simpler states of society, and whether Birmingham or Chicago is to be preferred to mediaeval Florence.

In *Progress and Religion* Christopher Dawson attempted an historical enquiry into the factors underlying the rise and fall of civilizations, and he came to the conclusion that it was not as Gilbert Murray said, *à propos* the decline of the Greek civilization, due to a 'loss of nerve' but in each and every case by the failure of life. Religion was the dynamic element in every culture, whether in ancient Egypt, Mesopotamia, China, Greece or Rome, and when the vision faded, the life went out of that civilization:

> Behind every civilization there is a vision – a vision which may be the unconscious fruit of ages of common thought and action, or which may have sprung from the sudden illumination of a great prophet or thinker. The experience of Mohammed in the cave of Mount Hira, when he saw human life as transitory as the beat of a gnat's wing in comparison with the splendour and power of the Divine Unity, has shaped the existence of a great part of the human race ever since.

Nowhere have the conclusions which Christopher Dawson reached in *Progress and Religion* been better summarised than by Vera Brittain, in reviewing the book for *Time & Tide*:

> Europe stands at the parting of the ways. Science alone is not enough, for 'science provides not a moral dynamic but an intellectual technique'. The civilization of Western Europe is faced with inescapable alternatives; it must either abandon the Christian tradition and with it faith in progress and humanity, or it must return, consciously and deliberately, to the religious foundation on which those ideas were based .... His conclusions are difficult to refute, for the achievements of material progress, which are our only argument against them, seem already to have carried us nearer to the abyss of disaster than to the mountain of salvation.[2]

T. S. ELIOT AND 'THE CRITERION'

Christopher's greatest literary output was in the early 1930s: he was deeply aware of new currents of thought both in England and on the Continent – particularly in France and Germany – and he felt the ever more pressing need to interpret history in the light of current events and ideas. He also felt the need to write about the spiritual reality of the Catholic faith which seemed barely apparent through the medium of its art and its Press; the latter, he wrote, 'somehow manages to be entirely out of touch with the real world – to live in the atmosphere of the sacristy – and yet at the same time to be thoroughly unsupernatural and materialistic.'

Much of Christopher's most profound spiritual writing was written for *The Dublin Review* during the late 1920s and early 1930s, and its editor, Algar Thorold, became a close friend. While they shared interests in mysticism and comparative religion, they were very different in background and character, Thorold being an ex-diplomat who had spent most of his life in Florence and Paris, a brilliant *raconteur* and conversationalist. He was also the nephew and biographer of the political journalist, Henry Labouchère. His father was the Bishop of Winchester, and it was said that he missed the See of Canterbury owing to his son's conversion to Catholicism. When Gladstone recommended him to Queen Victoria for the Archbishopric she was reputed to have said that a man who was so unsuccessful with his own son as to let him become a Roman Catholic could hardly be considered a suitable candidate.

Owing to Thorold's wide acquaintance in the literary world, *The Dublin Review* became the equal of any of its contemporaries in the political, literary or historical fields and stood alone above the rest of the Catholic Press. Through Thorold, Christopher came to know T. S. Eliot, who invited him to write for his review, the *Criterion*. In a letter to Christopher, Algar Thorold wrote on 15 August 1929:

> I lunched yesterday with T. S. Eliot. He said such gratifying things about *The Dublin* that I felt quite embarrassed. I naturally think that he is an extraordinarily intelligent man; you may find a further ground for his judgement (as I do also) in the fact that he is a great admirer of your work, particularly of *Progress and Religion*. He timidly asked if I should consider it an unfriendly act were he to ask you to write for the *Criterion* and remembering that in Spinoza's words: 'it arises from no accident, but from the nature itself of reason, that the highest good of man is common to all,' I encouraged him to do so. I hope you won't make me jealous! I really thought Eliot particularly nice, though looking ill.

This letter was followed by an invitation from T. S. Eliot to Christopher, written the next day, to write for the *Criterion*:

> Dear Sir,
> I have recently read some of your work and have had it in my mind some little time to write to you to express my interest. But have only been brought to the point at this moment by having had some

conversation about you yesterday with Mr. Algar Thorold and Father Burdett. I wish merely to express my conviction that *The Criterion* ought to publish some essay by you and I should be very grateful if you would write to me and make some suggestion.

Also I should very much like to meet you at some time when you are in London.

Yours very truly,
T. S. Eliot

This was the beginning of a long acquaintance – although the two men had so many intellectual interests in common, a certain lack of communication between them prevented a close friendship. David Jones, who knew Eliot well, said that the latter had told him how *Progress and Religion* had influenced his own ideas on religion and culture. There is surely evidence of this in a poem like *The Rock* where Eliot writes of the higher religions, the prayer wheels and 'affirmation of rites with forgotten meanings.'

The immediate outcome of T. S. Eliot's invitation was an article by Christopher Dawson for the *Criterion* entitled 'The End of an Age', published in April 1930. In the same year he wrote *Christianity and Sex* for the Criterion Miscellany, a series of pamphlets published by Faber & Faber to which D. H. Lawrence also contributed and this essay had something of Lawrence's influence. Both saw marriage and the family as the basis of social life – Lawrence argued in his last published work[3] that marriage was Christianity's greatest contribution to civilization, and that to destroy it would restore the pre-Christian dominance of the state as in Soviet Russia. They agreed too on the value of organic British society and distrust of suburban culture. It was natural that they should both oppose Bertrand Russell. Of his prophecy that the marriage of the future would be confined to those who seek parenthood for its own sake, Christopher Dawson wrote:

> But under these circumstances who will bother to marry? Marriage will lose all attractions for the young and the pleasure-loving and the poor and the ambitious. The energy of youth will be devoted to contraceptive love and only when men and women have become prosperous and middle-aged will they think seriously of settling down to rear a strictly limited family.

He foresaw an Orwellian situation developing with regulation

of parenthood by the state, with motherhood as 'one of the
chief branches of the public service.' But this would offend not
only Christians but the freedom in love demanded by the
reformers, and mankind would be no more than a stage in 'the
evolution of an ape into a machine.' Eugenics might avoid this
fate if it stood out against 'cranks and fanatics who are prepared
to castrate anybody who fails to conform to the accepted
standards of successful mediocrity.'

The romantic ideal of sex had set frustration above fulfillment and caused a natural reaction to the physical, treated by
Aldous Huxley with more disgust than pleasure, and the
rationalist was closer to pessimism than the Christian: St
Augustine, he wrote, was 'far from being the Manichean sex-
maniac that so many moderns imagine' and again:

> If Pascal views the world as a hospital, Voltaire sees it as a mad-
> house. Human nature has lost its dignity, without losing its cor-
> ruption.

Lawrence had shown that sex cannot be rationalised, but it
can be spiritualised as Christopher Dawson wrote:

> But if we once renounce the vain attempt to rationalise sexual life,
> we must be prepared to find in sex a mysterious element which is
> akin to the ultimate mysteries of life. The religious significance of
> sex has always been felt by man. Primitive religion regarded it as
> the supreme cosmic mystery.

This essay has been cited at some length because it shows so
clearly the force with which the historian of ideas can attack a
contemporary problem. The whole piece summarises centuries
of Christian and human experience as true today as it was then.

THE CATHOLIC REVIVAL IN THE 1930S

> Every culture is like a plant. It must have its roots in the earth and
> for sunlight it needs to be open to the spiritual. At the present
> moment we are busy cutting its roots and shutting out all light
> from above, and then we are surprised that it withers. Culture
> cannot live by its own superficial activity, any more than a plant
> can live by its stalk.
>
> Christopher Dawson (1928)

In the ferment of discussion following the second Vatican
Council, the existence of a Catholic intellectual revival in the
1930s has been largely forgotten. It had emanated first from

France, with writers like Claudel, Péguy, Maritain, Etienne Gilson, the medieval historian, and Pere Rousselot, the interpreter of St Thomas's thought, and then spread to Germany but it was not until the Thirties that this movement really penetrated to England.

English Catholicism had been a sadly insular affair, cut off from European thought, and dominated by the authorities at Westminster, the secular (mainly Irish) clergy and the Catholic Press. But now there were signs of a reaction from the past and a new breed of writers had appeared, nearly all of them converts, who deliberately set out to change the order of things and face the problems of the new age.

One of the key figures and organisers behind this movement was Tom Burns; his house, first in St Leonard's Terrace and then in Glebe Place, Chelsea, became a centre for discussion among Catholic writers, artists and intellectuals, the nucleus of this group being, in addition to Tom Burns himself, Christopher Dawson (on his rare visits to London), Martin D'Arcy, sj, Alec Dru, later the translator and editor of Kierkegaard, David Jones, Harman Grisewood of the BBC and Bernard Wall, a political journalist who was also an authority on Dante and Petrarch.

From St Leonard's Terrace, the journal *Order* was founded, which carried on its cover a woodcut of a unicorn by David Jones, especially commissioned for the review. It appeared under an anonymous monomark which ensured a freedom of expression on religious matters not otherwise possible in those days of clerical censorship. When the fear of Modernism was still very much a live issue in the minds of the clergy, Christopher wrote in a letter to Edward Watkin (undated):

> Re Modernism, it seems to me that the real trouble is not in the matter of freedom so much as in the dominant spirit. I mean the last two Popes are usually supposed to be more liberal than Pius X, but in spite of that, things seemed much easier in that time somehow. Likewise English Catholicism is generally supposed to be freer than French, yet here you got *The Universe* last week attacking Sir Arthur Keith for his harmless lecture on palaeolithic man, while in France the Abbé Breuil is one of the leading lights of 'L'Anthropologie', and I think Boale the editor is a Catholic too.

The aims of *Order* were both negative and positive: on the negative side it was directed against the old-time militant

Catholic who was fiercely anti-Anglican and enthusiastic for material, temporal and visible triumphs of the Church; aggressive and rigid in argument showing no sympathetic knowledge of human character. On the positive side it aimed to encourage more interest in the spiritual side of Catholicism, to foster a love of the liturgy and to recognise the value of all intellectual and creative work irrespective of religion.

The writers of *Order* also directed their attention towards the 'intellectual-militant' of the school of the 'Chester–Bellocian' and were to make the point that Catholicism was not always a jolly tavern, nor were Catholics necessarily medievalists and that Europe was not always the Faith. (This of course referred to Belloc's much-quoted remark: 'The Faith is Europe and Europe is the Faith.')

A confidential document which set out these aims summed up the situation thus. That:

> While the Chester–Bellocians *exeunt* fighting, the cultured Catholics and non-Catholics are at sea on most things connected with sex, other world-religions, the problem of evil, free will and behaviouristic psychology.

As for the Catholic Press, two words sufficed – *Delenda est* – (It is to be destroyed); its function should be clearly demarcated and be educative. At that time, *The Catholic Times* (now defunct) seemed to be trying to be the paper for the Irish ghetto and a *Church Times*; *The Universe* indiscriminately commented in leaders on national and sectarian matters; as for *The Tablet*, then under the editorship of Dr Oldmeadow, it was a journal of such un-ecumenical slant that Anglican Bishops were referred to by the title of 'Mr' in its columns. It was to be 'ridiculed until it bursts'.

The review continued for a few issues and was then replaced by a series of booklets entitled *Essays in Order*, published by Sheed & Ward in a hardback edition at the modest price of 2/6d each.

The first volume to appear was Jacques Maritain's *Religion and Culture* (1931) in which Christopher Dawson as co-editor with Tom Burns wrote a general introduction to the whole series. He said that the Catholic intellectual movement and its significance was not yet realised in England:

> The existence of Catholic philosophy is hardly recognised except

in academic circles, and it is still possible for writers like Dr. Coulton and Bishop Barnes, whose own mental outlook is entirely that of the past, to treat Catholicism as an exploded superstition which is completely out of touch with the mind of the present age.

The intention, therefore, in launching *Essays in Order* was to make the contemporary European movement of Catholic thought better known in England by introducing, for instance, such German philosophical writers as Peter Wust, Carl Schmitt, Theodor Haeker and Dietrich von Hildebrand. Dawson pointed out that in France particularly there had been a striking revival of Catholic activity in the field of pure literature, 'represented by poets and dramatists like Claudel and Henri Ghéon, critics such as Henri Brémond, Charles du Bos, Gabriel Marcel and Henri Massis, and novelists such as François Mauriac and Julien Green.'

From 1931 until 1938 contributions to this series appeared steadily from English, French, German and other continental authors on subjects ranging from politics to philosophy, sociology and religion. In addition to Maritain's *Religion and Culture*, titles included *Crisis in the West* by Peter Wust; *Christianity and the New Age* and *The Modern Dilemma* by Christopher Dawson; *The Bow in the Clouds* by E. I. Watkin; *The Russian Revolution* by Nicholas Berdyaev and *Form in Modern Poetry* by Herbert Read.

Editorial policy was conducted between the two editors in a somewhat haphazard manner that suited them both; ideas were thrashed out in correspondence but occasionally, when time permitted, Tom Burns roared down to Dawlish in a sports car of 1920s vintage or Christopher went up to London where he and Valery stayed at a gloomy private hotel in South Kensington, christened 'the mausoleum' by Tom Burns. The ideas for authors were mainly Christopher's while Tom Burns was responsible for making the contacts and consulted Christopher on the results.

It was originally intended that the series should enter the field of artistic reprints under the guidance of Eric Gill, but this idea, probably for financial reasons, never materialised. A cheap edition of Gerard Manley Hopkins's *Wreck of the Deutschland* illustrated by David Jones, which was one of the works proposed, sounds attractive but impracticable.

Both editors were working in the midst of diverse other activities: Tom Burns was selling books for Sheed & Ward as well as editing them; he also said he wanted to write himself and was thinking of a book on D. H. Lawrence, which however never got written. On one occasion he wrote to Christopher that he was 'just off to dine with Aldous Huxley under the hawk eye of Ottoline Morrell – intent on fomenting religious discussion. Ye Gods!'

Christopher was not only writing two *Essays in Order* (1931 and 1932) but had contributed two major essays to a commemorative volume on St Augustine for his 15th centenary. He was also writing *The Making of Europe* which appeared in 1932.

St Augustine, as Christopher often said, was, like Dante, one of his earliest heroes, so that when he came to contribute to *A Monument to St Augustine* in 1930 he was already an expert on the subject. His two essays, *The Dying World* and *The City of God*, make up nearly a fifth of the whole book (which was edited by Tom Burns) and they were later re-published in a book of collected writings *Enquiries into Religion and Culture* (1933).

The first essay deals with the age of Augustine and the part he played in it: first, he showed him as neither medieval nor classical:

> He is essentially a man of his own age – that strange age of the Christian Empire which has been so despised by the historians, but which nevertheless marks one of the vital moments in the history of the world. It witnessed the fall of Rome, the passing of that great order which had controlled the fortunes of the world for five centuries and more, and the laying of the foundations of a new world. And Augustine was no mere passive spectator of the crisis. He was, to a far greater degree than any emperor or general or barbarian war-lord, a maker of history and a builder of a bridge which was to lead from the old world to the new.

Into these two essays Christopher Dawson poured all his love of classical history and literature, which he had developed from the early days of his youth and his years of solitary study; of Tertullian's rhetoric, for instance, he wrote:

> .... it is at once exhilarating and terrific. It is as though one were to go out of a literary *salon* into a thunderstorm. His work is marked

by a spirit of fierce and indomitable hostility to the whole tradition of pagan civilisation, both social and intellectual.

Augustine himself, he said, remained an African more than a Roman, not having the devotion of a Prudentius to the Empire:

> St Augustine saw things otherwise; To him the ruin of civilization and the destruction of the Empire were not very important things. He looked beyond the aimless and bloody chaos of history to the world of eternal realities from which the world of sense derives all the significance which it possesses. His thoughts were fixed, not on the fate of the city of Rome or the city of Hippo, nor on the struggle of Roman and barbarian, but on those other cities which have their foundations in heaven and in hell.

'Not very important things' – that phrase embodies Christopher Dawson's serenity in his own view of history: he wrote in the same style through the Second World War and when he foresaw the years of chaos and confusion that were to come. He had Augustine's faith in another City – The City of God:

> A transcendent and timeless reality .... older than the world, as wide as humanity – nothing less than the spiritual unity of the whole universe, as planned by the Divine Providence and the ultimate goal of creation.

In his second essay, *The City of God*, he studied Augustine as philosopher and writer. Remarkably, as he pointed out, he was 'not only the founder of the Christian philosophy of history, but was actually the first man in the world to discover the meaning of time':

> His subtle and profound mind found a peculiar attraction in the contemplation of the mystery of time which is essentially bound up with the mystery of being. He was intensely sensitive to the pathos of mutability: 'For all this most fair order of things truly good will pass away when its measures are accomplished, and they have their morning and their evening.'
>
> (*Confessions*)

From this new Augustinian theory of time there followed a possible new conception of history and one which was of the essence of Christopher Dawson's own historical thought:

> If man is not the slave and creature of time, but its master and creator, then history also becomes a creative process. It does not repeat itself meaninglessly; it grows into organic unity with the

growth of human experience. The past does not die; it becomes incorporated in humanity. And hence progress is possible, since the life of society and of humanity itself possesses continuity and the capacity for spiritual growth no less than the life of the individual.

Finally, he ended with a reminder that Augustine was a reformer who in the West broke away from the tradition of an 'omnipotent sacred state and a passive people' and it was the 'Augustinian Theory, for all its otherworldliness, (that) first made possible the ideal of a social order resting upon the free personality and a common effort towards moral ends.' All the Western ideals that we are still striving for today – freedom and progress and social justice – stem in some measure from:

> .... the profound thought of the great African who was himself indifferent to secular progress and to the transitory fortunes of the earthly state, 'for he looked for a city that has foundations whose builder and maker is God.'

HISTORIAN OF EUROPE

Some time in the 1930s, Sheed & Ward produced a small booklet containing selections from Christopher Dawson's writings and it carried as its frontispiece a cartoon by Thomas Derrick, showing the author brooding over the skyscrapers of New York with aircraft circling overhead. The caption underneath read: 'Mr. Christopher Dawson, having emerged from a long study of the Dark Ages – or *The Making of Europe* finds little comfort in the modern world – or *The Modern Dilemma*.'

Both works appeared in 1932 and as the caption above suggests *The Modern Dilemma* interpreted his studies in ancient and medieval history in terms of the modern age. It was the second of his *Essays in Order*, subtitled *The Problem of European Unity*, and the material was taken from a series of talks given on the BBC in connection with a general programme on the forces of change transforming the modern world.

The essay was immediate in style and subject – the crisis of the day – for Europe, after only fourteen years of peace, was once more drifting towards war and revolution. It was, too, a plea for reality against outmoded thought. 'Current beliefs', he wrote, 'are always out of date', for they are those of a previous generation and it needed 'a considerable effort to see things as they are and not as other people have seen them.' The most outmoded idea, he considered, was the spirit of exclusive nationalism which was the true destroyer of European unity.

More than forty years ago, Christopher Dawson was writing almost prophetically of the need for a united Europe if civilization was to survive. 'The crisis of Europe is the crisis of the world', he wrote, 'but it is only in and through Europe that the new world can realise itself.' Its survival, he maintained, depended on four ideals: the Christian ideal, the ideal of humanity, the scientific ideal and the ideal of democracy.

A chapter on democracy dealt with problems which are as pressing today as they were in the 1930s. The evil of modern society, as the author saw it, was that the whole social order was directed towards economic instead of spiritual aims:

> The economic view of life regards money as equivalent to satisfaction. Get money, and if you get enough of it you will get everything.

In modern democracy it cannot be denied that both capitalists and socialists have accepted economic wealth as the end of society and the standard of personal happiness. But as Christopher Dawson wrote: 'The standard of life is really not an economic but a vital thing; it is a question of how you live rather than how much you live on.' He took as examples the cases of St Francis of Assisi and the poet Wordsworth: the one possessed no income at all but had achieved 'a complete measure of social adjustment', the other, a less extreme instance, had 'during the happiest and most productive period of his life an income of about £70 a year, and he would have been no better off with a million, because he had found the way of life that suited him.'

The fundamental issue of the modern dilemma, therefore, lay in the choice between the spiritual and the materialistic view of life: if civilization was to be saved there must be a return to a religious view of life. In today's terms, what we now realise is that the worship of technology and the greed for power has caused not only the catastrophe of the last war but the terrible possibility of a future nuclear war which could only mean the end of civilization.

Christopher Dawson thought that the political and economical revival of Europe was impossible without a spiritual revival of European culture:

> Christianity has not only given Europe its religious beliefs and its spiritual ideals; it has actually been the spiritual force that created the unity of Western culture. Before the coming of Christianity there was no Europe.

The idea in this last paragraph was central to his next book, *The Making of Europe*, which he subtitled 'An Introduction to the History of European Unity' and in the preface he again insisted that if our civilization was to survive 'it should develop a common European consciousness, and a sense of its historic and organic unity .... We must rewrite our history from the European point of view.'

From this point Christopher Dawson became and was seen as a 'European historian'; he saw the need for a united Europe and that we could no longer be satisfied with an 'aristocratic civilization that finds its unity in external and superficial things and ignores the deeper needs of man's spiritual nature.' The deeper traditions in Europe went back behind Humanism and behind the superficial triumphs of modern civilization to the fundamental social and spiritual forces which had gone to the making of Europe.

One of the aims of the book was to bring new light to the ages which had generally been considered 'dark' – the period between 400 and 1000 AD – that most neglected of historical periods, and probably for this reason, of all his books it has been the one most used by historians and students. As a Catholic historian he saw the Dark Ages as ages of dawn for they witnessed the conversion of the West, the foundation of Christian civilization and the creation of Christian art and Catholic liturgy.

In those six centuries, 'the foundations of Europe were laid in fear and weakness and suffering,' but the disasters of the time evoked an heroic spirit:

> This was the spirit of the great men who were the makers of the new age – of St Augustine, who saw the vanity and futility of the cult of human power; of St Benedict, who created a nucleus of peace and spiritual order amidst the disasters of the Gothic wars; of St Gregory, who carried the cares of the whole world on his shoulders while civilization was falling in ruins around him; of St

Boniface, who in spite of profound discouragement and disillusion gave his life for the increase of the Christian people.

The foundations on which he considered European unity had been built were four: the Roman Empire, the Christian Church, the classical tradition and finally the barbarian societies. All of these factors had contributed something, whether political, spiritual or intellectual to the commonwealth of Europe. The barbarians, he said 'provided the human material out of which Europe has been fashioned: they are the *gentes* as against the *imperium* and the *ecclesia* – the source of the national element in European life.'

Of equal importance in this book is the part played by the Eastern Empire and the renaissance of Byzantine culture as opposed to Western culture. Dawson thought that the latter had been a neglected subject even by 'the greatest of our historians of the Eastern Empire – Edward Gibbon' and that Byzantine culture was not merely a decadent survival from the classical past but a new creation forming the background of the whole development of medieval culture and even that of Islam, to a certain extent.

His conclusion was that by the end of the 10th century Northern paganism had passed away and the whole of Western Europe was incorporated into the unity of Christendom:

> And at the same time the long winter of the Dark Ages had reached its end, and everywhere throughout the West new life was stirring, new social and spiritual forces were awakening, and Western society was emerging from the shadow of the East and taking its place as an independent unity by the side of the older civilizations of the oriental world.

The illustrations in this book show the balance of the weakness and disasters of the period with the beauty of early Christian, Byzantine and Romanesque art. In particular the frontispiece of an Orante from the catacombs is used to illustrate the character of the 'New People', and notes by the author draw attention to the new creation of Christian art.

Writing in 1932 to G. K. Chesterton, to whom he sent a copy of the book as a tribute to the inspiration he had drawn from his poetry, Christopher said:

> Years ago when I was an undergraduate your *Ballad of the White Horse* first brought the breath of life to this period for me when I

was fed up with Stubbs and Oman and the rest of them. Unfortunately the boredom that is generated in people's minds by academic history leads to a positive anti-historicism which seems to me becoming characteristic of modern 'left-wing' thought. I have tried to write a history that does not leave out everything that matters, in the academic fashion, and that gives a proper place to spiritual factors. Unfortunately I am afraid that my book is in danger of falling between two stools – being too popular for the academic public and too abstruse for the general reader.

As it turned out, *The Making of Europe* was well-received in the scholarly world, not only by Catholics but also by eminent non-Catholics such as Dean Inge, Sir James Marriott and Dr H. A. L. Fisher, the last mentioned making the point that 'although Mr Dawson is a Roman Catholic, who quite rightly makes no concealment of his religious standpoint, he advances nothing from which even the most protestant historian, who knows his facts, need recoil.'[4] The unyieldingly anti-Catholic Dr Coulton, however, certainly did recoil in a scathing article he wrote for *The Cambridge Review*, denouncing particularly the idea that anyone should consider the Dark Ages as Ages of Faith.

Most gratifying was the tribute from the agnostic, Aldous Huxley, who wrote in *The Spectator*: 'The Dark Ages lose their darkness, and take on form and significance. Thanks to the author's erudition and marshalling of facts, we begin to have a notion of what it is all about.'[5]

ROME AND 'THE CONVEGNO VOLTA'

The great success of these first books was a cheering factor in Christopher's life, and 'Uncle Paul' seemed to have removed his unwelcome presence at least for the time being.

The most tangible proof that he was now accepted as a historian of European standing was an invitation from Signor Guglielmo Marconi, The President of the Royal Academy of Italy, to attend a conference – the *Convegno Volta* – in Rome on 14th November 1932; the subject was to be 'Europe'.

Politicians, historians, writers and intellectuals were invited from all over Europe. The British delegation was small, numbering only five: Lord Rennell of Rodd, who had been the British Ambassador to Rome from 1908 to 1919; Lord

Lymington; Sir Charles Petrie, the historian; Paul Einzig, the economist; and Christopher Dawson. Others who had been invited but did not accept were Winston Churchill, Lloyd George, Austen Chamberlain, Stanley Baldwin and Hugh Dalton among the politicians; the financier Norman Angell, and the economist J. M. Keynes, while writers included Rudyard Kipling and Hilaire Belloc.

Among the more outstanding participants from other countries were Count Apponyi from Hungary (who died the following year), Stefan Zweig, the historical novelist, Louis Bertrand, the French Academician, and Prof Daniel Halévy, whose work as a historian Christopher particularly admired. Last and certainly most sinister were the German delegates, Goering, who had been president of the Reichstag since August 1932, and Rosenberg, whom many later came to think of as Hitler's evil genius.

What most of the European delegates did not realise, and it was a factor which annoyed Christopher considerably, was that this was no historical or academic conference as they had been led to believe but a 'put-up job' by Mussolini's government to turn events to their own ends. Mussolini's Rome was disinfected of squalor and beggars and all the external signs of poverty but already there was the atmosphere of a police state; everywhere the delegates went they felt they were being followed and spied upon and even when Christopher and Valery finally left Rome for Siena, where they were meeting Valery's sister who was married to an Italian, they knew that someone was watching them at the station to see where they went.

The delegates were entertained in sumptuous splendour by the government and stayed at the Excelsior Hotel, which was and still is one of the most luxurious in Rome. The meetings of the *Convegno Volta* were formal occasions at which morning dress and top hats were *de rigueur*; for the evening functions it was full evening dress, uniforms and decorations for those who had them. Sir Charles Petrie remembered the pervading smell of mothballs from the uniforms of the French Academicians who were present. He also recalled an amusing incident, when Goering, who was a very bad linguist, misunderstood the announcement that decorations would be worn for a governmental dinner and turned up without them. Furious, as

he was extremely vain and loved parading in his medals, he
rushed away to put them on.

The opening ceremony of the conference took place in the
Julius Caesar Hall on the Capitol on 14th November with
short speeches to welcome the delegates by Buoncompagni,
the Governor of Rome, Marconi and Mussolini himself. The
meetings were held in the Farnese Palace (now the French
Embassy), a magnificent building of the high Renaissance
period, partly designed by Michelangelo.

At the opening meeting, Sir Charles Petrie spoke first on the
unity of European culture, then Christopher was called on as
the next speaker, the subject he chose being 'Interracial Cooperation as a factor in European culture'. His speech was a plea
against nationalism and racial hatred and as such could not have
pleased the Nazi element in the audience, particularly when he
delivered such statements as:

> The relatively benign Nationalism of the early Romantics paved
> the way for the fanaticism of the modern pan-racial theorists who
> subordinate civilization to skull measurements and who infuse an
> element of racial hatred into the political and economic rivalries of
> European peoples.

and

> If we were to subtract from German culture, for example, all the
> contributions made by men who were not of pure Nordic type,
> German culture would be incalculably impoverished.

Christopher always dreaded public speaking and it must
have been a particular ordeal before such a large and distinguished gathering; the speech, however, went off well and
Lord Rennell, perhaps realising his shyness, made a point of
congratulating him afterwards.

The tedium of the long meetings and speeches which were
often very boring was relieved by the social occasions. There
was a memorable garden party at the Villa D'Este, where, in
the magical surroundings of the famous fountains, the guests
were entertained with champagne and caviar. But the highlight
of these functions was the dinner given by Mussolini on behalf
of the Italian government in the Grand Hotel. Valery had the
doubtful honour of being placed next to Goering at the high
table and only two places from Mussolini – she also had to

submit to having her hand kissed by Goering when they were introduced. Conversation with him tended to be heavy going; not only was there the language barrier but his mind was evidently more in Berlin than in Rome at that moment. He was constantly leaning across the lady next him on the other side to talk excitedly to Mussolini about some impending event of great importance to him; eventually a telegram arrived for him in the middle of the dinner with the news of Von Papen's resignation as Chancellor of the Reichstag, which meant Hitler's rise to power, and after brief apologies he left to fly back to Berlin. The Austrian Minister, who was also sitting next to Valery, said he hoped Goering's plane would come down in the Alps!

Looking back on the occasion of this conference one can only be struck by the immense irony of a situation which brought together politicians, historians and intellectuals to discuss the historic and cultural unity of a Europe which the totalitarian powers were already plotting to destroy.

Christopher, with his dislike of formal gatherings, did not get much enjoyment out of the Congress, particularly when he became aware of its political undertones. Valery, who was more socially inclined, enjoyed the festive side of the proceedings, and she did not have to participate in the interminable meetings or listen to the speeches. Nor did Christopher have much liking for the new Rome Mussolini had created; it was organised, it was more hygienic – no traveller was likely now to contract the dreaded 'Roman Fever' which emanated from the undrained Pontine Marshes – but it had lost something of its earlier romantic grandeur which he remembered with nostalgia from his first visit to Rome in 1909. Lord Rennell remembered how, in the early days of his ambassadorship, the cardinals still drove in their carriages through the streets of Rome in their scarlet cloaks, with flunkeys carrying torches alongside. Most of the papal splendour had now gone and the carriages had been replaced by cars and trams, which made Rome one of the noisiest cities in Europe.

CHAPTER EIGHT

Return to the North

HOPES OF A PROFESSORSHIP

Only a few weeks before his departure for Rome, Christopher's mother died at the age of eighty-two, after a long illness. All his life he had been very close to her and felt the bond of their mutual interests in history and literature and the land of Wales. In an unfinished poem, written after her death, he wrote of her love of the rivers and the hills:

> The rivers of the West and the rivers of the North
>   The waters of Usk and Wye
> The land of Powys and the land of Dyfed
>   and the Black Mountain
> The habitations of old and the generations of the past
>   All these lived in her heart ....

His father continued living at Hartlington, with his daughter who had never married, but after his wife's death he became more silent and solitary as if he had no further wish to live. In February 1933 he died quite suddenly and Christopher only just managed to get to Yorkshire before the end came. He died as he had lived, a staunch adherent of the Anglo-Catholic faith and Fr Symonds, a Mirfield father, came over to see him just before he died. A terrible blizzard then descended on that part of Yorkshire and Hartlington was cut off from the outside world for four days so that it was only with great difficulty that the coffin and the mourners could reach the church for the funeral.

Christopher now inherited the house and estate in Yorkshire as well as his father's money and for the first time in his life at the age of forty-three he was reasonably well off, although he found this hard to realise after the years of scraping along on a small income. He once said how wonderful it would be to have money when one was young, but he never put this theory into practice with his own children, who were treated in exactly the same way as he had been by his father. I, for instance, received £5 a term pocket-money when at Oxford in the 1940s, which was a ludicrous sum even then.

The question now remained whether to resign from his post at University College, Exeter, and move to Hartlington in the Yorkshire Dales. Although he loved the house and the country, the climate, the lack of friends and intellectual contact were on the face of it a forbidding prospect for one who depended so much on these things. Walking was his only country pursuit and he had little or no interest in the affairs of estate management and lawyers – the latter were a constant worry to him. His mind was totally pre-occupied with his books and writing, and money and business affairs were to him an unwelcome distraction which if possible he handed over to Valery.

However, his mind seemed to be already made up for him when a professorship at Leeds University fell vacant for which it had been suggested he should apply. This was the Chair of the Philosophy and History of Religion, which was very much in his own line of country. The only trouble was his Catholic religion, which was a serious drawback, since the Chair had been endowed by an old Wesleyan lady and there was a strong Nonconformist and anti-Catholic faction on the committee for the appointment. His own application, which gave his *curriculum vitae* with his list of publications to date, sounded impressive enough and it was further supported by testimonials from six eminent scholars and academics. Among these were the Vice-Chancellor of Manchester University, Walter Moberly, who had formerly been Principal of University College, Exeter and who had a high opinion of his work both as lecturer and teacher as well as a writer and the Warden of New College, H. A. L. Fisher, who wrote:

> Mr. Christopher Dawson is the author of one of the most remarkable and original historical books, which has come out in the country during recent years. It is clear that he has in a marked degree the gifts of a teacher, for his perspective is admirable, his learning under strict control, and his arrangement a model of lucidity and force.

Dean Inge wrote a personal letter to Christopher and a very

characteristic one which emphasised the particular bugbear –
the religious difficulty:

> The one drawback is of course your religion. My distrust of the
> good faith of Roman Catholic scholars is almost as great as Dr.
> Coulton's, but honestly I believe that you are quite straight and if I
> were one of the electors I think I should support you, to the
> surprise of my friends who know my views.

The other supporters, particularly the future Bishop Barry
and John Murray, then Principal of University College,
Exeter, wrote testifying to the breadth of his religious views
but the most glowing praise he had was from his ex-tutor,
Ernest Barker, then Professor of Political Science at Cambridge. From two closely-written pages one can only concentrate on points of particular interest such as that in his view
Christopher Dawson had 'the mind and the equipment of a
philosophical historian above any other contemporary or
pupil' that he had ever known. He mentioned his Second Class
Honours Degree but added: 'I always knew that in intellectual
power, he stood alone among all the men I had ever taught.'
Finally he compared him as a Catholic thinker 'as being a
man and a scholar of the same sort of quality as Acton
and von Hügel'. He felt that he combined massivity and
insight.

These extracts are not given for the sake of eulogy but to
show the kind of backing he had for his application. Christopher himself felt encouraged, particularly when the Vice-
Chancellor of Leeds University invited him to lunch and
seemed favourable to his appointment. It was, therefore, all the
more disappointing, after having to wait two months for the
outcome of the committee's decision, to hear that the forces of
bigotry had won the day and had decreed that the Chair could
not be held by a Roman Catholic. According to Frank Sheed,
the Bishop of Bradford (the same who broke the embargo on
Edward VIII's affair with Mrs Simpson) said: 'A Chair in the
Philosophy and History of Religion should be held by a
member of the National Church'. Christopher had another
bishop in mind. When writing to George Every in August 1933
he said:

> It was a great disappointment about Leeds and I don't think it
> would have happened if it had not been for that wretched Bishop

of R .... and his sister, They had much the same attitude to Catholics as the Nazis have to the Jews!

The Chair ultimately went to Prof E. O. James, who held the appointment until 1945.

HARTLINGTON 1933–1936

After the disappointment of the Leeds professorship, Christopher was faced with a dilemma: whether to choose the prospect of intellectual isolation and a bleak climate for the sake of living in a house and place he loved, or whether to abandon it for an easier life in the south of England, perhaps near some centre of learning. At one time contemplating the magnificent view from the house over the fells, he would say he could never leave that place, but at another it seemed he could hardly bear to stay and face the cold and darkness of the northern winter and the isolation it entailed.

Proverbially writers are supposed to look for solitude and beautiful surroundings in which to work, and in the case of a Wordsworth this is certainly true, but the business of writing is essentially a lonely one and Christopher felt this more than most. 'Conversation is meat and drink to me', he once wrote in a letter to Edward Watkin, but no one who did not know him intimately would have suspected this for so often he seemed silent and withdrawn.

But it was not altogether surprising that he felt, in spite of the obvious disadvantages, a genuine desire to live at Hartlington, for it was there that he had spent some of the happiest years of his life and the thought of re-living those childhood years again with his own family must have weighed considerably in the balance. Always a lover of nature and the English countryside, and conversely a hater of towns and city life, Christopher felt that of all England this particular part of the country was the most beautiful.

Writing about this time to Edward Watkin, who was living at Sheringham in Norfolk with his wife and five children, he described the country in early summer as 'glorious with blossom. I have never been here before in time to see the bird-cherry in flower up the valley, and the bluebells and garlic flower in the wood are wonderful.' He enclosed a poem written in Chinese style – a *genre* he had studied when he was writing about the civilization of China. 'It is meant to ensure

your visiting us later', he wrote. Edward Watkin commented
that to anyone who did not know that it was written as a joke, it
would appear as an invitation to pure hedonism.

The Invitation of Ta-Sun

Climbing the limestone terraces
  Above the Western Paradise
My thoughts turn to my friend Wo-Ti-Kin
  And the days that we walked these paths together.

The sun still warms the rocks
  And the air is sweet with the scent
Of thyme, and the mountain primrose
  And the little thorny roses.
But my friend Wo-Ti-Kin is far away
  Beside the Eastern Sea.

'Pluck the flower, while the dew is
  fresh' said the sage Yang-Chu
For youth and time pass
  And in the shadow world no flowers grow.
A cup of wine and a garland of flowers
  Are better than the incense-sticks
of many dutiful descendants.

For the time being, Christopher and Valery decided to give
Hartlington a fair trial; the house was large and inconveniently
planned and even in those pre-war days it was difficult to run.
Worst of all was the heating problem in those cold northern
winters; Col Dawson had installed an early version of central
heating which sent warm air up through vents in the floor in the
old Roman manner, but the enormous boiler had to be stoked
twice a day and fires were lit in the bedrooms all through the
winter. Horton, the former coachman, now the chauffeur,
stoked the boiler; Beth, formerly the children's nurse, and
Martha, the parlourmaid, who had come from Wales many
years previously, lit the fires; and cooks came and went with
the seasons. One went mad and threatened to cut her throat
'from ear to ear' and another, hired through the columns of
The Universe, had religious mania and spent most of her time
praying in the chapel.

In that very un-Catholic part of Yorkshire, divided between
the 'Church' which was middle-of-the-road Anglican and the

'Chapel', which was Methodist, there was no Catholic church nearer than ten miles; in the circumstances the Bishop of Leeds gave permission for a chapel at Hartlington, which was a rare privilege, the only other chapel in the neighbourhood being at Broughton Hall, the other side of Skipton, where the Tempests, an old Catholic family, had had a chapel since pre-Reformation days. A priest came from Skipton on Sundays to say Mass at Hartlington and by degrees a congregation which seemed to spring from nowhere, composed of Irish hay-makers, mill-workers, summer visitors and the occasional tramp, assembled. Because the chapel was in an oak-panelled room and the house itself had by that time acquired an air of antiquity, many people who visited the chapel thought it was a pre-Reformation one and asked if there was a priest-hole in the house. The rector of Burnsall, unlike his predecessor, was of Low Church persuasion, and viewed all 'Romanist goings-on' with deep suspicion, while the Irish Catholic Canon from Skipton was narrow-minded in another direction. On one occasion, Christopher found himself defending some women holiday-makers, who turned up for Mass wearing trousers, against the censures of the parish priest; he argued that in many parts of the world such as Turkey and the Far East it was considered more respectful for women to wear trousers and that they would not be allowed into a sacred building in these countries wearing skirts; all depended on different cultures and customs.

All in all, the few years spent at Hartlington were happy ones, particularly in the holidays when the children came home from their respective boarding schools. They found the 'old house' (as they thought of it) re-furbished and much of the Victorian and Edwardian furnishings disposed of and replaced by the Sheraton and Chippendale furniture which had been inherited from Uncle William Dawson. The handsome portrait of Sophia Dawson painted by Romney still hung in the dining room where it had always been. Christopher set up his library in what had been the former drawing room, which faced south, looking over Burnsall Fell, and the hall with a huge open fireplace became the centre of family life. Here in the evenings there were games of charades, plays written and acted by the children, dancing to an old-fashioned gramophone and games of 'murder' in the dark passages upstairs. In all these activities

Christopher took part and in the winter joined in tobogganing on the steep snow-covered slopes. On a personal note, I remember asking him to compose a letter in Latin which I had been set for a holiday task by my school, and he produced the following lines:

> Hic frigas erat magnum et durum, nos autem jubilantes ibamus in montes et sedentes in curru qui barbaris vocatur *Toboggan* ferebamur magno impetu a vertice montis in profundam vallem. Boum!

Christopher, as might be expected, never settled happily into the role of a country gentleman and landowner. The estate was more of a worry to him than a pleasure or an interest and beyond putting in an appearance at the local Agricultural Show he took no part in county activities. While his father was never a typical country squire, he took an active interest in the affairs of the district, being a justice of the peace on the local Magistrates Bench and a churchwarden of Burnsall Church. As a writer and intellectual Christopher was considered eccentric by some of his more conventional neighbours; some thought he was a pacifist because he had not fought in the war, while one formidable lady told him that his beard made him look like a Bolshevik!

None of this worried him unduly; there was always a nucleus of friends among the neighbours he had known since his boyhood, with whom visits were exchanged and often friends came to stay from further afield – Edward Watkin and his daughter Teresa, who was Christopher's goddaughter and a great friend of his own three children; the Sheeds, Tom Burns, Bernard Wall, who was just starting a new quarterly, *Colosseum*, to which Christopher became a contributor; and David Jones.

In July 1935, David Jones stayed some weeks at Hartlington during which time he painted a picture from the house; he was then a comparatively unknown artist and Christopher commissioned the picture as a friendly gesture, paying him about £100 for it. In a letter of 2nd July 1935, David Jones was writing to his friend René Hague:

> This is a *simply heavenly place. I do wish you were here.* It's exactly like Capel in many ways – but more prosperous and less instinct with the waste land feeling, but the general formation of

river, tree, hill slope, tumbled-stone-wall, sheep-thing – remarkably similar – all private to young Kit Dawson – very nice. This house is solid, comfortable and Victorian and filled tight as tight with books so that you don't know which to read at all. So as usual you find yourself reading something you might read anywhere – *The Listener* or Burke's Peerage.[1]

At that time Christopher was in worse health than usual and was plagued more than ever by insomnia and in the same letter David Jones wrote: 'Just heard Kit put out his electric light (midnight). Poor Kit never sleeps without Sedormid & Co. and then hardly at all . . . . I do wish he could be made well, he is so nice.'

While David Jones was staying at Hartlington, his friend Mgr John O'Connor (Chesterton's *Father Brown*) came over to lunch from his Bradford parish, sending a fine salmon ahead of him for he was quite a *gourmet*. Indeed there was the embarrassing occasion when he was travelling up to Yorkshire with David Jones and, displeased with the food provided in the dining-car, suddenly hurled a plate of spaghetti at the astonished waiter.

Another time Evelyn Waugh came on a visit and Valery remembered an enjoyable expedition to Stonyhurst in his car. They found him a thoroughly good-humoured and amusing guest. Christopher had always enjoyed Waugh's novels and had they met again in later life, when changes in the Catholic liturgy they both loved so well were taking place, they would have had even more in common.

A very different kind of visitor was Eric Gill, who spent some time at Hartlington in 1934 when he was carving the inscription on Christopher's parents' grave-stone. His unusual appearance with his beard and sculptor's smock caused the village children to run into their school saying they had seen Christ in the churchyard. According to David Jones, Eric Gill and Christopher never really got on well together: Gill said, 'Christopher can never forget that he is a gentleman' while it could also be said that he himself had a conscious desire to identify with the 'working man'.

'THE SPIRIT OF THE OXFORD MOVEMENT' (1933)

One might have thought that the disruption of leaving his job at Exeter, and the disappointment over the Leeds pro-

fessorship, added to the turmoil of moving house, might have
also disrupted Christopher's work. But the case seems to have
been reversed, for in 1933 alone he had produced an essay on
William Langland's poem, *The Vision of Piers Plowman*, a
study which combined the literary, historical and religious
aspects of this poem, brilliant in its analysis of that age and of
the unique quality of Langland's work; various articles in
such places as *The Dublin Review*, *The English Review* and
The Spectator and a book *The Spirit of the Oxford Movement*, a commemorative essay for the centenary of the
Oxford Movement. A volume of selections from his work
Enquiries into Religion and Culture was also published in
that year.

Of all Christopher Dawson's books, short as it is, I think
The Spirit of the Oxford Movement was the subject in which he
felt most at home. The age itself attracted and influenced him;
it was the age of Coleridge and Wellington, of Nelson and Jane
Austen, of Shelley and Newman, who was only junior to
Shelley by nine years:

> It was that unique moment in the history of our culture when
> English society had emerged from the stability of the Georgian
> world and had not yet become set in the mould of Victorian-
> ism. That comparatively short period witnessed an extraordinary
> flowering of the national genius such as England had not known
> since the Elizabethan age. . . . . The English mind was more adven-
> turous, more alive to ideas, less stodgy and provincial than either
> before or since.

He had moreover an intimate personal knowledge of the
Oxford Movement for he had been brought up in its traditions
which had a direct influence on his own religious life, as he
emphasised later in his Harvard Lectures.

In this book, he was also able to use his powers of description to the full, not only in his portraits of the leaders of the
movement, Newman and Froude, Pusey and Keble particularly, but in his evident feeling for the old Oxford of Newman's day so different from our own:

> We who know only the modern town which sprawls its ungainly
> length from industrialised Cowley to suburbanised Wolvercote
> can hardly realise the character of the little city which lay among
> its rivers and meadows . . . . it was more beautiful perhaps than any

other place in England which was still rich in beauty: and consequently it could still inspire loyalty and affection.

In the preface he apologised for adding to the 'already copious supply of literature that had been called forth by the
centenary of the Oxford Movement' but he felt there was still a
need for a work of historical interpretation for few things were
more difficult to understand than the mind of the immediate
past. He thought this fact was only too clearly shown by
Geoffrey Faber's book *Oxford Apostles* which he described in
a letter to George Every as 'pitiable' and he could not understand how T. S. Eliot could have allowed the dedication of it to
him.

This book was concerned with the psychological interpretation of the Oxford Movement from a Freudian viewpoint:

> Seen through Freudian spectacles the severe moralism of the Trac-
> tarian ethos dissolved into an orgy of morbid emotionalism. The
> history of the Oxford Movement becomes an essay in sexual
> psychopathy.

He defended Hurrell Froude against Faber's accusation of
homosexuality:

> The unwary Freudian who regards Froude's anguished self-
> accusation as evidence of some typical perversion may be dis-
> concerted to find that he is dealing not with some dark hidden
> sensuality but with an unmortified desire for roast goose or with a
> secret brooding over the pleasure of a day's yachting.

And he concluded that it was the confusion of moral and
medical values which was the besetting sin of the literary
psychologist.

Although this short book was written within certain limits,
only dealing with the early years of the Oxford Movement, one
is left with the feeling that it would have gained enormously if it
could have been extended into a longer work going on to deal
with Newman's conversion to Rome and his later development, a task which Christopher Dawson was well equipped to
perform. Instead he kept himself firmly to his primary aim – to
write a purely historical study of the Movement: 'In all this
Oxford Movement essay', he wrote in a letter to George
Every, 'I have been careful to keep my own beliefs out of it and

have simply tried to put myself into the skin of the Tractarians and to see things with their eyes.'

He realised how in that more religious age passions and feelings ran high:

> If (today) religion no longer arouses passion, it is because our minds are no longer alive to religious issues. When life still flows strong in economics and politics, there is no lack of hatred, and hatred that has no spiritual principle to restrain it from evil. It is since religion has gone out of European life that the era of pro-scriptions and persecution has returned. Hence we have little excuse for assuming an attitude of moral superiority towards the past.

In the concluding chapter he dealt with the true significance of the Oxford Movement and with the issue of Modernism which was the great and burning question of the age; it was not the Modernism of a man like von Hügel, who while sharing the views of the Modernists in critical matters wholeheartedly accepted the dogmatic principle of Catholicism, but the Modernism of those to whom 'man is the measure of all things and the spirit of the age is the spirit of God.' In the eyes of such a Modernist there are no eternal truths and no divine law other than the law of change.

This was the historical significance of the Oxford Move-ment: according to Christopher Dawson 'it stood *pro causa Dei* against the apostasy of the modern world.' In the 19th century, after the victories of Liberalism and material progress, men had 'the illusion that all was for the best in the best of all possible civilizations, and that the traditional opposition between the Church and the World had lost its meaning':

> The Tractarians were not deceived by these illusions. They read the signs of the times better than the men who professed to be in sympathy with the spirit of the age. They knew where the world was going and they would not have been surprised by the atheism of modern Russia or the materialism of modern mass-civilization. They believed that Christianity was once more faced with the prospect of persecution and that it must be prepared for a long struggle against the powers of the world.

This short work received a pertinent salute in *The Concise Cambridge History of English Literature*, a revised edition of which was published in 1970, the year of Christopher's death.

À propos Lytton Strachey's *Eminent Victorians* it was stated: 'The truth (about Cardinal Manning) is contained in Dean Church's *History* or in Christopher Dawson's characteristically excellent work *The Spirit of the Oxford Movement*'. His name was also rightly mentioned among 'the ranks of distinguished historians who are also men of letters'.[2]

CHAPTER NINE

Crisis in Europe

MEDIAEVAL RELIGION

The year 1934 saw the end of one line of Christopher Dawson's thought, that of his historical and particularly medieval studies, and the beginning of his writing as an interpreter of political situations arising through the new ideologies. In that year he gave the Forwood Lectures at Liverpool University which appeared in book form as *Mediaeval Religion*, later expanded in 1953 to *Mediaeval Essays*. The essays extend from Augustine to Piers Plowman and from the Moslem culture of Cordova and Cairo to Northern feudalism and Norse epics, yet persist in a unity of theme and argument – the learning is nowhere more evident, yet there is a tone not of polemic but of protest against a false view of the whole period.

This is an important and a difficult point, not of religious controversy, nor of historical fact, but of culture and definition. The whole medieval period had been so distorted by partial views on either side that the central vision had been obscured: even the term 'Dark Ages' was partly an effect of this distortion. Christopher was concerned to break down the artificial barriers between periods erected by such terms. For instance, the history of the Roman Empire and the barbarian invasions was often studied to the complete neglect of the Christian Empire and Byzantine culture: so too the Renaissance and the Reformation were exaggerated to the neglect of the much earlier revival of learning and the Cluniac and papal reforms of the Church. History was woven without a seam, but it had been divided into periods and shared out between nations with hardly less cynicism than the partition of Poland.

On the other side were the Romantic distortions, the 19th century dreams of knighthood and chivalry and troubadours, Germanic forests and taverns and Merry England, confused with Catholic illusions about the Ages of Faith, which he rejected more strongly because they had been exaggerated in the generation immediately before his own.

These were only less false than the national myths which had so glorified France, Germany, and Britain that European culture was viewed as Western, whereas at least until the year 1000 and beyond, the higher culture was in the Moslem and Byzantine East and in the Mediterranean. To correct this he devoted two essays to the Oriental Background and the Moslem West, to show that such cities as Cairo and Cordova were most civilized when Western Europe had least urban life and was a feudal or tribal society:

> Western civilization in the tenth century was still, no less than in the days of the Roman Empire, practically identical with the Mediterranean world. Three great powers dominated and shared this world: The Byzantine Empire in the Balkans and Asia Minor, the Fatimid Khalifate in Africa and Syria, and the Spanish Khalifate in the far west; and their capitals – Constantinople, Fustat (Old Cairo) and Cordova – were the three foci of Western civilization.
>
> At that date no one could have guessed that these great empires were on the eve of their decline and that the future lay with the barbarians of the North.

(Mediaeval Essays)

A third essay considers the origins of the Romantic Tradition, and this persists in the same direction, for he traces them beyond Provence and the troubadours to Moslem Spain and Oriental society: and once his attention is drawn to it, even the casual reader can clearly detect in verse derived from the troubadours the accents of the Arabian Nights – the adoration of beauty, the passion, the melancholy, and the fatalism. In fact, this is now widely accepted, but it was this essay which pointed the way, to reveal another facet of its author's influence.

Here too are fascinating glimpses of that strange Jewish, Moslem, Christian Mediterranean culture which extended from the East to Cordova and through Barcelona into Provence. Here from the 9th to the 13th centuries the three religions debated, exchanged ideas, translated each other's works, consulted, taught, and learnt, in philosophy, in medicine, in science, and in manners. So far from being a dark age, this was more open in its criticism than the 18th century.

In the same year (1934) Christopher gave a notable lecture to the British Academy on Edward Gibbon; Algar Thorold, who heard the lecture, said that it was worthy of Gibbon himself. He appreciated Gibbon as a master of style, 'stately and ornate as a Roman triumph', and a master of history; he saw him as the last of the humanists and a typical man of the 18th century: 'He stood on the summit of the Renaissance achievement and looked back over a waste of history to ancient Rome, as from one mountain to another.' He pointed out also that Gibbon was indebted to another tradition – and one to which he was spiritually hostile – that of the Catholic Church and he made full use of its resources:

> It is here and not in humanism that we find the true highway that leads from the ancient to the modern world. By this road we can travel without a break from Eusebius and Jerome and Augustine to Bede and Marianus Scotus and Otto of Freising, and the patristic culture which supplies the key to the mind of the later Empire also forms the intellectual background of the monastic annalists and historians of the Middle Ages.

Even Gibbon could see how the stream of classical culture continues to flow by the use of Latin in the Church so that, as he himself wrote, 'the flame of science was secretly kept alive to enlighten and warm the mature age of the Western world.'

THE CHURCH AND THE DICTATORS

With the respect and reputation acquired by his first works, Christopher was pressed by publishers, editors and the BBC to contribute his views on subjects extending from sociology through politics to religion. He was the more valued in such matters because while he clearly and firmly expressed a Christian view, his temper was more ecumenical than controversial, and he had more command of his subject than some publicists.

In the spring of 1934 Christopher was asked by *The Catholic Times* to write four articles on 'The Church and the Dictators', and they appeared at the end of April and in the first three issues of May. The editor was confident that they would be widely discussed and he was not disappointed.

The first considered the emergence of Fascism, the second

Catholic social teaching, especially that of Leo XIII, the third the Totalitarian State, and the last the position in England.

Two statements in the first article aroused controversy: 'Fascism stands above all for the creation of a social order which is neither that of Communism nor that of Capitalism.' The other was a quotation from Paul Einzig: 'To a very great extent, Fascism *is* Socialism.' The central thesis was in the third article:

> A Europe divided among 24 nations each determined to decrease its imports and to increase its armaments cannot survive. What we need is not a suicidal nationalism that ignores the spiritual community of civilization, nor a cosmopolitanism which ignores historic realities .... but a European order. Some form of European organization is necessary, and we can only attain it if we return to the old tradition of Christian Europe and recognise a higher spiritual loyalty than that of blood or class.

This theory, a mixed economy, was then associated with the corporate state, on which much of the controversy turned: whether this could be given a Christian form, or whether it would necessarily be forced into a totalitarian mould. Those most opposed to it claimed that Dawson was a Fascist or had Fascist sympathies. Charges of Communism and Fascism were made freely in those days, often to denote no more than opinions about Soviet Russia. But in 1934 Russia was judged more soberly than Italy or Germany when Fascists and their shirts appeared comic, when Mussolini and Hitler were favourite butts of the cartoonists.

That Christopher had from the first viewed them less lightly was evident from a letter he had written to George Every in the October of the previous year:

> The German Revolution has depressed me exceedingly. It entirely blocks one line of advance, and it opens up a whole vista of horrible possibilities that are rapidly becoming probabilities. It is no good our washing our hands of it. We are all implicated. I do not mean that we in England are likely to start Jew-baiting – but there are other possibilities no less disastrous.

He judged Fascism more soberly in this perspective of horror, and, with his usual care, uncovered the origins of its ideas and the sources of its power. To those ignorant or

contemptuous of it, not forseeing the millions of lives and
deaths involved, this was itself a fault, though in fact he studied
and set out the principles of Marxism with no less care.

Some attacks were so unjust that they exasperated even his
serenity, and in a letter to *The Catholic Herald* he pointed out
that 'to recognise that the enemy is strong is a very different
thing from regarding him as a friend.' That was well enough,
but he then permitted himself a flippancy which aroused flames
of indignation:

> Finally, I would say that I object to being called a Fascist because it
> is apt to make people suppose that I am a follower of Mr Oswald
> Mosley or some such leader; if, however, the word is used to mean
> someone who has awoken to the fact that Mr Gladstone is dead,
> then, of course, I have no objection to being described as one.[1]

Irony is always dangerous in journalism, as it is often taken
out of context – there were people to say: 'A Fascist? He admits
it himself.' The point he emphasised by this reference to a
changed world was one he had made in *The Catholic Herald*
earlier, in answer to criticism: 'The fact is that there is hardly
any political party at the present day which does not, implicitly
or explicitly, treat the state as a final end.'

All this fell into perspective in his next book *Religion and the
Modern State* (1935) when he was able to develop the argument
at more length. Part of the book had already appeared in print,
for some of it was taken from articles written in reviews and
newspapers, but the style was more direct as a result rather
than the reverse: one reviewer wrote that it told the plain truth
which every political person should know, put forward with 'a
very unacademic vigour made pungent with epigrams (e.g. the
machine gun is 'a symbol of the age of plenty which has made a
thousand bullets fly where one flew before.').

As the author said in his introduction an eagerness to seek a
scapegoat typified the state of mind in Germany then, while
everywhere appeared a readiness to blame a single cause,
whether Fascism, Democracy, Capitalism, or Communism, as
the root of all evils. In fact the evils were not confined to one
country, for the modern state mechanised all human life. But
the fault was less in this machinery of the state than in the spirit
which controlled it.

Israel with its detachment from all the empires of the world was the basic tradition for Christians, who could accept no social system as an end in itself:

> Civilization is a road by which man travels, not a house for him to dwell in. His true city is elsewhere.

Any system, whether a Roman Empire, a Nazi Germany, or a Soviet Russia, which demanded the whole allegiance of man, frustrated his religion:

> If religion loses its hold on social life, it eventually loses its hold on life altogether. And this is what has happened in the case of modern Europe. The new secularised civilization is not content to dominate the outer world and to leave man's inner life to religion; it claims the whole man.

This was the general theme of the book – the essential dualism between the City of God and the City of Man. The idea of building an earthly Jerusalem in England's green and pleasant land was an empty hope which could never be realised:

> We must recognise that this determination to build Jerusalem at once and on the spot, is the very force which is responsible for the intolerance and violence of the new political order. There are it is true quite a number of different Jerusalems: there is the Muscovite Jerusalem which has no Temple, there is Herr Hitler's Jerusalem which has no Jews, and there is the Jerusalem of the social reformers which is all suburbs: but none of these is Blake's Jerusalem, still less that city which the Apostle saw 'descending out of heaven like a bride adorned for her husband'.

Christians could therefore best serve mankind in detachment from the pride and glory of worldly systems:

> When the Church possesses all the marks of external power and success, then is its hour of danger; and when it seems that no human power can save it, the time of its deliverance is at hand. Christianity began with a startling failure, and the sign in which it conquered was the Cross on which its Founder was executed.

In writing this book Christopher seemed apprehensive of the kind of reception it would get from the Press and public opinion generally. 'Writing on a matter like this', he said in a letter to George Every, 'one is sure to find points of difference with everybody and to represent no one but oneself,' and in the preface to the book he had written that it was only through the problems which had become so insistent during recent years that he found himself forced almost against his will to write it. As it turned out the book was an immediate success, but when Frank Sheed wanted to print a second edition as the first had sold out, Christopher refused with a maddening obstinacy which he could show at times and nothing would make him change his mind. His publisher then suggested that he should take out certain passages which could be misinterpreted but he refused to allow this either, saying that people would then think he had changed his views.

In a way perhaps he was right for it turned out that his ideas could be misinterpreted by even the most perceptive and sympathetic of writers and this was shown in a dissertation on Christopher Dawson's political thought written in 1950 by Prof Bruno Schlesinger, later, in America, to become one of his closest friends. Like the readers of *The Catholic Times* articles, Prof Schlesinger thought that *Religion and the Modern State* was an exposition of Dawson's pro-Fascist views and wrote:

> Convinced of the impending breakdown of the nineteenth century order of democracy and capitalism, Dawson views Fascism as the ascendancy of a new social order fitted to the needs of the twentieth century. In enumerating certain characteristic traits of Fascism, he follows a highly selective method of underlining the good features while neglecting the evil ones; wherever possible Dawson gives Fascism the benefit of the doubt. In doing so, he overlooks altogether the basic negativism of Fascism, which is primarily an anti-democratic, anti-capitalistic, anti-liberal, and anti-semitic movement.[2]

This was strong stuff, and in a letter of 24th January 1950 written to Prof Schlesinger on the subject, he equally strongly defended his views. He pointed out that in *Religion and the Modern State* he had never departed from the views stated in his earlier books and it represented only the reapplication of the ideas he had always held and still did; also that Prof Schlesinger had taken his exposition for the case of totalitarianism for the author's own views while in fact the book was essentially anti-totalitarian. He underlined again the central thesis of this work and quoted his own words:

> The issue is not simply one between two rival economic or political systems; it involves a spiritual issue that is deeper and more

complex. It is the choice between the mechanised order of the absolute state, whether it be nominally Fascist or Socialist, and a return to a spiritual order based on a reassertion of the Christian elements in Western culture.

BREAKDOWN

Between the years 1936 to 1939 Christopher produced no major published work. He contributed a number of articles to *The Tablet* of which he was on the Board of Directors for a short time – his fellow directors being Douglas Woodruff (the editor), F. W. Chambers, Arthur Pollen and Tom Burns. He resigned his directorship in 1937, not because of a disagreement on matters of policy but because he felt he had not enough say in the running of the paper. In a letter of 21st July 1937, Christopher wrote to Douglas Woodruff:

What I feel is that if I cannot take any active part in the direction of the paper or the determination of policy, I do not want to give the public any ground for thinking that I do. Nor do I want to be bound in any way as regards obligation of contribution or rights of republication, otherwise than as an ordinary contributor. (Actually I think I am more likely to provide you with useful stuff, if I am free to send in anything that strikes me as suitable at the moment than if we tried to settle for series of articles beforehand.)[3]

Christopher had started to write a book on the French Revolution,[4] when at the beginning of 1936 he had a serious illness. Having always been a semi-invalid, he was now really ill, suffering from a combination of heart strain, chronic insomnia and severe mental depression, and for the first time in his working life he found himself unable to write; this was a considerable setback for him as he had no other interests outside his work.

Less and less time was spent at Hartlington for he felt he had to get away from the extreme isolation of the place and in the spring of the same year he and Valery decamped to Sidmouth in Devonshire where they took lodgings for some months. David Jones was living there at the time, in a nearby hotel, recuperating from a nervous breakdown, and they renewed their friendship, going for long walks together and discussing Welsh literature, Celtic mythology and the traditions of Greece and Rome. Indeed, it was in his preface to *The*

Anathemata, the poem which is so closely bound up with these subjects, that David Jones expressed his particular debt to Christopher Dawson's writings and conversations.

It was at Sidmouth also that Christopher acquired the nick-name of 'Tiger': one day, David Jones was walking along Sidmouth sea-front with his friend, Prudence Pelham, when they met Christopher and talked to him for a time; as they went away, Prudence Pelham, shattered by his learning, exclaimed: 'My God, what a tiger!' Ever after he was known among his friends as 'Tiger Dawson' but he was never addressed as such to his face. This story was recounted to me by René Hague, David Jones's friend and editor of his published letters. It may well be that Christopher had no knowledge of the nick-name himself, for he certainly never mentioned it to his family.

One of the reasons for his persistent insomnia was that he was constantly worried that his books did not reach a wide enough public. David Jones remembered him rushing round at an early hour to his hotel (while he was still in bed) and telling him how he had been awake all night worrying about this: 'No one reads my books', he said. David Jones, in an attempt to calm him down, told him how he had heard some dean preaching in a cathedral and quoting from one of his books, but Christopher replied: 'I don't care what that wretched dean said about me – it's the kind of people who read the *Daily Mirror* I would like to be read by.' He failed to understand that his books could never be 'popular' in that sense.

In the same context, George Every remembered him saying to him with great passion: 'The Church is the World'. This had something to do with 'a certain sense of his own incapacity for wielding the kind of influence that is open to a layman. It was one of the puzzles of his life that he always wanted to be an influence, and was very influential, especially in the long run, but felt powerless.'

As Christopher felt that he could no longer face another Yorkshire winter, he and Valery decided to spend six months in Italy where they went in the autumn of 1936. They stayed first at Bordighera near the French border and then went on to S. Margherita near Rapallo. Here through Fr Desmond Chute, a friend of David Jones and Eric Gill, they met Ezra Pound who also lived in Rapallo and at that time was writing the *Cantos*.

Christmas was spent in Rome, where they re-met Bernard Wall and his wife Barbara (also a writer), who were staying there. Bernard was now well-established as both a writer and political commentator and also edited his own review, *Colosseum*, to which Christopher often contributed. He and Christopher saw eye to eye on the question of British sanctions against Italy, which they thought would, far from stopping the Abyssinian war, only strengthen the unholy alliance between Mussolini and Hitler.

In 1936 came the outbreak of the Spanish Civil War. From the distance of today it looks less like a war waged by heroic Republican idealists or holy crusaders against Communism, which is how the two sides and their supporters then presented it. The atrocities on both sides were so appalling that it is impossible to sustain such a black-and-white view. But at that time, for Catholics particularly, the issue was seen as one between Communism and Catholicism, and Christopher felt that had the Communists got a foothold in that part of Europe the results would have been disastrous.

In an article written for *The Catholic Times* on the Spanish Civil War he wrote:

> It is not merely a conflict of brute force, as in the days of the Turkish invasions, it is a battle of wills and beliefs, and it is in Spain, which has always been the bulwark of Christian Europe and bore the brunt of the battle with Islam in the past, that the battle with the new enemy of Christendom is being fought out to-day. It may well be that the issue of the struggle in Spain will decide the fate of Europe.
>
> The victory of Communism in Spain would be a victory for Communism in its most dangerous aspect, for it would not be a victory over capitalism, which is relatively unimportant in Spain, but over Catholicism, which is the very root of the Spanish tradition. And Spain is not a country for half measures; if she abandons Christianity, she will do it passionately and thoroughly. On the other hand the recovery of Christian Spain might well mark the turning point in her own history and that of Europe.
>
> If Spain could find herself once more, after the dreary century of disunion and weakness – if she could once more take the place to which her history and her genius entitles her – then it will be a victory not only for Spain but for Europe. It will bring back to the European society an essential element without which European civilization has become one-sided and incomplete. And we must

hope that the spirit which saved Europe from Islam and turned the tide of the Reformation is not dead: that out of the agony and destruction of the present crisis Spain will be reborn.[5]

In Rome that winter, Christopher met a number of priests and high-ranking officials of the Curia; their impression – conveyed via the English College to Fr Desmond Chute, who subsequently passed the information to David Jones – was that Christopher Dawson was a very brilliant man but he was much too interested in German theology and would probably end up a heretic! The ghosts of von Hügel and Tyrrell were not yet laid in their minds but in the case of Christopher they could not have been more wrong.

Back in England in 1937, Christopher was no more settled in his work or in his habitation. It was almost as if the turmoil of the crisis in Europe had its effect on his own life and for the last few years before the war the Dawsons were constantly on the move. Hartlington Hall was shut up and between 1937 and 1938 they lived in as many as six different rented houses ranging from Sussex to Surrey to Hampstead and thence to Kent. This life-style was neither logical nor economical, for with no settled home Christopher's work became disrupted and Hartlington was standing empty. But it was another of the puzzles of Christopher's life that, with his brilliant and logical mind, he found practical decisions almost impossible, whether they were about money, houses or family life.

Frank Sheed told the story in later years of how one day Christopher was worrying about his son's future career as he seemed to have difficulty in settling to anything. Frank told him that in the 18th century the eldest son was always given a house. It was a brilliant idea because the historical connotation immediately appealed to Christopher and he gave his son a most interesting but dilapidated 17th century house (known as 'The Folly') at Settle in Yorkshire which had been in the family for more than 200 years but had never been occupied by them since the early 18th century. With considerable expertise and imagination Philip restored this semi-ruin to its pristine glory, and it became the centre of much local interest and a setting for a number of important functions. At one time part of it was used as the headquarters of the National Trust in that part of Yorkshire.

'BEYOND POLITICS'

In 1938 Frank Sheed was anxiously pressing Christopher to finish his book on the French Revolution but he was to be disappointed for by this time he had turned again to solving the problems of the day in a successor to *Religion and the Modern State* entitled *Beyond Politics* which was published in January 1939. Again, like *The Spirit of the Oxford Movement*, it was a short book but according to Canon V. A. Demant who reviewed it in an article in the *Nineteenth Century*, subsequently published in a book, it deserved to be read by all Englishmen with any public influence and particularly by all religious leaders. 'While nearly everybody', he wrote, 'is sheltering behind the international smokescreen and saying that we cannot do anything about our home problems until foreigners cease to be so tiresome, Dawson calls attention to the strains within the national community.'[6]

By this time the threat to Europe was so grave that Christopher wrote again of the threat of the new 'socio-political ideologies' whether Communist, Fascist or Democratic. In particular he studied how England could preserve her liberty in the face of the totalitarian menace. In a sense, too, it is a very topical book for this present time since he foresaw a possible future situation in which the political involvement of the trades unions in parliamentary life could lead to a totalitarian order:

> If all the workers are embodied in the unions, and if the TUC decides the policy of its parliamentary candidates, it is obvious that the English party system could no longer exist, and the whole political order would be subordinated to an organisation based on industry and governed by purely economic considerations.

Modern societies were trying to reconstruct a genuine community to take the place of the Christian community of the past and this gave them both an opportunity and a justification. He wrote:

> For the greatest danger that threatens modern civilisation is its degeneration into a hedonistic mass civilisation of the cinema, the picture paper and the dance hall, where the individual, the family and the nation dissolve into a human herd without personality, or traditions or beliefs.

Nor could religion be used as a 'social tonic' for times of

national emergency 'to extract a further degree of moral effort from the people;' the greatest service the Church could perform for Western civilization was to preserve her own inheritance and not allow herself to be used as an instrument of secular power or politics: 'Religion serves a higher creed than man can comprehend.'

The book was about the historical crisis of those times which is unfortunately still our crisis today. An analysis of the spiritual purpose in history describes the world in which we live as 'submitted to forces which are both higher and lower than reason':

> There are forces of nature in the strict sense and there are higher forces of spiritual good and evil which we cannot measure. Human life is essentially a warfare against unknown powers – not merely against flesh and blood, which are themselves irrational enough, but against principalities and powers, against 'the Cosmocrats of the Dark Aeon', to use St. Paul's strange and disturbing expression powers which are more than rational and which make use of lower things, things below reason, in order to conquer and rule the world of man.

The book ended: 'To the Christian the world is always ending, and every historical crisis is, as it were, a rehearsal for the real thing.'

At the time of the Munich crisis of 1938, Christopher wrote an article for *The Tablet* on the subject: 'The Moral of Austria.' From this it is clear that he thought that Chamberlain and the Baldwin Government had got the worst of the bargain and were totally ineffective against Hitler's diplomatic manoeuvres.

> There is no virtue in a peace which consists in sitting still till our enemies are strong enough to destroy us. The only peace worth having is one that is based on a common understanding and the will to cooperate within definite limits to safeguard common interests.

But given the situation of the Munich agreement he thought the only possibility was to take advantage of the time in hand and to arm as quickly as possible.

The year before war broke out Hartlington was let to the Leeds Grammar School for an indefinite period and the Dawsons rented an unfurnished house in Cambridge. This was a considerable upheaval, for moving from a large house into a much smaller one meant storing some of the library and the furniture. Again it was an experiment which proved to be only a temporary solution; the house was on the outskirts of the town and Christopher was only on the fringe of university society. Naturally he met more people than if he had stayed in Yorkshire with only infrequent visits to London, but he still felt he was something of an outsider.

About this time he became friendly with Dr J. H. Oldham who ran *The Christian News-Letter* and also organised a group called 'the Moot' which discussed questions relating to Christianity, politics and culture; the other members were T. S. Eliot, Dr Karl Mannheim, J. Middleton Murry and Prof R. A. Hodges of Reading University. Christopher attended these meetings only occasionally but it is evident from a letter he wrote to George Every that he felt somewhat out of sympathy with their views:

> Eliot is a great stand-by and I am very fond of Oldham but I have not got much out of his Moot so far; – possibly because I have only been able to go once, but more I think because it tends towards that alliance of religion and politics which seems to me definitely the wrong path. One of the troubles with English religion is the strong Philistine element which has a natural affinity with the Philistine element in English politics and business – deep calling to deep. I don't mean that the Moot itself embodies these forces but I don't think Oldham etc. quite realise the danger of a Philistine dictatorship – a triumvirate consisting of Mr Caliban MP, Lord Caliban and Dr Caliban DD.
>
> It is terribly difficult to oppose any effective resistance to this – one can only do what one can. I agree with you that the cessation of *Criterion* is a serious set-back and I want to do all in my power to keep at least one independent Catholic review going with a cultural programme and not a sectarian one.

This last remark referred to a project he had in view with Bernard Wall to found a review to be called *Europe* which was to take the place of *Colosseum*, which was already in financial difficulties. It was hoped that Sheed & Ward might finance the new review. The war brought an end to any such venture but his own ambitions as an editor were realised when he was invited to edit *The Dublin Review* in 1940.

CHAPTER TEN

A Writer's War

EDITOR OF 'THE DUBLIN'

Only a state of emergency could galvanise Christopher into settling down to live in one place. The first was a domestic crisis, when in the 1920s he had to start providing for his growing family; the second was the national emergency created by the Second World War. Now he wanted to be at the centre of some intellectual activity rather than on the edge of things as he had been in the last desultory year at Cambridge. Various friends suggested Oxford as being within reach of London but not, so far, considered a bomb target. Once more the removers and packers arrived and the furniture and library of about 5,000 books went into store until a suitable house was found. This was not easy since Oxford, the former home of lost causes, became the home of exiles and evacuees, government departments engaged in secret activities and others less secret. Balliol College was given over to Chatham House, the Institute of International Affairs, with Arnold Toynbee as its Director and a staff of experts on every country in Europe. In fact, Oxford was no longer the peaceful seat of learning of the pre-war years but a hive of activity and a metropolis on its own.

After another succession of furnished houses, this time in Oxford, Christopher and Valery rented an unfurnished one at Boars Hill, where they had started their married life. After the war they bought this house and stayed there until 1953 when they moved back to Devonshire. If one was to describe Boars Hill as a suburb of Oxford it would be true but perhaps unfair, but it is certainly an adjunct. It was once a small village on the edge of Berkshire and Oxfordshire and being only three miles from Oxford it was almost impossible that it should not be developed as a residential area. In its heyday, between the wars, it became the abode of the intellectual elite – Gilbert

Murray, the eminent Greek scholar, lived there as did two poet laureates, Robert Bridges and John Masefield, and Robert Graves in his early days as a struggling poet and writer kept the village stores and post office. Sir Arthur Evans, the archaeologist, built himself a stately mansion overlooking a lake while Lilla McCarthy, the actress and friend of Bernard Shaw, had a tithe-barn moved from Herefordshire to Boars Hill, in which there was a minstrels gallery from which she and her friends declaimed passages from Shakespeare.

This Parnassus-like state did not survive for long and by the 1940s most of this distinguished company had departed, and their places were taken by retired captains of industry or ex-Indian civil servants. There among the dripping pines and overgrown foliage, they found large houses grand enough to suit their taste and some sort of substitute for Poonah and the India of the 'Memsahibs'.

The house which Christopher bought, built beside a small wood and known as 'Copse Side', was neither large nor grand, but a modest family house of the 1914 vintage: its chief merit was an uninterrupted view over the Berkshire Downs. But it was also close to the RAF airfield at Abingdon and far from being a peaceful, bomb-free place, night after night the sirens wailed and the German bombers droned overhead on their way to Coventry and other industrial targets. In the event, no bombs were dropped on Oxford – Hitler, it was said, wanted to take an honorary degree there – but there was considerable panic among the dons as the war went on and many of them sent their children to the USA or Canada to be educated. Christopher's family were nearly all grown up: Juliana had enlisted first as a nurse then as a driver in the army. Christina, the present writer, was studying to go to Oxford University while Philip was still at school, at the Oratory near Reading.

The breakthrough that Christopher needed came in 1940 when he was appointed editor of *The Dublin Review* in succession to Algar Thorold. The gift of the appointment was in the hands of Cardinal Hinsley who had a great admiration for Christopher's books and in this he was upheld by his friend and adviser, Dr David Mathew, himself an historian of distinction.

Founded in 1836 by Cardinal Wiseman, in co-operation with Daniel O'Connell and Michael Quin, 'The Dublin' had known its peaks and its doldrums: Newman once described it as 'a dreary publication .... which wakes up to growl or lecture and then goes to sleep again,'[1] and Maisie Ward recalled that Father Tyrrell wrote to her father, Wilfrid Ward, when he took over the editorship: 'You will have more worry over it than it is worth, I have seen death in its eyes for many a long day.'[2] Algar Thorold's editorship, as already noted, was one of the peaks of its existence and Christopher Dawson's in wartime was notable in quite a different way.

In July 1940, he composed an Editorial Note, reissued in the following number as the events of that summer had reinforced its theme; in this he underlined the need for 'all the positive intellectual and spiritual forces of Western culture' to unite to defend their heritage:

> It is here that Catholics have a special responsibility .... They are the heirs and successors of the makers of Europe – the men who saved civilisation from perishing in the storm of barbarian invasion and who built the bridge between the ancient and the modern worlds.

But it was not only an appeal to Catholics and to the Allies but to all Christians and to all the Western powers, whether they were involved in the war or not, to 'face the consequences of the totalitarian challenge.' It was the aim of the new *Dublin Review* to make public opinion alive to the issues at stake and to build up a defence for Western Christendom.

His strong articles over five years of war, later resumed in *The Judgement of the Nations* (1943), cost him as he wrote them 'greater labour and thought' than any other, but they were by no means his only work for the review. Constantly in his own articles he insisted on the unity of European culture and the need to find a form for this, but he practised this no less consistently in his choice of contributors. It was a brilliant stroke to cable to Georges Bernanos in Brazil and to get from him the famous *Lettre aux Anglais*, to publish pieces of Maritain, Fumet, Sertillanges. But the French were allies: more remarkable were the articles accepted in the height of war from prominent Germans, such as Hermann Rauschning, Franz Borkenau, J. P. Mayer, Prof Gerhard Leibholz and other exiles. They appeared side by side with the work of Polish and Spanish writers, and in the isolation of Britain under siege *The*

Dublin Review became the one truly European periodical, its contributors united in defence of their common culture.

This unity was also ecumenical, for not only all Christian communions were admitted, but all scholars who had something to contribute to the common cause, from the Master of Balliol, A. D. Lindsay, to American, Russian and Hungarian writers remote from Oxford.

Douglas Jerrold, whose politics were, if anything, rather to the right of General Franco's, did not see eye to eye with Christopher, and he disapproved of him publishing articles by Maritain and Bernanos who had not supported Franco in the Spanish Civil War. Even before Cardinal Hinsley's death, he tried to get Christopher removed from the editorial chair, but on that occasion the cardinal, who did not mince his words, threatened to move 'The Dublin' to another publisher if Christopher's position there was not secured. Cardinal Hinsley died in 1943 and the following year, Jerrold, by a manoeuvre, which Robert Speaight described in his autobiography, *The Property Basket*, as 'anything but pretty' ousted Christopher from the editorship. Barbara Ward had been Assistant Editor and her supposedly 'left-wing' politics were likewise distrusted.

'THE SWORD OF THE SPIRIT'

Almost simultaneously with his appointment as editor of *The Dublin Review* Christopher Dawson was invited by Cardinal Hinsley to be Vice-President of a new movement he had founded after the fall of France called 'The Sword of the Spirit'. This was in July 1940 and Christopher readily accepted. On 1st August the cardinal launched the movement with an appeal for unity and in his opening address he said:

> We must not obstinately rush into or stick to any extreme. The Right is not always and wholly wrong, and the Left is not always and wholly right. *Virtus stat in medio* – perfection is the golden mean. No extreme can claim a monopoly of wisdom and justice – Unity through charity is our battle-cry! Christian charity embraces all parties and all races.

And in a letter of 20th July he had written to Christopher on the same theme of a unity of the centre:

Archbishop's House,
Westminster, London, S.W.1.
20. VII. 1940

My dear Mr. Dawson,

Best thanks for your letter. I agree absolutely. This is the sort of thing we want.

Unity. The last words Pius XI said to me when he sent me here were these:

'Take to England and to my people the message I gave to French Catholics: Avant tout l'unité, partout l'unité, en tout cas l'unité, a tout prix l'unité'. That we must have now and here.

The extremes of Right and Left among Catholics are disastrous to the essential cause.

Because we are Catholics we must be loyal and reasonable patriots. If the Latin Catholic Bloc is against our country we are against that Bloc, because it is setting up a false principle – i.e. exaggerated nationalism – against true loyalty to Fatherland.

We must insist on the one thing necessary – to resist the philosophy of racialism, of class hatred etc. which seeks to dominate and enslave.

Not tanks, airborne forces, mines, torpedoes but strong manly faith will unite our nation and win victory. Politicians plus moral degeneracy plus treachery have brought about the collapse of France. What has impressed me in this crisis is the readiness of so many Britishers to accept religion as the only real basis of our strength.

I rely on your help in the crusade of 'The Sword of the Spirit'. The title, adopted by my friends and helpers, seems to me to express just the needed motive for our activity.

> With kindest regards and every blessing
> Yours devotedly in Christ
> A. Cardinal Hinsley

That Christopher held the same central political position is evident from a letter he wrote to the editor of *The Catholic Herald* a few years later, 30th September 1945:

With regard to my political position, I do not think it is any longer permissable to divide Catholic opinion by Right and Left. There was some justification for the distinction when the Left stood for the freedom of the individual and the Right for the authority of the State. But today when the totalitarians of the Left deny freedom and the totalitarians of the Right reject Law, the old distinctions have become meaningless and Catholics are obliged to unite in order to defend principles far more vital than the issue of the Left-Right party dog-fight. This was the object for which The Sword of the Spirit was founded and I do not think the need is any less grave today. The fact is that the problem transcends politics; and the old political attitudes and party alignments are as inappropriate as the old military tactics are in regard to the atom bomb.

It will take a long time for men's minds to adjust themselves to the new situation and unfortunately we have not got much time. I only wish that what I have written since 1935 may help to stop Catholics talking in terms of Left and Right and to understand the situation that we have got to face, whether we are united or whether we are divided.

Arthur Hinsley, like Churchill, was a man for the time; in fact, Churchill admired him and it was said that when the question of appointing a new Archbishop of Canterbury arose, he said, 'A pity we can't have the old man at Westminster'!

Although so different in many ways Christopher and Cardinal Hinsley had in common their Englishness and their Yorkshireness and when they met they recognised these qualities in each other. Hinsley was the very antithesis of a wily Roman prelate: when he spoke it was directly and from the heart and this was what endeared him to people. Of humble origin (his father had been the estate carpenter at Carlton Towers in Yorkshire, the home of the present Duke of Norfolk), he was no intellectual but he could appreciate the gifts of intellect in others. Likewise he was absolutely free from bigotry, from cant and all hypocrisy – in short he was a *good* man, who radiated kindness to all around him. The tragedy was that, already old when he came to Westminster, he did not live long enough to bring his work to fruition. He might have achieved, if he had had the co-operation of the rest of the hierarchy, a Second Spring in the Catholic Church in England of much the same kind as Newman had envisaged in the Oxford Movement.

'The Sword of the Spirit' was the first Catholic attempt to found an Ecumenical movement in England and apart from Cardinal Hinsley himself, it was at the outset entirely a lay movement. Afterwards, because of difficulties with the other bishops who were demanding some form of censorship in the bulletins, Fr D'Arcy was called in as an adviser and other priests were asked to write and lecture. The Board, with Cardinal Hinsley as President and Christopher Dawson as Vice-President, consisted of Richard O'Sullivan, KC as Chairman, with Barbara Ward and Prof A. C. F. Beales of London University as Joint Honorary Secretaries. Manya Harari, the future co-founder of the Harvill Press, although not a member of the Board, was a leading light in the movement. Robert Speaight described 'The Sword of the Spirit' as:

> Launched by Cardinal Hinsley, animated by Manya Harari, put into operation by Barbara Ward and intellectually nourished by Christopher Dawson .... Faith was strong in both these remarkable women and Christopher Dawson leaned heavily upon them, as they – for different reasons – leaned upon him. He was then living near Oxford, and since his delicate health kept him away from London the 'Sword of the Spirit' owed a great deal to the Great Western Railway and journeys that were 'really necessary.'³

Indeed, it was a remarkable trio: never a 'committee man', Christopher's administrative powers were decidedly limited; he was far too intellectual for down-to-earth discussions and all the *minutiae* which committee work involves. He would have done better not to have taken it on at all but instead to have confined himself to being the 'brains' of the movement. Barbara Ward, with untold energy and vivacity and many public and professional activities already occupying her time, did most of the administrative work for *The Dublin Review* and a good deal for 'The Sword of the Spirit' with assistance from Prof Beales, while Manya Harari provided the European contacts which were necessary. A White Russian emigrée, half-Jewish by birth and married to an Egyptian financier, she had a certain air of almost Eastern mystery with her long cigarette holder and the romantic black cloak which she often wore. Less practical than Barbara Ward, she had perhaps more understanding of Christopher's brilliant but sometimes eccentric mind and his tendency to often cancel an engagement at the last minute.

David Jones, in a letter to his friend, Harman Grisewood, described a meeting he had with Christopher in wartime London, written on 'the Glorious First of June, 1942' from 12, Sheffield Terrace, London, W.8.:

> I saw Tiger D. a few days ago, had dinner with him in what Tom used to call the 'mausoleum' in Queen's Gate Terrace – I must say it is a gloomy place. The Tiger had just had tea with the Arch-

bishop of Canterbury, the Bishop of London and Miss B. Ward – what an astonishing party. It was heavenly seeing the old Tiger again and he was not so bad, and sent you a lot of love. He was very funny in his own way. A bit severe and frightening in the way deep learning is apt to be – but by chattering about this and that and all the odds and ends I could think of, I drew from him some remarks I was pleased to hear .... He'd read Powys's *Owain Glyn Dwr* (of course! what's he not read?) and we chuckled together about the things in it, and we discussed a bit the resurgence of cruelty, torture, police-state & Co – agreed that historically it's a very complex subject indeed – I mean vis-a-vis the Christian Church etc. He said he found that Catholics, in his experience, since he became a Catholic, were getting far more, not less, 'institutional' (in the bad sense) and mechanical, so to say. That the age of von Hugel, the 'belief' in the Holy Ghost, in the subtlety of where truth resides etc. seemed far away – and a belief in effecting things by organisation and formulas etc. etc. (among Catholics) growing rather than lessening. In short, that 'propaganda' is universally dominant in the Church as outside it, and once you yield interiorly to the propagandist attitude you're sunk. We talked about how that one of the 'condemned propositions' of Luther was 'that the burning of heretics is offensive to the Spirit' – well that the burning of heretics *is* offensive to the Spirit is obviously true – condemnation or no condemnation. Yet rather than make this admission they go in for all kinds of beating about the bush to justify the papal absurdity – all of which is a pity and *quite* irrelevant to the truth of the Catholic Religion.[4]

This letter is included as the only verbal record of one of the many conversations between Christopher and David Jones. Christopher was very much alive to the seeming paradox between religious and historical fact: he would never try to explain away the evil and corruption that had existed in the Church but at the same time he was aware that it had something unique in the holiness of its saints. Frank Sheed recalls a conversation between Christopher Dawson and Edward Watkin: 'They were discussing some of the grimmer facts of the Church's history. It was a scarifying experience. After a silence Dawson said, "But there's something there." '[5]

While Christopher was completely orthodox in his Catholic belief he took his own line on some of the more legalistic aspects of the church. Censorship was one of them – his advice to Edward Watkin was: 'It is really much wiser not to try and

wangle things with ecclesiastics. As a rule if you leave them
alone they will leave you alone.'

'The Sword' (as it was commonly called) produced a bulletin
twice monthly and Christopher usually wrote the first three
pages of this. One of his more unusual contributions was a
poem, written in 1942, called *Prayer to St. Michael* which is
reproduced below:

Angel of God
Ruler of light
Whose arm holds back
the ancient night
See how darkness
Falls on the land
and the People of God
Fail and are few.

Our armies are broken
The saints are dead.
The prince of evil
Lifts up his head.
In the dark hour,
In the deep night,
Come down and help us,
Where help is none.

When first the Father
Fashioned Mankind.
Foreseeing all
With changeless mind,
He chose thee champion
To guard His own.

Heavy the charge;
For man's life is frail –
A cobweb spun
Between heaven and hell,
A perilous bridge
On which to ride
The high horses
Of human pride.

Yet on that bridge
Is set the strife
Of all the powers

Of death and life.
For there alone
Evil has power
to ruin and ravish
The creature of God.

Michael the prince
Come to our aid
The earth is shaken
Heaven is afraid.
Weigher of souls
In the last hour
When the bridge breaks
Hold fast thy charge.

'The Sword of the Spirit' was not intended originally to be only a Catholic movement but to unite all men of goodwill in the crusade against totalitarianism. The other churches soon joined in the movement led by Dr Bell, Bishop of Chichester, backed up by the Archbishop of Canterbury, the Archbishop of York and the Moderator of the Free Churches. Cardinal Hinsley's idea was to have a joint movement for Christian co-operation – reunion was not even suggested at this stage – but the rest of the hierarchy with the exception of Bishop David Mathew who upheld Cardinal Hinsley's principles were against any form of co-operation from the start and would only consider a separate 'non-Roman' branch of the Sword of the Spirit. It seems pitiable now that Catholic bishops were not only arguing about saying the Lord's Prayer with other denominations but even vetoing the idea of getting together to discuss social questions. The worst offender in this respect was Dr Amigo, the Archbishop of Southwark; even the Arch-bishops of Valladolid and Lisbon were more liberal than he on the question of Christian co-operation (for the Sword of the Spirit had also become an international movement). To a polite letter from the Bishop of Chichester asking that Catholics in the Diocese of Southwark should join in a week of Christian witness to discuss such general topics as 'Religion and the Home', 'Religion and the School' and 'Religion and Industry' Archbishop Amigo replied that as the Catholic Church alone had divine authority to define what Christian principles were, he feared that 'in a joint gathering opinions would probably be expressed, with which we could not agree, but which by our presence we should appear to countenance. Moreover The Catholic Church cannot consent to be grouped with other bodies as "one of the churches".[6] In a word there was to be no dialogue: he decided that it would be better for the Catholic sector to 'act separately' and to arrange their own series of lectures the following week. This chilly rejoinder was a great blow to the Bishop of Chichester, who was already assured of the goodwill of Cardinal Hinsley and of the Catholic laity (he was a personal friend of Christopher's). In a letter to Christopher he wrote:

> The fact that the R.C.s are going to have a separate show the following week – 'It is better for us to act separately' – makes the *non*-co-operation all the more marked. Is there anything to be done? it is a great disappointment.

Christopher, likewise, in a letter to Barbara Ward, wrote that he 'was dismayed by the correspondence between Southwark and Chichester' and Cardinal Hinsley in an earlier letter to him of 30th August 1941, had quite clearly stated his own views on co-operation between the churches:

> I am against rigidity, except of course regarding revealed truth and the necessary Church discipline to guard the same. We cannot compromise our Catholic principles. So I said at the General Meeting – our co-operation is not for 'Reunion' (here we must be guided by *Mortalium Animos*) but for the realization of the practical principles of the Social Encyclicals (*Rerum Novarum* and *Quadrigesimo Anno*).
>
> In the Army, Navy, Air Force, on Public Bodies, Charity Commissions etc., we are already co-operating in practical work. Why not extend the sphere of our practical co-operation to natural measures of a wider application?
>
> It is hard to make oneself understood in writing, yet I am so anxious about this question which is vital to the success of the Sword of the Spirit. Please do not be discouraged by these difficulties. There is no question so intricate in Moral Theology as this problem of co-operation in the various incidents of life! A difficulty somewhat parallel to our present problem confronted me in the Mission field. One school of missionaries would isolate their converts in Native villages, kept carefully reserved and away from contacts with paganism etc., The other school insisted that, if the converts were made 'strong in faith' they would be a *leaven* in the

native villages or kraals. I am wholeheartedly with the idea of *leaven*.

I hope I have written something that will help, and that will encourage you in your splendid work. There is a priest in whom I have perfect trust, and whom I recommend to you – Rev John Heenan PhD DD of Manor Park. (later Cardinal Heenan). He knows his theology and he knows my mind.

> Warmest regards and every blessing
> A. Cardinal Hinsley.

N.B. The native villages were a failure.

In 1942 Cardinal Hinsley resigned from the Presidency, owing to illness and pressure of work. These were the reasons given in the Press. It was a bitter blow to his friends and most of all to his Anglican ones, such as the Bishop of Chichester. The latter wrote in a letter to Christopher on 5th March 1942:

> It is, however, the end of your letter which fills me with sorrow. I had no idea that the Cardinal was resigning the Presidency of the Sword. It is indeed a calamity. I accept what you say as confidential, but what can it mean? Just as the movement for Christian co-operation was coming to a really promising stage, and a joint announcement was to be made public at Lincoln's Inn Hall on March 19th, can the Cardinal really be withdrawing: I am sure he does not want to withdraw. I wonder what has caused it all?

In all probability what caused his resignation was a directive the Cardinal received from Rome that only Roman Catholics could be full members. Frank Sheed describing the event wrote that he remembered his sick feeling and Cardinal Hinsley's sick face, as he told him of it:

> Something vital and hopeful withered in that moment. The Sword continued, an Anglican society was formed with the name Religion and Life . . . . But, as a movement drawing all men of good will to 'the unity of the Spirit' in the bond of peace, it was over that afternoon.[7]

In 1943 Cardinal Hinsley died and Christopher Dawson wrote an obituary in the Sword of the Spirit *Bulletin* under the title *A Champion of the Spirit*, in which he said it was difficult to estimate the loss that the Church and the nation had suffered by his death for 'he represented the central tradition and the essential quality of English Catholicism to a degree that has rarely been equalled.' He stressed the qualities of his 'intense national and local patriotism which, as an Englishman and a Yorkshireman, in no way contradicted or limited the width of his human and Christian sympathy with other nations and with the cause of suffering humanity throughout the world.' He might as well have also written the obituary of the Sword of the Spirit for without the cardinal's spiritual leadership it soon foundered among the rocks and shallows of political and social aims and there were already a large number of organisations dealing with these more secular activities. In terms of a movement towards Christian co-operation it was a great opportunity lost at a time when the nation had a sense of common purpose. And the fault, it must be admitted, was on the Catholic side.

Increasingly, Christopher Dawson found he had to write down to what he called the 'parochial' level and to shelve all the deeper spiritual issues. In 1947 he expressed his views in a letter to Fr John Murray, SJ (the official Ecclesiastical Assistant) saying that 'the movement was left in a state of suspended animation, unable to go on and unable to stop.' He had always rather felt that he was the fifth wheel of the coach and now he was the fifth wheel of a broken down coach without a driver!

Prof A. C. F. Beales, contributing to a controversial discussion in *The Times* letter columns ('Catholicism Today', 8th November 1949) summed up the remarkable achievements of the Sword of the Spirit in war-time Britain. He recalled the famous joint letter to *The Times* of 21st December 1940, signed by the leaders of all the churches, which drew up a programme for a remarkable Christian campaign in this country during the war. It resulted in two important events: first, the meetings at the Stoll Theatre of 10th and 11th May 1941, when Cardinal Hinsley presided on the first day and the Archbishop of Canterbury on the second and then the joint statement on co-operation promulgated in May 1942, which, excluding such divisive questions as doctrine and Church order, called for a united stand by all Christians on ten points of social and international order which had been set out in the original letter to *The Times*.

The momentum of that wartime drive had slackened, he wrote, but the whole episode showed what could be done together by those who wish, fundamental differences notwithstanding.

Peace brought with it other problems, for the agreement at Yalta, where Churchill and Roosevelt were overruled by Stalin, was felt by many people to be a betrayal of the oppressed countries, particularly Poland, in whose cause Britain had declared war on Germany. Christopher felt strongly about the handing over of Poland to Russia and realised that the first of Pius XII's five Peace Points of December 1940 had already gone by the board: 'There is no room for the violation of the freedom, integrity and security of other states, no matter what may be their size or their capacity for defence.' Likewise, when the terrible deportations of Russian nationals took place after Yalta he helped the Bishop of Chichester prepare his speech, calling attention to this tragedy in the House of Lords, by providing historical data. Cardinal Griffin also wrote a letter to the press on the subject so that at least it cannot be said that leaders of Christian opinion were entirely silent on these atrocities.

Christopher was also associated with Bishop Bell in his efforts to convince the British government that it was necessary to co-operate with the anti-Nazi resistance movement inside Germany during the war. A close friend of Christopher's was Prof Gerhard Leibholz (brother-in-law of Dietrich Bonhoeffer) who, being Jewish, had escaped with his family from Germany just before the war and settled in Oxford.

'THE JUDGEMENT OF THE NATIONS'

Christopher Dawson wrote one book during the war – *The Judgement of the Nations* (1942) – and it bore the scars of war not only in its title. The first part was 'The Disintegration of Western Civilization', its first chapter 'The Hour of Darkness' and there was the moving Foreword:

Four years have gone to the making of this book – years more disastrous than any that Europe has known since the fourteenth century. Small as it is, it has cost me greater labour and thought than any book that I have written.

I dedicate it to all those who have not despaired of the republic, the commonwealth of Christian peoples, in these dark times.

The horrors of the war were such that only the power of the spirit could overcome them:

> We are passing through one of the great turning points of history –
> a judgement of the nations as terrible as any of those which the
> prophets described. We see all the resources of science and tech-
> nology of which we were so proud devoted methodically to the
> destruction of the world. And behind this material destruction
> there are even greater evils, the loss of freedom and the loss of
> hope, the enslavement of whole people to an inhuman order of
> violence and oppression. Yet however dark the prospect appears
> we know that the ultimate decision does not rest with man but
> with God and that it is not his will to leave humanity to its own
> destructive impulse or to the slavery of the powers of evil.

The book was better received by Anglicans than by Catholics: particularly by Dr Bell, Bishop of Chichester, who,
when making a speech in the House of Lords, held the book up
recommending it to everyone to read.

But it also had some criticism from the agnostic Left and the
Catholic Right: in answer to a letter of Douglas Woodruff's
suggesting that Christopher should write a reply in *The Tablet*
to an attack on this book by Harold Laski, he wrote:

> It is difficult to make a reasoned reply to Laski's thesis, which is, I
> gather, that we are to replace faith in Christianity by an act of faith
> in Russia. I know that the cult of the Sacred Bear played a great
> part in primitive Arctic cultures. But at any rate they had the
> satisfaction of eating the bear, whereas in the new cult it is the bear
> that eats us – and if your Yugoslav correspondent is to be believed,
> that is already happening in grim earnest. I only hope his facts are
> exaggerated: nothing is more uninteresting than atrocity statistics.
>
> P.S. While Laski is attacking my book from the Left, the
> theologians are starting an offensive on the other wing. Did you
> see Fr. Beck's article on it in this number of the *Clergy Review*?[8]

The Rev Andrew Beck (later Archbishop of Liverpool) criticised the author of *The Judgement of the Nations* for being too
much 'influenced by the Old Testament and especially by the
prophets'; he found the suggestions made about the problem of
reunion 'startling' and thought that it was neither just nor fair
to non-Catholics to speak of 'common beliefs'.[9] Later, as
Bishop Beck, writing in *The Times* in 1949, he proclaimed the
impossibility of a Catholic and a non-Catholic saying the

Lord's Prayer together with united minds: 'The Catholic saying for example "Thy Kingdom come," would be praying for
the conversion of all men to Catholicism; the non-Catholic
evidently would not subscribe to this petition.'[10]

In view of his subsequent role when as Archbishop of Liverpool he played a leading part in the Ecumenical Movement, he
must have been embarrassed if he ever thought of his former
statements on the subject of joint prayer such as the one in the
same letter where he said:

> It would pain the Bishop of Winchester that Catholics should be
> dubious about his giving a blessing at a joint meeting. But their
> attitude is the logical outcome of their belief that, so far as they are
> concerned, and from their point of view, the Bishop of Winchester
> is a layman.

It is astonishing to consider now, not so much that the
hierarchy have changed but that they have changed so much,
performing an 'about turn' that has taken ordinary Catholics
completely by surprise. Christopher never changed his views.
As a Catholic he often attended Evensong at Christchurch
Cathedral in Oxford. When the Dean, who was a friend of his,
asked him if his Church allowed him to do this, Christopher
replied: 'I never ask'. Similarly, at the beginning of the war, I
was attending a non-Catholic school and during school prayers
it was expected that I would sit outside with a Jew and an
atheist. My father thought this was ridiculous and advised me
to attend prayers with the others.

In the 1940s Christopher held that the most pressing need of
the time was 'without any compromise of principles or any
narrow exclusiveness' to unite against antichrist, on the deepest and most spiritual grounds. Antichrist was totalitarianism
in whatever form it manifested itself and the fact that Russia
had become our political ally did not mean that we should
share her ideological beliefs. Antichrist could also mean the
total organisation of human society on anti-Christian principles.

In the light of all this it can be seen that Christopher was far
ahead of his contemporaries in the Catholic church in his views
on Christian unity. He pointed out in *The Judgement of the
Nations* that the greatest causes of Christian disunity were
political and sociological:

To the average Protestant, Catholicism is not the religion of St. Thomas and St. Francis de Sales and Bossuet; it is the religion of Wops and Dagoes who worship the images of the Madonna and do whatever their priests tell them to. And the same is true of the average Catholic, *mutatis mutandis*.

He believed that the time in which he was writing was more favourable to the cause of unity than any since the Middle Ages. When Christianity is a minority and a persecuted religion it becomes a reality and 'a centre round which the scattered forces of Christendom can rally and reorganise.'

He looked forward as he did in his first writing, *The Nature and Destiny of Man*, and in his last Harvard Lectures, to a universal spiritual society which would be above schisms and heresies and the efforts to secularise religion bringing it down to the level of material society, and in the unpublished notes for *The Judgement of the Nations* he wrote:

> The more our religion rises above the level of human idea and human behaviour into the sphere of the supernatural and the divine, the nearer we come to the attainment of unity.
>
> In other words, we have lost unity by departing from God. The more we make our religion a human thing, the more deeply it is involved in the temporal, this worldly sphere, the more we lose the spirit of unity. Schism is the breach which results from the collision between the spirit of the age and the spirit of God.

Forty years ago when Christopher Dawson wrote *The Judgement of the Nations* he prophesied the end of the age of schism and argued that all the living elements of Christian life and thought would be drawn together into organic unity. He saw no need to talk about the ways and the means, for he held that 'the ways of the Spirit are essentially mysterious and transcend human understanding'. Christians, he thought, might even be forced together in spite of themselves by the very strength of the opposing forces.

Several years later, talking to an American Methodist who had come to interview him about his views on Christian unity, Christopher Dawson stressed the point he had made in *The Judgement of the Nations* that true unity could only come about in the first place, by the recognition of Christ as King – organisation was secondary. If we could think of Christ as Lord, and Pope as Servant, then the Papacy could be seen as a necessary symbol of a unified Christendom.[11]

This vision of unity was not merely to be seen as a kind of Christian Utopianism; it was a living spirituality comparable to the unity of the human race in the natural order. He believed that the creation of this divine society was of infinitely greater importance than anything else in human history and the spirit of this society, which was charity, was the only power which was capable of giving new life to our civilization.

The last chapter of the book was devoted to European unity, and in this he considered a federation of European nations. He pointed out that 'the USA is a federation which has become a national unity, while the British Commonwealth and the USSR are empires which have developed into federations.' The League of Nations had failed to take account of these larger groups, yet it was essential to proceed from existing realities:

> At the present moment the ideal of a United States of Europe may seem Utopian and unreal, but it seems the only solution capable of reconciling the national freedom and cultural autonomy of the Western European peoples with the tradition of European unity and the needs of world order.

He reached this conclusion with a foresight shared by the Austrian Count Coudenhove-Kalergi who in that same year, 1943, held the fourth Pan-European Congress in New York.

CHAPTER ELEVEN

A Wider Public

THE GIFFORD LECTURES

On 12th March 1945, Christopher Dawson received a letter from Edinburgh University asking if they could submit his name for appointment as Gifford Lecturer for the next term of the lectureship, 1946–47, the first to be given since 1940. It was rumoured that it was his friend, Dr Bell, the Bishop of Chichester, who had put his name forward. The Gifford Lectureship, one of the most coveted and distinguished in Great Britain, was in Natural Theology and was defined in the Deed of Foundation as follows:

> For promoting, advancing, teaching and diffusing the study of Natural Theology in the widest sense of that term, in other words, the Knowledge of God, the Infinite, the All, the First and Only Cause, the One and Sole Substance, the Sole Being the Sole Reality, and the Sole Existence, the Knowledge of His Nature and Attributes, the Knowledge of the Foundation of Ethics or Morals, and of All Obligations and Duties thence arising ....
>
> The Lecturers appointed shall be subjected to no test of any kind, and shall not be required to take any oath, or to emit or subscribe any declaration of belief or to make any promise of any kind: they may be of any religion or way of thinking, or, as is sometimes said, they may be of no religion, or they may be so-called sceptics or agnostics or free-thinkers, provided only the patrons will use diligence to secure that they be able reverent men, true thinkers, sincere lovers of and earnest enquirers after truth.

The appointment was for two years, in each of which one course of ten lectures had to be delivered. Christopher accepted, though not without some trepidation – from the start he seemed nervous of committing himself to a programme which he might not be able to complete – and he proposed to take 'Religion and Culture' as the general theme for his course of lectures.

After working on them for a year, a sudden fit of despondency seemed to overtake him and he decided that he would be unable to deliver the lectures the following term. One day in June 1946, Frank Sheed visiting Christopher found him, much to his horror, in the middle of composing a letter tendering his resignation as Gifford Lecturer, and nothing it seemed would persuade him to change his mind. The letter, addressed confidentially to Prof John Baillie, went off on 7th June and was intended as a preliminary to his formal letter of resignation, which would be addressed to the Committee. It read:

Copse Side,
Boars Hill,
Nr. Oxford,

June 7, 1946

The Very Rev. Professor John Baillie,
9, Whitehouse Terrace,
Edinburgh, 9.

Dear Baillie,
I am sorry to say that my work for the Gifford Lectures has not been going well and I fear that I shall not be able to deliver them. I am writing to you personally – however I thought that I should write to you confidentially before I take any step to send my resignation to the committee.

The fact is that for many years now I have been out of touch with philosophical studies and with the currents of philosophical thought in the universities and I have found it much harder than I expected to recover contact. I find for example that the only book I have read recently which deals expressly with Natural Theology is Austin Farrer's – entirely incomprehensible and far from my own way of thinking. No doubt there are other more competent students who are no more sympathetic to Farrer's approach than I am, but I am not even in a position to criticize him as I do not even understand the background against which this present discussion of the problem of Natural Theology is being carried on.

In addition to this difficulty, I have had the protracted difficulty of ill-health which has stopped my writing almost entirely since February. This, I hope, is only a temporary hold-up, but it has taken the time which was essential for the preparation of the lectures, so that apart from the intellectual difficulty I see no present hope of completing the course, even the first part of it, in time for the coming university year. I need not say that this is a grievous disappointment to me, for there is no distinction I should value more than that of being a Gifford Lecturer but under the circumstances I do not see any alternative but to resign.

I only hope it will not cause great inconvenience to the Trustees and to the University. Can you tell me to whom I should write on the subject and whether I ought to do anything besides sending a formal letter of resignation?

Yours very sincerely,
Christopher Dawson.

Prof Baillie wrote back taking a firm and reassuring line. He said that he had consulted with his colleague, Prof Kemp Smith, and they both considered that the facts he had set out did not warrant or necessitate resigning the appointment, or at least being in a hurry to do so. They also thought that he was taking the provisions of Lord Gifford's will too conscientiously; some lecturers had perhaps rather unscrupulously ignored these but some of the best courses had been purely historical rather than philosophical. They also thought they would far rather have something in the field of the history of culture and ideas, which was what was proposed, than a course of a more systematically philosophical or theological nature. In any case it was far too late to appoint another lecturer for the period already assigned since two years notice had to be given. They agreed however to postpone the lectures if necessary for another eighteen months or even that Christopher should give only one course.

This touch of firm reassurance was just what Christopher needed to give him the impetus to go ahead with the lectures and any fears he had were further allayed after Prof Baillie had read the first five lectures and wrote in another encouraging letter: 'Your lectures are so little abstract philosophy, and so much historical, that I am now a little puzzled that you should have had doubts as to their competence and sufficiency.'

After this uneasy start the lectures were duly finished and Christopher delivered them in Martin Hall, New College, Edinburgh. The first course of ten lectures, *Religion and Culture*, was given in April and May 1947 and the second, originally entitled *Religion and Culture in Medieval Europe*, in November 1948. His shy manner and quiet intonation, combined with a lack of confidence in his own powers, must have made him seem the most unassuming of Gifford Lecturers, and of course, the deepest thinkers are not invariably the best speakers – 'the gift of the gab', the histrionic powers of the actor, the orator or the preacher are often alien to the academic mind.

The Gifford Lectures were published by Sheed & Ward in two volumes: *Religion and Culture* (1948) and *Religion and the Rise of Western Culture* (1950). In the first book, he resumed the themes of his earlier work, notably *The Age of the Gods* and *Progress and Religion*, and further developed his key thought that 'religion is the dynamic element in culture.'

The second Gifford lecture, 'God and the Supernatural', contains the most concise definition of religion made in recent years. Christopher proposed a new historical approach and quoted from Calvin's *Institutes* – 'some sense of the Divinity is inscribed in every heart'. To those who argue that religion was born of man's early fears and hopes, the lecturer replied that 'primitive man in his weakness and ignorance was nearer to the basic realities of human existence than the self-satisfied rationalist who is confident that he has mastered the secrets of the universe.'

Man faces two unknowns, his own nature and the nature of the universe. To the spiritual mystery of man's nature there is 'an immense body of testimony from East and West and from all the great traditions of the world religions' and Indian philosophy is based on this transcendental intuition. The mystery of the universe is the other unknown, for 'Man is born into a world that he has not made, that he cannot understand and on which his existence is dependent.' This sense of cosmic transcendence finds its classical expression in the Book of Job. This is no less important, especially for primitive religion.

The cosmic sense leads to a pluralist or polytheist theology, whereas the intuition of transcendent spirit tends to a unity, even to a denial of existence for anything but the One. So a transcendent quality in the cosmos was recognised by primitive man, however diffused as in the Polynesian conception of Mana, 'most easily understood as a pagan analogy of the Christian conception of grace'.

This religious intuition inspired culture: 'The temples of the gods are the most enduring works of man'.

Priests of the temple founded a tradition of learning based on a spiritual principle, while intellectuals – the clerics of modern society – more often advanced a material principle and reduced its religious character. The contrast is between the Oni of Ife in Nigeria who in this century claimed that to interrupt his sacrifices would endanger the universal course of nature:

> It is still too early to say whether this change is permanent. It is not impossible that a century hence the people of Ife may regard the atomic bomb not as an evidence of scientific progress but as an unfortunate by-product of the abandonment of the theocratic order and the neglect of sacrifice.

If there is irony here, there is too a reminder that primitive thought has its own insight, for the modern idea of nature is more abstract than the idea of God. Primitive thought starts with gods and things and events, not nature. So too an advance in culture may bring a religion of pure contemplation to renounce society, so that the unity of archaic culture is destroyed:

> Thus the world of culture is gradually weakened and finally deserted, like the great Buddhist cities of ancient Ceylon where the jungle has returned and swallowed up palaces and monasteries and irrigation tanks, leaving only the figure of Buddha contemplating the vanity of action and the cessation of existence.

This tension between religion and culture creates both the great societies and great revolutions, for the religion which formed a society becomes a disruptive force in times of social change. Too close a union between religion and culture is 'fatal to the universal character of religious truth':

> If this identification is carried to its extreme conclusion, the marriage of religion and culture is fatal to either partner, since religion is so tied to the social order that it loses its spiritual character, and the free development of culture is restricted by the bonds of religious tradition until the social organism becomes as rigid and lifeless as a mummy.

Here is a more forcible reminder of the distinction already noted between religion and culture. It was this rigidity of structure that Christopher Dawson criticised in the Oriental sacred monarchy and in the modern Communist state, for in both, control of the mind and control of government were one and the same.

The first series ended with a forecast of what could happen if mankind lost the religious foundation for his social way of life:

We are faced with a spiritual conflict of the most acute kind, a sort of social schizophrenia which divides the soul of society between a non-moral will to power served by inhuman techniques and a religious faith and a moral idealism which have no power to influence human life. There must be a return to unity – a spiritual integration of culture – if mankind is to survive.

If *Religion and Culture* reflects the main themes of his first two books, the second series of Gifford Lectures, *Religion and the Rise of Western Culture*, is an extension of the ideas first expressed in two other major historical works, *The Making of Europe* and *Medieval Religion*. It was a longer book than the first volume and was illustrated. While *Religion and Culture* dealt exclusively with the world religions, the second volume was devoted to the history of Christian culture from the birth of Western civilization after the downfall of the Roman Empire when the Northern barbarians were converted to the Christian faith, down to the later Middle Ages – the age of Dante, St Francis and St Dominic and in England, William Langland, the author of *Piers Plowman*.

He wrote of the dynamic character of Western Culture and its transforming influence on world history, the continuity of the western development which owed its unity to a common religion, the formative period in the Middle Ages, and finally the bearing of this study on the problems of the life and death of civilization. Of the Dark Ages he wrote:

> Inevitably these ages of the death and birth of cultures are furthest withdrawn from the light of history. But where, as in the case of the origins of our own culture, we are able in some degree to penetrate the darkness, it is possible to see something of the creative process at work in the depths of the social consciousness; and however incomplete this knowledge may be, it is of very high value for the student of religion and the student of culture.

Just as David Jones made the central theme of his poem *The Anathemata* the importance of the Roman liturgy and the ancient mythology of the saints in the continuity of our Western tradition, so in the second volume of Gifford Lectures Christopher Dawson pointed out how much we have to owe to both in the formation of Western Culture. He stressed its missionary aspect which was older than Christianity since it went back into the remote past beyond the beginnings of recorded history. He quoted the Romans 'who were not unconscious of it' and Virgil himself who 'chose for his hero not the typical heroic warrior but a kind of pilgrim father, the pious long-suffering Aeneas who was charged with the providential mission to found a new city and bring the Gods to Latium.'

He wrote of the cult of the saints in the Dark Ages, and how it was very difficult for the modern mind to enter this world of popular Christian imagination. The saints were not merely intercessors but they were supernatural powers and watchers over countries and peoples, for in many cases the local pagan cult had been deliberately replaced by the cult of a local saint. This was something far from the mysticism of the late Middle Ages or the metaphysical religion of the age of the Fathers, but it was still Christian in spirit although of a Christianity 'striving against the all-pervading influence of a barbaric environment'. It was a twilight world where the Christian and the barbaric were brought together:

> It was inevitable that the Christian ascetic and saint should acquire some of the features of the pagan Shaman and demi-god: that his prestige should depend upon his power as a wonder-worker and that men should seek his decision in the same way as they had formerly resorted to the shrine of a pagan oracle.

One reaction of an enthusiastic reader is recorded in a letter from C. S. Lewis, who had been sent a copy of the first volume. The letter, undated, was written at Magdalen College, Oxford:

> I embarked on it at once and indeed by greedily reading it at lunch and splashing it with gravy have already deprived the copy of some of its freshness. I have now finished it (for the first time). It was exactly what I wanted, going of course, far beyond my knowledge but often linking up with the little I do know – always the most exciting kind of reading, I think. It also was strangely 'corroborating' – I don't quite know how or why. So much for subjective reactions. What makes me feel that it must also be good (*simpliciter* as well as *mihi*) is that on the Humanists, where I am least out of my depth, it seems to me particularly sound. What a lot of error about them is still in circulation! The bit on p. 17 about the relation between Hegelianism and Darwinism is most important. How many people notice that the two great mythical and poetical expressions of Developmentalism (Keats' *Hyperion* and Wagner's

Ring) are both pre-Darwinian? P. 31 about the most primitive and most sophisticated minds (and the gap in between) is new to me and excellent. P. 193 is a magnificent ending. But I mustn't go on regurgitating plums from your own cake. Thanks very much: you have given me a great treat.

THE VICTORIAN TRADITION

Ten years elapsed between the Gifford Lectures and the Harvard Lectures of 1958–62 and during this time Christopher Dawson held no other university appointment. But he was much in demand for lecturing, broadcasting and reviewing for various journals, such as *The Tablet*, *The Month* (the Jesuit periodical), *Blackfriars* (produced by the Dominicans), *History Today* and *The Times Literary Supplement*.

In the spring of 1948 he contributed to a BBC series in company with G. M. Trevelyan, Bertrand Russell and Lord David Cecil on *The Ideas and Beliefs of the Victorians*.

In the first talk he described theirs as 'a great revolutionary age', which Marx maintained was transforming the world. They achieved social peace through their passion for compromise – 'the work of idealists and the more intense and sincere was their idealism, the stronger was their devotion to compromise'. This was no less true of their theorists than of their politicians:

> The beliefs of early Victorian England may seem to us a strange compound of mutually inconsistent orthodoxies – the bleak rationalism of the Utilitarians and the narrow pietism of the Evangelicals, but they were like flint and steel to one another, and from their contact there sprang that spirit of moral idealism and that passion for reform which burn like fire beneath the hard surface of the age of iron and steam.

In his second talk he amplified this by a discussion of the Humanitarians, largely devoted to the Christian reformer Shaftesbury of the Factory Bill and the strict Benthamite, Chadwick of the new Poor Law. They were allies against bad drains, bad housing, and vested interests, but their motives and ultimately their effects differed sharply.

The Utilitarianism of Chadwick produced 'the anti-humanitarian philosophy of Herbert Spencer who regarded the miseries of the poor as part of the Law of Progress'. Spencer attacked the notion that 'all social suffering is removable and

that it is the duty of somebody or other to remove it. Both
these beliefs are false'.

To this Shaftesbury replied:

> There is nothing that is so economical as justice and mercy
> towards all interests – social and spiritual – of all the human race
> .... our bodies, the temples of the Holy Ghost, ought not to be
> contaminated by preventable disease, degraded by filth, and dis-
> abled for His service by unnecessary suffering.

Christopher Dawson concluded:

> Here, I believe, it was Shaftesbury, the religious pessimist and the
> political reactionary, who voiced the humanitarian conscience of
> Victorian England better than Herbert Spencer, the rational
> optimist and the philosophic liberal.

Following on this study of the Victorian age Christopher
Dawson proceeded to write about his own Victorian childhood in an autobiographical memoir which he called *Tradition
and Inheritance*, on which I have relied, as already stated, for
the first chapter of this book. It was originally written at the
request of Neville Braybrooke for his literary review *The Wind
and the Rain*. This was a remarkable publication founded
originally by Michael Allmand when he was a schoolboy at
Ampleforth. After the war and Michael Allmand's heroic
death at the age of 20 in the Burma Campaign, for which action
he was awarded a posthumous V.C., his friend, Neville Braybrooke took on the editorship of the review and assembled
contributions from a number of distinguished writers and
poets.

Christopher's two articles were printed successively in the
spring and summer of 1949 and were reprinted posthumously
in America in booklet form by the Wanderer Press (1970).
Both Fr D'Arcy and Fr Gervase Mathew thought that this was
one of the best things Christopher ever wrote, but at the same
time it was one of the least known. Several friends urged him to
extend it into a book but this he would never do, chiefly
because he had no inclination to write about himself. In his first
introduction (unpublished) he wrote:

> I am not attempting to write the story of my life. It seems to me an
> almost impossible task even for the few whose lives are intrinsi-
> cally significant. It is very doubtful whether man possesses the

faculty of spiritual introspection, and without such insight how can we dare to write of our own lives?

According to his unpublished notes he first intended to call this memoir *Notes on My Early Life: Social and Spiritual Background*. It was to be a study of family tradition – of people and places and the roots of his own spiritual inheritance. In the first draft he introduced the memoir with a quotation from St Paul taken from the Latin Vulgate: 'Quis enim te discernit? Quid autem habes quod non accepisti?', which in his own translation read: 'For who maketh thee to differ from another? And what hast thou which thou didst not receive?' (1st Corinthians IV. 7.)

He deliberately set out to write against the stream of modern autobiography which actually rejected any idea of cultural inheritance and showed a positive antipathy to family tradition. He decided to reverse the attitude and write about 'the cult of parents and kinsfolk and native place'. He went on:

> Piety in the classical sense of the word is not a matter of sentiment or social tradition, it is a moral principle that lies at the root of every culture and every religion, and the society that loses it has lost its primary moral basis and its hope of survival.

FRIENDS AND ACQUAINTANCES

Since 1944 Christopher had used the Society of Authors as his literary agent and through the efforts of Anne Munro-Kerr of its Foreign Rights Department his books were translated into nearly every European language. Through Sheed & Ward's New York office also his books were published in America and became well known there and Frank Sheed himself brought publicity to them on his frequent lecture tours throughout the USA. Subsequently his work became better known on the Continent and in the New World than in his own country. Eventually more visitors to Boars Hill came from abroad than from Oxford itself.

It must be admitted that this was partly Christopher's own fault for he was not lacking in invitations to dine at All Souls' College or at Campion Hall where Fr D'Arcy was Master. But his shyness made him dread these public occasions and as often as not he would put off an engagement at the last minute on the pretext of illness; there was no doubt that he much preferred talking with one friend he knew well to meeting strangers at a party. One frequent visitor to Copse Side was the Dominican, Fr Gervase Mathew, from Blackfriars in Oxford.

Gervase, brother of Archbishop David Mathew, was in his own way immensely learned as a Byzantine scholar, an archaeologist and a medievalist. He was eccentric in the true Oxford tradition. A tramp-like figure with an old hat crammed down on his head, a rucksack on his back and his inevitable walking stick, he was as arresting in appearance as G. K. Chesterton and even more vague. He had a wide acquaintance, ranging from the very grand to the most humble, and his friends included Prof Tolkien, C. S. Lewis and the 'Inklings'. On his archaeological travels he often had incredible adventures which he dismissed lightly. He was awarded the OBE for quelling a native riot and survived a plane crash into the sea when returning from a visit to Africa. Once, when driving through Libya in a jeep, he was jeered at as a priest and called a 'Nazarene'. 'How wonderful,' he commented, 'to be mocked at in the same words as were used to our Lord.'

Other Oxford friends of Christopher's were the Dominican, Fr Victor White, a theologian and an expert in Jungian psychology, and Prof Evans-Pritchard, the anthropologist, in both of whose subjects Christopher had a great interest. Fr Thomas Corbishley, SJ, who succeeded Fr D'Arcy as Master of Campion Hall in 1945, was also a frequent visitor to Boars Hill and often brought visiting scholars from America to meet Christopher. One of these was Fr Clement McNaspy, SJ from New Orleans, who studied with Christopher in the late 1940s when he was writing the Gifford Lectures. They struck up a long friendship which continued during the time when Christopher was at Harvard. At Oxford, Fr McNaspy recorded, they used to go for long walks over the Berkshire Downs and Christopher would point out 'from his encyclopaedic, fingertip knowledge, spots of prehistoric or historic interest. A walk with him was worth volumes.'

Although Christopher was a contemporary of Arnold Toynbee's both at Winchester and Oxford, he did not come to know him until the years between the wars. At Boars Hill he saw him more frequently, since he was the son-in-law, by his first marriage, of Gilbert Murray, who was a neighbour. When Christopher reviewed the final volumes of Toynbee's *magnum opus*, *The Study of History*, he said that any historian would gain new insights from this 'scholar of immense learning and universal cultural interests'. But on other aspects their ways parted: Christopher could not share Toynbee's belief in the identity of the higher religions, in view of the divergence between the historical and the mystical. But he found more common ground with Toynbee on his theory of civilizations. He wrote to John Mulloy in a letter of 25th September 1954:

> I am just finishing my two articles on Toynbee's new volumes. You will be interested to see that he has scrapped his original theory of the equivalence of civilizations and has substituted a theory of progressive stages leading to the world religions very much in the style of my old 'Cycles of Civilization' (*Enquiries*), except that he makes it culminate in religous syncretism, not unlike Northrop's view. I cannot help thinking that he has been influenced by my theory, which was published as an article ten years before his first set of volumes, but he makes no reference to it, so I must assume that it is a case of coincidence.

On his side Arnold Toynbee also appreciated Christopher as a historian while not sharing his Christian views; after his death he wrote to me:

> He was a most original-minded and sincere-minded thinker, and he made his great contribution to the understanding of history in spite of having to contend with bad health .... We differed in religion – I am an agnostic – but we agreed in trying to see history as a whole and also in believing that religion is at the heart of human life.
>
> (15th November 1973)

Visiting scholars were often surprised when they came to see Christopher Dawson at his home on Boars Hill to find not the remote and severe intellectual they probably expected but a warm and friendly man who never talked down to the young or his intellectual inferiors but met them at their own level. As often as not, arriving in the afternoon, they would find him engaged in hacking down nettles in the wood or on some other vigorous gardening pursuit or just returned from a long trudge in the country. His gardening efforts were all of this kind whether he was damming up streams in Yorkshire or clearing the undergrowth at Oxford; conventional gardening, such as weeding and lawn-mowing or even planning and planting, held no attraction for him.

The winter of 1951–52 brought a Spanish interlude for Christopher and Valery for he received an invitation from the British Council to lecture in Madrid and Cadiz. This had been arranged by a Spanish friend, Dr Esteban Pujals, who had long been an admirer of Christopher's work and later wrote a study of it. They spent the rest of the winter travelling in Spain; they visited Granada where Christopher was struck down with a severe attack of 'flu at Christmas and then went to the warmer climate of Malaga to recuperate.

From Malaga he wrote to Edward Watkin:

> It is a kind of glorified Torquay with villas and rock gardens very much in the same style. But it also has a splendid Renaissance cathedral where we had a fine Pontifical High Mass this morning. It is not at all Baroque – mid-16th century with the coat of arms of Philip and Mary in it. What pleased me most here was the feast of the Immaculate Conception at Seville where the ceremonies were performed perfectly with the old Cardinal (Segura) presiding and in the evening we saw the boys dancing before the High Altar which I have often heard of. There is nothing at all oriental about it – a kind of northern square dance, very slow and stately and the singing rather like the English Tudor music. I think Seville is a perfect town and it would have made a much better capital than Madrid with its traditions of St. Ferdinand and Alfonso El Sabio. I was disappointed with Madrid which has not even got a Cathedral. I should have thought Philip II and his successors would at least have provided one, but while Granada and Malaga have fine Renaissance cathedrals, Madrid has nothing. I wasn't able to get out to the Escorial or to see Toledo, so my impressions of Spain are rather one-sided. I found Granada depressing, probably because I was ill. But it does not seem a living city like Seville.
>
> What is so strange about this place is that one goes round a sort of Torquay road like Lincombe Drive and one finds at intervals little tablets commemorating the priests who were shot there in 1935 and 1936: it seems so extraordinarily incongruous.

(i) *The Makers of Christendom*

Between 1949 and 1954 Christopher worked hard to promote with Sheed & Ward a great publishing venture of Christian biography and history extending to thirty-three volumes, from the Acts of the Apostles to the Life of Blessed Maria Christina, wife of King Bomba, 1812–36. This magnificent project ran into the usual difficulties known to all with experience of publishing.

The first aim of such a series is to be comprehensive, but this at once raises questions for publisher and editor. The publisher finds that some of the central figures, a St Thomas More or a St Teresa, have been treated so recently or so often that there is no public for further works, while the editor has the opposite problem with neglected figures, that texts are inaccessible and untranslated. The greater figures are too well known, yet cannot be ignored: the lesser are not known well enough, yet cannot be exaggerated.

Compromises are made, texts obtained, translators and editors of volumes approached. Some are unwilling or unable: they and publisher and editor have other work and, as time passes, the series gets that appearance of a half-built monument which so strangely resembles a ruin.

What in fact wrecks such ventures, especially today, is the large capital they require. Only a great private endowment, university, or other institution could support it. Granted that, Christian biography would be a monument of the highest quality.

Just to read the list – one volume might contain four or five lives – gives a measure of Christopher Dawson's immense learning. It extends from the early Fathers to the Anglo-Saxon missions in Germany, from Snorri Sturlasson's Life of St Olav to the Jesuit missions in Japan, from Raymond Lull to the Life of St Benedict.

What remains of this great attempt is Christopher Dawson's own introduction to the series and six volumes, under the general title of *The Makers of Christendom*, one of them being *The Mongol Mission*, which he edited. It is an account of the extraordinary venture recorded in the 13th and 14th centuries by the Franciscan missionaries who travelled into the wild and uncharted wastes of Mongolia and China to visit the court of the Great Khan, who ruled over one of the most savage races in history. It is also the first known record of an attempt to bridge the gap between East and West.

(ii) *Understanding Europe*

In 1952 came the publication of a new book, *Understanding Europe*, which had a continuous theme that 'our system of education should give a larger place not only to the history of Europe but still more to the study of Christian culture.'

The war not only destroyed the work of men's hands, from homes to schools and hospitals, but devastated no less their minds and memories. Facing the ruins as his hero Augustine had done, Christopher Dawson saw that the conflict between German and Russian versions of absolutism which had broken Europe came from state control of the mind – and ultimately, therefore, from education.

The professors of German nationalism and Russian autocracy were inhuman in their defiance of freedom and independence:

> A great war is not a matter of human choice. On the contrary, it marks the point at which events pass out of human control. It is a kind of social convulsion – an eruption of the forces which lie dormant like the subterranean fires of a volcano on the slopes of which man builds his cities and cultivates his fields.

None of the great wars of history, the Thirty Years' War or the wars of the French revolution, had the results imagined or desired by their leaders – and Hitler's aim of a greater Germany ended in one smaller and divided.

Efforts at reconstruction after the damage of war were not measured to the forces which had produced the conflict:

> The activities of the modern planners and international reformers bear the same relation to the world crisis as the activities of a mining engineer or even a plumber to a volcanic eruption. They are sensible and rational and scientific, but they belong to an essentially different plane from that of the forces which they are attempting to master. The foundations of our world are shaken and we shall not save it by replanning the superstructure.

Much needed reforms in education, to teach the lessons of European culture, had been too superficial:

> The result was that the modern world has been inundated by a shallow flood of universal literacy which destroyed the old traditions of popular culture and increased the mass-mindedness of modern society without raising its cultural standards or deepening its spiritual life.

A society without a conscience could not counter the forces of conflict, because it failed to know its own mind, its own strength – its origins and its principles. The work of Christopher Dawson after the war was directed towards restoring the conscience of Western society.

(iii) *The Dynamics of World History*

In 1953 there was an important meeting with an American Mr John J. Mulloy, who had long been a devoted admirer of Christopher Dawson and had come over to England expressly to meet him and make a further study of his work and ideas, and out of this meeting and the series of talks they had together came a scheme for a book, which was to have a widespread influence in America.

The Dynamics of World History, which appeared in 1956, was compiled from the works of Christopher Dawson by Mr Mulloy, who arranged his choice in two parts, the first, *Toward a Sociology of History*, the second, *Conceptions of World History*.

The first part consists chiefly of excerpts from books, early *Sociological Review* articles and others, some of which had been collected in *Enquiries* (1933) – long out of print and rare. The second part included reviews and judgements on historians from periodicals as far apart as *History Today* of London and the *Criterio* of Buenos Aires.

From his long acquaintance with Christopher Dawson's work, Mr Mulloy was in a good position to make his choice and arrange his material, to satisfy his own interest as an American sociologist and to fit this into a frame which embraced other elements of history and culture. Even apart from this synoptic view, his book has a unique value in that it brings together much material never before reprinted.

Since the excerpts from books and *The Sociological Review* articles have been noticed earlier, it is more useful here to consider the second part of the book, that on *Conceptions of History*, then Mr Mulloy's own essays which introduce and conclude the book.

This second part opens with an important piece on *The Christian View of History* to show that the decay of philosophic idealisms had prejudiced other conceptions:

> Thus the Christian view of history is not a secondary element derived by philosophic reflection from the study of history. It lies

at the very heart of Christianity and forms an integral part of the Christian faith. Hence there is no 'philosophy of history' in the strict sense of the word. There is, instead, a Christian history and a Christian theology of history, and it is not too much to say that without them there would be no such thing as Christianity.

Another piece, *The Kingdom of God and History*, confirms that some view of history is always envisaged, as without this it would be impossible to interrelate facts:

> The essence of history is not to be found in facts but in traditions .... A visitor from another planet who witnessed the Battle of Hastings would possess far greater knowledge of the facts than any modern historian, yet this knowledge would not be historical for lack of any tradition to which it could be related; whereas the child who says 'William the Conqueror 1066' has already made his atom of knowledge an historical fact by relating it to a national tradition and placing it in the time-series of Christian culture.

The Christian tradition is always a sacred history, distinct from secular events, the old opposition between the chosen people and the Gentiles, or the new between the Church and the world. Yet this dualism is never absolute, for the hand of God falls also on the Gentiles, most remarkably in the case of Cyrus, prophesied by Isaiah as chosen by God to deliver his people. Similarly the Church prospers or endures by standards other than those of the world: 'She wins not by majorities but by martyrs and the cross is her victory.'

A piece on *The Problems of Metahistory* defends Toynbee and historians of culture and society against the attack of an academic historian, Mr Alan Bullock (now Lord Bullock):

> The academic historian is perfectly right in insisting on the importance of the techniques of historical criticism and research. But the mastery of these techniques will not produce great history, any more than a mastery of metrical technique will produce great poetry.

Some larger vision is found in great historians, such as Tocqueville or Ranke, and this 'lies very close to the sources of their creative power'.

A piece on Gibbon included the brilliant introduction to the *Decline and Fall* written for the Everyman edition which applied to Gibbon the line on his favourite Emperor Julian:

Perfidus ille Deo quamvis nonperfidus Urbi (Unfaithful he may have been to God but not to the City). Gibbon too had his vision, lost to later history:

> It no longer shares that sense of living membership in a great tradition and a classical order which Gibbon with all his limitations of spiritual vision and historical imagination still possessed.

Similarly, a review of the *Outline of History* showed that Wells too had a vision greater than his defects:

> Nevertheless, Wells had a real gift of historical vision and a power of synthesis that many eminent historians have lacked. This was due above all to his religious faith, to his conviction that history was not a record of dead events, but a creative process out of which a new world and a new humanity must ultimately emerge.

His defect in recent history was neglect of any history of science to which his whole work led, through immersion in politics.

Fuller treatment was naturally given to the vision behind Arnold Toynbee's masterpiece, *The Study of History*, because it was a subject so close to his own heart:

> Dr Toynbee has been guided in his immense task by two parallel motives; first by the Hellenic philosophic quest for a *theoria* .... and secondly by the Hebraic prophetic mission to justify the ways of God to man .... Both these motives are so deeply rooted in the tradition of Western civilization that we can none of us ignore their force. But there is always a danger that the philosopher will be tempted to simplify the irrational multiplicity and idiosyncrasy of the world of history.

With all his respect for this great work, Christopher felt that this temptation had not been avoided, particularly in too sharp a distinction between primitive and civilized societies, in the equivalence given to higher religions and civilizations, to the prejudice of cultural borrowings and interchanges which resulted in super-cultures. He concluded:

> Nevertheless, a telescopic survey of the whole field of study also has its value, especially when it is carried out by a scholar of immense learning and universal cultural interests like Dr Toynbee. And I do not think that any historian or social anthropologist can read his work without gaining new insights into the nature of the problem of the relations between civilizations.

Mr Mulloy in his lucid introduction to *The Dynamics of World History* emphasised the scope of Christopher Dawson's thought, not only in the history of culture, sociology and anthropology but also in comparative religion which, he aptly noted, is treated as mankind's religious experience. The much longer essay at the end of the book, *Continuity and Development in Christopher Dawson's Thought*, has the further interest of excerpts from his letters to Mr Mulloy. One of these, written in 1952, compares the spread of Hellenism over the ancient world with that of Western culture over the modern world:

> As the unity of the ancient world was finally broken in two by the rise of Islam, so the modern world is being broken in two by the rise of Communism.

Another, of 1955, comments on an age of technology:

> Even if, *per impossibile*, all the spiritual traditions of culture could be temporarily suppressed, it could only lead to a nihilist revolution which would destroy the technological order itself ....
> Orwell's *1984* is a good picture of a purely technological order and the only fault I find with it is that he seems to believe it is a possibility.

The Dynamics of World History was extensive in scope for it covered thirty-five years of writing, and as one reviewer in *The American Historical Review* pointed out, it was 'an anthology – not an abridgement – of Dawson's writings on the history of civilisation'. In England *The Times Literary Supplement*, in a front-page review summed up the essential quality of Christopher Dawson's work as:

> An opening up of frontiers, a broad integration of isolated disciplines in the crucible of a human and passionate mind, an unfreezing of cold abstractions into the human realities: love, enthusiasm, faith, anger, death.[1]

The title of *The Times Literary Supplement* article was 'God and History'. A much less favourable review was given in the *Spectator* under the title 'The Church, Marx and History' by Christopher Hill, later Master of Balliol but at that time an assistant lecturer in that college. Rashly assuming that the author was dead, he gave the book a scathing review, which included some generally contemptuous remarks about the book coupled with an attack on Christopher's professional standing as an historian. 'The late Mr. Dawson,' wrote Hill, 'was not a great historian: he was a diligent Roman Catholic publicist with a considerable and genuine interest in history'.

To this Christopher made a characteristically philosophic reply in a letter to the editor dated 24th September 1956.

> Sir,
>
> My attention has just been drawn to the article in your current issue by Mr. Christopher Hill on 'The Church, Marx and History', in which he states that 'the late Mr Dawson was not a great historian'.
>
> I do not wish to assert that I am 'great' but I do most emphatically deny that I am 'late', and I feel doubtful whether a writer who is unable to discover the truth in a contemporary matter of fact which is easily ascertainable is competent to survey the vast field which he has embraced in his article.
>
> It seems to me that there is no more sense in asking, like Mr Hill, 'What *is* the use of history' than in asking what is the use of memory. An individual who has lost his memory is a lost individual, and a society that has no history and historical consciousness is a barbarous society. It is as simple as that,
>
> Yours etc.
> Christopher Dawson

It is interesting that the last remark was echoed unconsciously by Mr Alexander Solzhenitsyn twenty years later when he ended his terrifying warning to the West with these words: 'A people that no longer remembers has lost its history and its soul.'

Christopher's letter brought an apology from the reviewer to which the letters editor gave the title of 'Manalive'. His explanation was that as the book had been edited by an American with no word of introduction by the author and the essay on his historical work seemed to aim at being definitive, he concluded that the author was dead.

BUDLEIGH SALTERTON, DEVON

In 1953, after thirteen years at Boars Hill, the longest time they had lived in any one place, Christopher and Valery decided to move house again. The place they now chose was Budleigh Salterton, on the South Devon coast about fifteen miles from Exeter. In a way it seemed like a leap from the

frying pan into the fire; many of Christopher's friends had left
Oxford after the war to return to London and his university
connections were few, but at Budleigh Salterton their circle
was even more limited, for most of Christopher's former colleagues at Exeter had retired or moved elsewhere.

Practically speaking, it was sensible to move to a smaller and
more convenient house for the family had all left home; in
1952, Juliana, the eldest daughter, had entered a convent, the
Assumption order, and this was a considerable blow to Valery.
At that time, before the relaxations brought about by Vatican
II, becoming a nun meant becoming 'dead to the world', and
while she was not shut away behind a grille, Juliana was never
allowed to come home except in the last resort of a death or
serious illness in the family. Valery never became reconciled to
the loss of her eldest daughter – it was almost like a death to
her. Christopher kept silent on the whole issue, but perhaps
they both felt that a move to a new life in another place might
prove some compensation.

Their new house was called 'Hermitage' (after the border-
land castle where Mary Queen of Scots was imprisoned in the
early days of her captivity). It lay on the outskirts of the town
in an attractive garden with distant views of the red cliffs and
the River Otter which wound its way down to the sea. Every
afternoon, winter and summer, Christopher took long walks
by the river or the sea; the country and the warm climate
weighed against the disadvantages of the move.

When they first went to live at Budleigh Salterton there was a
railway to connect it with the outside world, but the journey
from Waterloo via Sidmouth Junction and Tipton St John was
a long and tedious one and there were not many visitors to
attempt it. Even Frank Sheed, who had travelled most of
England on his visits to Christopher, thought twice before
making this journey. Finally, the branch line to Budleigh
Salterton was suspended, and it became even more isolated for
anyone without a car (neither Christopher nor Valery could
drive) and Exeter was the nearest station. But on the whole,
they were both happier in this place than they had been at
Boars Hill and they settled for a quiet life, little knowing that in
a few years time they would be uprooting themselves once
more to start a new life in America.

It was only to be expected that Christopher would find few

friends with similar intellectual interests in Budleigh Salterton:
Edward Watkin, who was living at Torquay, sometimes came
over to stay for a few days, but otherwise he knew only one
other writer, Ralph Ricketts, the novelist who was also a
Wykehamist and a convert to Catholicism like himself. After
Christopher's death, Ralph Ricketts recalled some of his
impressions and memories of him from those days:

I first met Christopher Dawson in 1954 or 1955 when he must
have been about sixty-five. He was very different from what I
expected; nothing pompous, pontifical or professional about him.
He gave an impression of fastidiousness which was embodied in
his slight, neat figure, his clothes and demeanour; his light, quick
movements; his voice and thin white hands. I recall a mixture of
venerability and youthfulness; his courtesy; the infectious
appreciative little laugh he gave when he was amused, and the
slightly petulant gesture with which he would turn away his head
if he was displeased! I remember the unusual combination of
fragility and virility, the impression of loneliness in his incongruous setting; he, who was supreme in his own intellectual sphere,
exiled in a world of tea cups and retired colonels. But it was a
voluntary exile, and I think the explanation may have lain in his
extreme sensibility: he might be bored to tears in Budleigh Salterton but he would not be hurt.
    Christopher preferred a tête-à-tête to general conversation.
When we went to visit them, my wife would be detained by Valery
in the first room and Christopher would lead me into his library
which opened out of it. (It was always very warm in the library,
sometimes too warm for my taste!) As one would expect, the
room was full of books, they covered the walls, were piled on
tables; there were papers also but without untidiness, no litter. We
would seat ourselves – there was always a slight element of formal-
ity – in two armchairs facing one another with, in winter, a bottle
of claret and two wine glasses on the hearth between us. Behind
Christopher's armchair was a French window leading into the
garden.
    I have heard it said that Christopher was difficult to talk to;
certainly he had little interest in small talk or in filling in the gaps in
a conversation. I found him stimulating, perhaps partly because he
so completely understood what one was saying before one had
finished saying it: there was never any need to explain, to cross a 't'
or dot an 'i'. His large, brown eyes were almost feminine in their
liquid expressiveness, revealing his thought and feeling: they
would glint with an almost mischievous amusement, grow bright

with interest or opaque with apathy or disapproval. Devoid of
pedantry, he was interested in everything of an historical, literary
or social nature, and enjoyed odd little scraps of information
about this or that. He was essentially well bred in every sense of
the word: *fin*. He was very modest and seldom spoke of his work.
Reserved, low-keyed, his conversation was not 'brilliant': no
verbal fireworks. He was never malicious; you felt he would have
considered it demeaning. Beneath his sensibility he gave an
impression of balance, even of stoicism; but he could be touchy.
To some extent, you had to bend to his mood and wishes: if he was
tired or bored, he made little effort to disguise it; in fact, he made
little social effort of any kind. He was completely natural, like a
child.

One other close friend was living nearby: this was Margaret
Geidt (née Houghton) whom they had known at Dawlish
when she gave the children their first lessons. She often accompanied Christopher on his walks and remembered his great
appreciation of the scenery – the sea and red Devonshire cliffs,
which he would clamber down by pathless ways which could
be daunting. He also liked to walk on Woodbury Common, a
wild moorland tract where the remains of ancient British
settlements could be found. She remembered once asking him
why with his obvious feeling for places and the beauties of
nature he had never written about it in his books. He replied
that he had, first in *The Spirit of the Oxford Movement* and
then more expansively in his autobiographical memoir
Tradition and Inheritance.

The intellectual isolation, which Christopher felt most
keenly in the years following the war, caused him to depend
increasingly for correspondence to exchange ideas and views.
The war had brought new challenges for him and the stimulus
of being in touch, through his work on *The Dublin Review* and
The Sword of the Spirit, with leading intellects both in England
and abroad. Now, he said, rather enigmatically that he was
working 'at the centre of a vacuum' presumably rather like a
man on a desert island might be.

He was not altogether happy with the state of the Catholic
Church in England during the 1950s, for he saw the Church
moving away from the spiritual and intellectual revival which
he had envisaged twenty years before into a more materialistic
and activist age. These were the first stirrings of a movement

which seems to have firmly taken hold in the present climate of Catholic thought. As Christopher often pointed out, ideas take about twenty years to germinate and therefore current ideas are always those of a past generation.

In 1956 he was writing to Edward Watkin of the 'evils' inherent in the church at that time:

> .... extroversion, legalism, activism and also an excessive concentration of attention on controversial theology and all sorts of stunts like vernacular liturgy etc. Legalism and controversialism are permanent problems, but the rest seem to me either new or far more prominent than in the old days. There is an amusing example of activism in *The Catholic Herald* this week – the reviewer of Père Grou's book writes as though the Dark Night of the Soul was a luxury reserved for the leisure classes and says that the depths of spiritual experience are 'incompatible with the demands of one's daily occupation.'

In 1958 Christopher was concerned to defend Baroque Catholicism against neo-Protestant attacks within the Catholic Church itself. He could not agree with Fr Louis Bouyer (c.f. *Du Protestantism a L'Église*)[2] in his idea that the Church of the past was wrong and now at least *we* are right ....:

> He (Fr Bouyer) even goes so far as to speak of the Scylla of Protestantism and the Charybdis of Baroque Catholicism, thus practically equating them in error. He does not realise the great achievement of Baroque Catholicism in mysticism and the interior life. He seems to think that the Church exists for the liturgy rather than vice versa, and personally I would rather see a few St Teresa's or St Philip than a whole tribe of Mass dialogians! .... No one could love the vernacular Bible more than I (especially the good old Authorised Version) but I think it is ludicrous that the later medieval Catholics were Pelagians till Tyndale came along.

Edward Watkin, to whom these words were addressed, was writing a book on *Roman Catholicism in England* and had asked Christopher's opinion on some points relating to the Reformation.

Christopher viewed these changes of thought as largely due to a Puritan movement within the Church. The Baroque spiritual ideal proclaimed its message through the mediums of art and music, poetry and mysticism, and it was in fact the inspiration of his own conversion. Imagination, he once wrote, was just as much a part of the soul as the intellect and will and he could not understand what he called 'the philistine and patronising' attitude to Baroque Catholicism expressed by certain Catholics at that time. It was a view of the Victorian protestant of the most narrow and bigoted kind.

In 1956 Christopher was invited to contribute to a commemorative volume in honour of Pope Pius XII's eightieth birthday. He took as his subject 'The Teacher of the Nations' for he maintained that no Pope in recent years had expounded the teaching of the Church more profoundly and more universally. The Pope's birth in 1876 was the text for a contrast between the old Europe and a new world where Popes spoke no longer to rulers but to peoples: the reign of Pius XII was 'one of the most momentous in the history of the Church.'

He drew attention to the Pope's work for peace – as a diplomat in the First World War and as Pope in the Second – and maintained that the Papacy stood as the one supra-national power which could speak to the nations the words of peace and reconciliation:

> The 20th century has been a catastrophic period . . . . but it has also seen the dawn of a new hope for humanity. It foreshadows the birth of a new Christendom – a Society which is not confined as in the past of a single group of nations and a single civilisation, but which is common to every people and language.[3]

About this time Christopher was engaged in a correspondence with the Benedictine, Dom Bede Griffiths, on the subject of Indian religion; Dom Bede was then living in India, as he still is, and had made a deep study of the relationship between Hinduism and Catholicism. In his autobiography, *The Golden String*, he wrote of how much he owed to Christopher Dawson for all his ideas on comparative religion and civilizations:

> I found in him a mind as wide in its range as that of Spengler, who had first attracted me to the study of history or as that of Arnold Toynbee, who has since made himself a master in that field.[4]

They discussed the wide gulf that separated the Hindu and Christian religions and Dom Bede thought that it was due to the complete separation of the Christian communities from Hindu life and thought. Today this has been largely overcome by the creation of *Ashrams* or prayer centres where the two

A picnic on Blubberhouses Moor (circa 1935): Christopher and Valery Dawson with their daughter Christina, the author.

Christopher and Valery Dawson at Torquay in 1932.

At Oxford, 1951: Christopher Dawson receiving the Christian Culture Award of the Assumption University of Windsor, Ontario.

Christopher Dawson talking to some of his American students.

Valery Dawson, with Christopher, after she had received the Ll.D. degree at Regis College, Weston (Mass.).

On his
seventieth
birthday:
Christopher
Dawson talking
to Alec Guinness
at Boston
College in 1959.

Christopher Dawson at
Harvard in 1959.

contemplative traditions meet and in which Dom Bede Griffiths has played an important part, but thirty years ago the situation was very different. In a letter of 19th April 1957, Dom Bede wrote:

> The average Christian has been taught to regard Hinduism as a 'pagan' religion, polytheist, idolatrous, superstitious. The Hindu is supposed to be living in darkness and ignorance and though he may be tolerated as a human being, his religion is despised and hated. I think this is scarcely an exaggeration of the attitude of the average Catholic. There is a total ignorance of the realities of Hindu religion and philosophy even among priests. Is it to be wondered at that the Hindu retaliates with a complete contempt for Christianity and a confidence in the wisdom and goodness of his own religion?

On his side, Christopher thought that the root of the trouble lay in nationalism, and in the fact:

> .... that men are Indians or Englishmen first and Christians afterwards, and that we have failed to bring home to people concretely and actually that the difference between Christian and non-Christian is infinitely greater than the difference between East and West, so that African, Asiatic and European Catholics are really all the same.

He agreed that the missionary tradition had certainly stressed the negative side of the religious differences of East and West – the evils of polytheism, idolatry etc., but it had also failed to convey the positive aspects of evangelism enough: 'It certainly seems unfair,' he wrote, 'that while the East rejects Christianity as the religion of the West, the Westerners should spend their time explaining the inferiority of Christianity to the religions of India.' (27th April 1957.)

In an earlier writing he had maintained that the Catholic Church by reason of her ambiguous position, committed neither to East nor West, stood as the one mediator between them. He wrote:

> She alone possesses a tradition which can satisfy both sides of man's nature, and which brings the transcendent reality of the divine Logos into relation with the tangible and visible facts of human experience.[5]

AN INVITATION FROM AMERICA

Between the years 1953 to 1958 Christopher Dawson was absorbed with the idea of introducing the study of Christian culture into higher education and in these years he wrote a volume of correspondence to Mr John Mulloy who helped him to publicize the idea in America. It was not a new departure for Christopher as is clear from his Edward Alleyn lecture given in 1944 and published in 1947 in *Our Culture* edited by Canon Demant. His first words then reflected his past work and disclosed more to come:

> I do not think there is any need for me to insist on the fundamental thesis that the present crisis of Western civilisation is due to the separation of our culture from its religious basis. I have been saying little else for the last fifteen years. But I think people are still not sufficiently aware of how great the responsibility of education has been in this disastrous process.

Religious education had to be deepened for today, he wrote, it was apt to be considered 'a kind of extra insecurely tacked on to the general educational structure, not unlike a Gothic church in a modern housing estate.'

One aphorism showed a fine awareness of human limits in line not only with Aquinas but with Irenaeus: 'The problem concerns the future, the human soul and God: three things which we cannot understand.'

In lectures given at Oriel College, Oxford, University College, Dublin and the University College of North Wales in Bangor he outlined his scheme for a programme of Christian Culture – a parallel could be drawn with Newman's 'Idea of a University' – and he further developed it in articles published in the American Catholic Review *Commonweal*, which was conducting a symposium on the subject, for *Lumen Vitae* in Brussels, and many more American journals.

Mr Mulloy, in an article of 1954, cited the three lectures as a new approach to the study of Christian culture and pointed out that it was in America where the greatest opportunities lay for the development of such a study. The new discipline would study the three main phases of Christian culture: (1) Its origins in the age of the Fathers; (2) Its development in the Middle Ages when Christian culture achieved classical form in the philosophy of St Thomas and St Bonaventure, the poetry of

Dante and the art of the Gothic cathedral and (3) Its flowering in the vernacular cultures and literatures down to the 17th century. Christopher Dawson thought, as he wrote in his article in *Lumen Vitae*, that the neglect of this study had been the root cause of the failure of modern education as a unifying force in the modern world:

> The time has come to repair this mistake. If we deliberately perpetuate it, now that we know what it is at stake: if we consciously permit the guidance of the modern world to pass from the leaders of culture to the partisans and the political ideologists, then we shall have a heavier responsibility than the politicians for the breakdown of Western civilisation.[6]

In America there were critics of the idea as well as supporters: the critics, many of them Catholics, thought that it was impracticable and perhaps rather reactionary, the supporters were eager to get something started at once. The first move came from Notre Dame University, Indiana, when in the summer of 1957 St Mary's College received a grant from the Lilly Foundation to inaugurate a programme of Christian Culture Study and Christopher Dawson, among other scholars, was invited to be a consultant. The new enterprise was launched by Sister Madaleva of St Mary's College under the chairmanship of Prof Bruno Schlesinger. In December of that year, Christopher also received and accepted an invitation to give a course of lectures the following summer at Gonzaga University, a Jesuit foundation in Spokane, Washington.

But it still came as a complete surprise and an unlooked-for honour when he was invited to become Harvard's first Professor of Roman Catholic Studies in 1958. It was even more of a surprise because ironically what was to be the most important letter he was ever to receive never reached him, for it was sent to his former address at Oxford and not forwarded. On 20th February 1958 he received a telephone call 'out of the blue' from Dr Douglas Horton, Dean of Harvard's Divinity School, who had just arrived in England, inviting him to lunch in Salisbury (which was half-way between London and Exeter) the next day, to discuss an offer he had made in a letter of 6th February. Christopher agreed to meet Dr Horton on the proposed date and during the meeting he was given the letter of invitation, the text of which read as follows:

Harvard Divinity School
February 6, 1958

Dear Mr. Dawson,

On Thursday, February 20th, I hope to be in England, and on that day or the next, if you are at home and willing to see me at Oxford, I should like to call upon you to present an invitation which is beyond doubt the most important I have ever had the honor of carrying.

Mr. Chauncey Stillman, a well-known Catholic layman and a warm friend of Harvard University, has just endowed in the Divinity School a 'Guest Professorship of Roman Catholic Studies,' the purpose of which is 'to cultivate the understanding of the theology and closely related studies of the Roman Catholic Church.' Since this unprecedented gift has not as yet been made public, I shall ask you to keep the news of it confidential until it is published on this end.

The incumbent of the chair would normally remain in Harvard for five years, with the possibility of re-appointment if mutually desired. The 'theology and closely related subjects' may be 'Dogmatic Theology, Patrology, Scripture – Old Testament or New Testament – Fundamental Moral Theology, Church History, General Theology of the Church, or the Theology of Redemption with its implications for the modern mind.' The range of the guest professor's interests is not exactly restricted!

You, sir, are the man we want to be the first to fill this chair. Even if you would wish to make the term much shorter than five years, we should still want you. On details of this sort I could speak at length when I saw you.

Though we cannot reproduce in Cambridge, Massachusetts, the lovely green of the Oxford lawns, we do have gardens, and there is opportunity for those who will to read and study and write. No more burdensome schedule of classes or meetings would be laid upon you than you yourself were willing to undertake. We think you would enjoy the experience.

It is not on this ground, however, that we are asking you to come to us. We appeal to you as a son of the Church. Never before in the history of the United States has there been anything resembling this professorship – a chair of Roman Catholic Studies in a university divinity school Protestant in tradition and Protestant in outlook. Archbishop Cushing of Boston has approved the new departure, and we really expect that future historians will look back upon it as the beginning, after centuries, of an era of happier relationships between the two great groups. We here at Harvard at least intend to provide for the venture the most favourable auspices.

I write with the knowledge and approval of President Pusey and our ranking faculty committee. I hope the idea touches your imagination, not to say your heart. May I come to see you?

Yours faithfully,
Douglas Horton
Dean

Christopher's response to this invitation was to accept at once and for the full term of five years. If he had been surprised by the contents of the letter, the Dean was even more so by this whole-hearted acceptance from a man who was advancing in years and of reputedly frail health; it came as a shock still more to Valery, who was present at the interview, for she knew well Christopher's nervous and hesitant nature. He said to her at the time, 'it is a call', meaning that he felt it was his destiny to continue his work for the cause of Christian culture in America.

One condition he made was that he might bring his books with him. To Dr Horton's question, 'How many books would that be?' he replied vaguely 'Oh, about 2,000.' The Dean's face registered astonishment, wondering perhaps why Harvard's library said to be the largest in the world, would not suffice for his needs, but nevertheless he agreed to the request.

In a letter of 25th February Christopher wrote to Dean Horton informally accepting Harvard's invitation. It could not be a formal acceptance because the news of the Chair had to be kept confidential until 14th April when it was to be ratified by Harvard's Board of Overseers.

Hermitage,
Budleigh Salterton,
Devon

The Rev. Douglas Horton,   25th February 1958
Harvard Divinity School.

Dear Dr. Horton,

When we met at Salisbury on Friday I was quite unprepared for the invitation that you brought me, since your letter of 6th February had most unfortunately failed to reach me. But, in spite of this,

I hope I was able to make clear to you how sensible I was of the honour such an invitation involves and how interested I was in the prospects that it opens up. Nothing, in fact, could be more attractive to me than the opportunity of initiating a study of this kind at Harvard and under the auspices of the Divinity School.

Of course I do not feel that I am competent to cover the range of studies that you outline in the third paragraph of your letter. But for some years now I have been feeling that there was a need for a fuller study of Christian culture than has hitherto been found in our higher education. The historians have not provided it because they lacked the necessary theological understanding and the theologians have not done so because their historical studies were too specialised. I think a Chair of Roman Catholic studies in a Protestant University might provide a good opportunity for investigating the possibilities of such a study, especially as it seems to have considerable irenical value.

Perhaps these are questions which should be postponed until we have an opportunity for more informal discussions. But meanwhile I have no hesitation in accepting your generous invitation and promising that I will do my best to co-operate with your plans for the new Chair.

> Your sincerely,
> (signed) Christopher Dawson

The only person whom Christopher told about the invitation, while it was still confidential, was Frank Sheed who replied by return of post: 'Please, Please, PLEASE accept it,' not knowing that he had already done so.

The formal printed announcement followed after 14th April which stated that after a meeting of the President and Fellows held on 7th April 1958 he had been appointed Charles Chauncey Stillman Guest Professor of Roman Catholic Studies to serve for five years from 1st July 1958 and that consent to this had been given by the Board of Overseers at their meeting of 14th April.

The financial arrangements were that he was to receive a salary of $12,000 a year and return passages, or flights, for the Professor-elect and his wife (as well as removal of the books) would be paid by Harvard.

As Dr Horton had said in his letter, the Stillman Professorship was a completely new departure for Harvard. Only through the generosity and vision of Mr Chauncey Stillman could it ever have been founded for up to that time Catholics had no status at Harvard and Mr Stillman, a convert to Catholicism and a Harvard man himself, thought that Catholics should be represented. Soon after Christopher had been elected to the Chair, Mr Stillman wrote to him:

> You are right in assuming that 'Harvard like Oxford has always held Catholicism at arm's length.' Calvinist founded, then Unitarian in the last century and now heavily secular, Harvard has always considered Catholicism intellectually contemptible, socially negligible, and dangerous politically. Nevertheless Catholics have increased numerically until even at Harvard they comprise I believe, 14%. The Church continues to produce scholars who cannot be ignored. It is an encouraging sign that we are outgrowing our provincialism and that the present Harvard administration has at least consented to giving a voice to historic Christianity.

There was indeed a strong Protestant tradition at Harvard, but no one perhaps envisaged the enormous reaction there would be to Mr Stillman's proposal and that it would become the centre of what was later described as 'one of the great discussions of the century' at Harvard.[7] While President Pusey himself was strongly in favour of the Catholic Chair from the first mention of it, a strong tussle developed between the professors who were largely Quakers and Methodists, not only for and against such a Chair but also where it should be: whether it should be part of the faculty of Arts and Sciences, which Mr Stillman favoured since undergraduates would then benefit from the course, or whether it should be a graduate course in the Divinity School. The supporters, led by Prof George Williams, who headed the committee which favoured the Chair, eventually won the day and it was decided to establish it in the Divinity School.

Another subject of discussion was who should be chosen as the first Stillman Professor and the search ranged from America to Europe and finally to England. The names of Gilson and Maritain had been put forward and there were strong forces for the former against the latter. It was Mr Stillman, advised by his friend, Fr John Lafarge, SJ, who had attended some of the original meetings when the Professorship was first mooted, who suggested the idea of an English Catholic, and the name of Christopher Dawson was proposed. There was very little debate about his appointment and in the

Press, both Catholic and secular, it was greeted with universal acclaim. Prof Francis Rogers, of Harvard, wrote to Christopher of the enthusiasm with which the news had been received, particularly by Archbishop Cushing of Boston, who told Dean Horton: 'You could not have made a better choice.' Fr Martin D'Arcy would like to have been chosen for the post as he said later to a friend: 'There were two appointments which Christopher held which I would have liked to have had – one was the Gifford Lectureship, the other was the Harvard Chair of Roman Catholic Studies.'

Prof Rogers wrote warmly of the superb way in which President Pusey and Dean Horton had handled the announcement of the creation of the chair and of Christopher Dawson's appointment. Enquiries were already being received from Protestant students from all over the country about the possibility of studying with him.

Even before the appointment was ratified, acting on Dr Horton's advice, Christopher booked passages on the S.S. *Caronia* for 24th June to arrive in New York on 1st July. The idea was to spend one night in New York before going on to Gonzaga University to deliver the lectures he had already agreed to give. This posed a serious problem for it meant delaying the start of his lectures by two weeks and cutting the course to six lectures and seminars instead of the twelve which had originally been planned, but he and Valery felt that the uprooting from England, the disposal of their house and the storage of their furniture, not to mention preparing the lectures both for Gonzaga and for Harvard, could not be achieved before the end of June.

Fr Leary of Gonzaga University was aghast when he heard the news (which was early in March) and one can sympathise with his predicament. He had already instituted nation-wide publicity for the summer session and put Christopher Dawson's name at the top of the list of distinguished speakers. People were coming from as far afield as Boston, Toronto, New Orleans, New York City (which was 3,000 miles from Spokane), Chicago and Los Angeles and many leading professors would have already made their plans for the summer accordingly. The chairman of the History Department at Gonzaga was particularly disappointed; Fr Leary put off telling him the news at first in case Christopher could be prevailed upon to change his mind but when he eventually broke the news 'he almost went through the ceiling'.

It was an embarrassing situation on both sides but worse was to follow. Christopher had applied for an immigrant visa in April and although he realised it would be a slow business he did not foresee any trouble in obtaining one. To his dismay, early in June he heard that the results of his medical examination had been unsatisfactory and the authorities were unable to grant him a visa to work in America. After a chest X-ray, the US Public Heath authorities declared that there was evidence of tuberculosis at some earlier date and it might still be infectious. The English doctors whom Christopher had consulted were strongly of the opinion that this was not so and that the scarring of the lungs shown on the X-rays were due to the chronic bronchitis he had had over a lifetime. His specialist consultant sent a long and detailed report to the Chief Medical Officer at the American Embassy but they refused to accept it and asked for further long and exhaustive examinations after which they would re-examine his case. The forecast was gloomy not only for Gonzaga University but for Harvard also. In view of the long delay Christopher was forced to cancel the passage for the end of June and to cable Fr Leary that he would be unable to make it in time to deliver the lectures. This was the last straw for Gonzaga University for it was too late to engage a substitute lecturer; all they could do was to ask Christopher to send the lectures and to get someone else to deliver them. In the event, Mr John Mulloy read them for the first two weeks of the course and conducted the seminars while the remainder were delivered by teaching members of the university staff. Up to the last moment Fr Leary did not give up hope of getting Christopher to come out to Spokane by trying to organise a short-term visa on what was known as the famous person quota but Christopher on his side did not dare leave England while his medical case was still *sub judice*.

There was further agitation at Harvard when it was learnt that after a re-examination a visa had been refused for the second time. It was then realised that only Washington could overrule the decision and Harvard brought all its influence to bear on the problem. Senator John F. Kennedy, as he was then, was persuaded to take up the cudgels on behalf of Harvard's new professor elect and so was the other Massachusetts

Senator, Leverett Saltonstall. Mr Stillman also wrote to Mr John H. Whitney, the American Ambassador in London.

All these efforts bore fruit for on 2nd September when Christopher had almost given up hope of ever getting to Harvard, he heard that he was going to be granted a visa immediately and so the long agony of waiting was over. Although Kennedy took the credit for the successful outcome of this affair it was Senator Saltonstall (a Protestant, incidentally) who actually and forcefully persuaded the Surgeon-General of the United States to overrule the decision of the Medical Officer at the London Embassy.

Passages were again booked on the S.S. *Caronia*, this time for 23rd September arriving in New York just in time for the beginning of the academic year at Harvard. In a press release Dr Horton said that the new professor would take up his duties right away and added: 'He'll leap from the deck to a classroom.'

CHAPTER TWELVE

American Adventure

HARVARD PROFESSOR

As if the delayed departure had not been enough, the *Caronia* ran into a hurricane in mid-Atlantic and they were buffeted in a storm for several days. But Christopher, elated by the prospect of his new venture, was in remarkably good spirits when the ship docked at New York on 30th September and he saw the famous Manhattan skyline for the first time. Describing that scene when he was lecturing in the States he said:

> No one from the Old World can land at New York without being immediately impressed by this spectacle of gigantic material power .... There is nothing like it in Europe or I think anywhere else. It seems to mark the coming of a new age and a new civilization.[1]

According to the Harvard Divinity School Bulletin he was 'chatting amicably with the Boston press' less than twenty-four hours after his arrival. When asked how he felt undertaking the role of first lecturer on Catholic thought at a Protestant divinity school he said: 'It's different isn't it? It's an adventure. I look forward to it very much.' He explained how after turning down many previous offers to come to America, he accepted the Stillman Chair because of its uniqueness and its adventurousness. He said that it was one of the major problems of the time to bring the non-Catholic world to an adequate understanding of the Church's position.

Such was the hurry of the departure from England that there had been no time to find a flat or house in Cambridge before their arrival and so Christopher and Valery started their life there in an apartment at the Hotel Continental not far from the Divinity School. Soon afterwards, they moved into a flat in Traill Street – while they were in America they seemed to move annually after the summer vacation. Christopher was given a

study in Andover Hall next to the Divinity School and here he
was able to house his books. If he had any disappointment it
was that the Divinity School was isolated from the rest of
Harvard and was not part of the Faculty of Arts and Sciences;
he would have liked to have had more contact with the History
School at Harvard.

Christopher was nearly sixty-nine when he entered upon the
most active period of his career, and he had never before held a
full-time university post. His professorial duties amounted to
two lectures and two seminars a week but in addition to this the
following year he took on a heavy programme of lecturing
during the vacations all over America, for from the moment
when his appointment was first announced he had been
deluged with lecturing requests. He also produced three books
during his time in America.

The invigorating air of Cambridge gave him a new lease of
life and in the words of *The Harvard Theological Review*'s
official Minute published after his death, 'Dawson would
prance out to classes when he was in a condition that would
have confined him to his bed when in England.' The physical
energy of the frail-looking English professor was a continual
source of astonishment to his American friends: one of them,
Fr Francis Sweeney, SJ, of Boston College, remembered him
climbing half-way up a hill, then having forgotten his glasses
thought nothing of rushing back to fetch them and returning
for the rest of the climb. At Cambridge he missed the opportunity for country walks that he had in England and his usual
walk was round a deserted cemetery; one day to his surprise he
met his old friend, Robert Speaight, approaching from the
opposite direction.

In a recent letter to me, Fr Sweeney recalled:

> The many happy hours I spent with your parents in Cambridge
> (tea on Sunday was a ritual that became a joyful part of my life),
> my trips with them to various parts of Massachusetts (especially
> our visit to the Trappist Abbey in Spencer, where they were
> received like nobility, as in the peerage of the spirit they were), to
> Newport and to the Philbrook Farm in upper New Hampshire.

If any of the professors of the Divinity School had been
alarmed at the prospect of having a Roman Catholic in their
midst, their fears were soon allayed when they realised that

Christopher Dawson's appointment was not the first step towards a Roman Catholic take-over. He never tried to inflame interest in Roman Catholicism and he always took great care to defend non-Catholic scholars. But from the beginning he was something of an enigma to his Harvard colleagues, for although they were aware of his lack of teaching experience they were not quite prepared for his quiet and unobtrusive approach and his total English reserve. They had experience of English scholars at Harvard before, who had showed eccentricity in one way or another (there was the case of one visiting professor who could only communicate matters of importance on the telephone), but perhaps they had never met one who appeared to live on a different plane above the practical questions of examination papers, faculty meetings and general administration. He always read his lectures in his usual quiet voice and never raised it to reach the back of the hall, and when it came to seminars, of which he had no previous experience, he lacked the cut and thrust to get a discussion under way. The difficulty was largely overcome by the appointment of an assistant, Mr Daniel Callahan, who fulfilled the office of interpreter for the professor.

When a student asked such a question as whether economics affected a particular period, Christopher might give a monosyllabic reply, or one which was simply out of their depth. Mr Callahan would then have to expand or explain. It was not an easy working relationship because, as Mr Callahan was the first to admit, their views did not coincide for he found himself highly unsympathetic towards Christopher's more conservative thought. But some bridge had to be built between the professor and his students who found his massive learning terrifying, a fact of which Christopher was totally unaware.

Writing in The *Commonweal*, Mr Callahan described the situation:

> For his students .... Mr Dawson was frightening. Unlike most Englishmen of Oxford education, Mr Dawson came to America with a number of illusions about American students: that they knew, as a matter of course, French, German and Latin, world history, the classics; that they were prepared to read three or four books a week for one course; and their term papers would be models of scholarly research.
>
> It was my painful duty to insinuate that, as a matter of fact,

nothing at all could be taken for granted about American students. And when I had a chance, I had to let the students, their faces blanched, know that if they read only eight hundred of the five thousand pages for the week they could probably get by. Eventually these problems worked themselves out: the students read two hundred pages, I read two hundred and one, and Professor Dawson of course read all five thousand.[2]

Part of Christopher's misapprehension about his students may have been due to the knowledge that he was to lecture to a graduate audience who would be at least twenty-one or twenty-two years old. The majority of them would be working for advanced graduate degrees, the Th.M. (Master of Theology), the Th.D. (Doctor of Theology) and the Ph.D. (Doctor of Philosophy) in the History and Philosophy of Religion. It could safely be assumed that being Divinity students, they would be interested in and favourably disposed towards religion but their knowledge of Catholicism would probably be limited to a vague and general knowledge of Church history and philosophy. Christopher Dawson's formidable task was to interpret Catholicism to this largely Protestant audience.

Although after the first impact his classes dwindled in size, he was rewarded by the quality of the students who stayed the course and he found their interest and enthusiasm stimulating. Both he and Valery warmed to the friendliness of the Americans, and although naturally enough she often felt homesick for England and the family ties there, for the first time she was able to have some share in his life, travelling with him to lecture appointments in far distant places and meeting new and interesting people. Students were often invited round to continue discussions over tea, which arrangement Christopher preferred to the more formal atmosphere of the Seminar.

In spite of his lack of teaching experience, Harvard felt well satisfied by Christopher Dawson's presence there and it was generally thought that with his quiet but persuasive personality and his learning he was the right occupant for the first Stillman Chair. The Catholic community at Harvard felt particularly proud to have him in their midst and looked on him as a *rara avis*, a representative of the wider world of European culture and scholarship. A Boston University student magazine referred to Christopher Dawson as 'not only an effective ambassador of Catholicism .... but a refreshing antithesis to the American conception of "stuffy" Englishmen and ivory towerish intellectuals', adding that he could converse 'with the vigor of a collegian, but with the true mark of an intellectual – humility.' People had been amazed by his range of topics, his perception of people and his sense of humour. This latter was illustrated by a story he had told about a meeting he had had with G. K. Chesterton at lunch in the Café Royal, in London, when G.K.C., completely unselfconscious of his surroundings, had sung one of his rollicking ballads to Christopher's son, who was then a small boy.[3]

His lectures on 'Catholicism and the Development of Western Culture' under the general title of *Christendom* were the climax of his lifetime work on the history of culture. The first series, *The Formation of Christendom*, provided a parallel course to the Gifford Lectures and an extension of *The Making of Europe*. Beginning like the Gifford Lectures with a definition of religion and culture he went on to discuss the origins of civilization. In the beginning was the word: language was the gateway to the human world and was the single factor that distinguished man from the animal kingdom. As man was formed by the word, so civilization was based on the sacred. Here again was the original thesis running like a thread through all his books, that religion is the dynamic element in culture:

> The world civilizations are the great beaten highways on which man has travelled through history and in every case man believed that they were following a divinely appointed path.

For the Harvard students who had the perseverance to follow the course through, it was an experience in education extending far beyond the scope of a single university course. Religion was shown in another dimension beyond belief and theology: it was the inspiration that lay behind all the creativity of man – the key to history, philosophy, Christian art, music and literature. The last lecture in the first series was devoted to the idea of a universal spiritual society as the goal of history, not as according to Arnold Toynbee's idea of a consensus of the great world religions of East and West but in the spiritual leadership of the one universal Catholic Church which would fulfil its role in history by healing the divisions of humanity and bringing back the nations into spiritual unity.

The second series of lectures, *The Dividing of Christendom*, have importance as Prof David Knowles wrote in his preface to the English edition as 'the only presentation by a mind of Dawson's calibre, of the stretch of modern thought and sentiment between Italian humanism and the French Revolution.' As a historian Christopher Dawson was convinced that the main sources of Christian division between the Protestant north and the Catholic south had always been cultural rather than theological and it was only by a combined study of the history of Christian culture and the study of theology that the nature and extent of the problem could be understood. The lectures covered the period from the breakdown of the medieval unity through the Renaissance and the Reformation right up to the 18th century and the age of the Enlightenment.

The third and last series of lectures, *The Return to Unity*, were unfinished and unpublished. The period covered was the 19th century and they dealt with the movements of Catholic revival in England and France, the Oxford Movement and the movement towards Christian Unity in the 19th and 20th centuries. Before he left Harvard Christopher presented the working drafts for all three volumes to the Divinity School where they are filed in the Andover-Harvard library.

THE CAUSE OF CHRISTIAN CULTURE

In spite of his strikingly and unmistakable English characteristics, Christopher had a great and unbounded admiration for America and the Americans and while he was a firm supporter of the European Movement he was nonetheless a NATO man. He came to America fully acquainted with its history, its politics and its literature and while he appreciated classical writers like Thoreau, Emerson and Herman Melville, he was equally at home with Thornton Wilder, Hemingway and Faulkner. He was also surprisingly up to date with American thrillers which he read in his leisure hours.

He summed up many of his ideas on American subjects in an interview he gave to Frank Sheed for an American magazine[4] just before his departure for Harvard. Of T. S. Eliot he said: 'England could not have produced him. It was not England that produced Henry James either; like T. S. Eliot he *became* a British citizen.' Questioned on the differences between American and European thought he said that basically there were none. Europe was the fountain head from whence came the belief in democracy, American idealism and the philosophy of natural law and America had remained truer to the last of the three than Europe. He said that Maritain had done much to bring European thought to America. There had been a great Protestant recovery of theology in Europe headed by such men as Karl Barth. Reinhold Niebuhr and Paul Tillich had made this theological development widely known in America – in fact, Tillich, he said, was 'a sort of Protestant Maritain!' Tillich, as it happened, was to be one of his colleagues in the Harvard Divinity School.

His belief in and admiration for the cultural power of American Catholicism was demonstrated whenever he spoke to Catholic audiences in America – his lectures extended from Chicago to Texas and Notre Dame University, Indiana. Staying at Pittsburgh with Bishop John Wright (the late Cardinal Wright) he was interviewed by the Press and spoke on the great opportunities in America for the cause of Christian culture, saying that he was convinced that young Catholic America was spearheading a 'cultural renaissance' but in spite of this 'awakening' American Catholics were not yet aware of the great opportunity of the part it was theirs to play in the American civilization of the future.

On this same visit to Pittsburgh, but on a lighter note, the late Cardinal Wright (in a letter of 20th February 1978) told me of the occasion when Christopher was detected in a scholarly error by his gardener:

> I had a gardener in Pittsburgh who was always delighted when 'intellectuals' were visiting at the house. He used to creep up behind them, hat in hand, when they were sitting in the garden and try to surprise them with his erudition. One day your father was enjoying a bit of sun in our garden and Jim came up to him with elaborate deference and said to him: 'Mr. Dawson, sir, I have heard it said that great scholars sometimes have to rely on students to check their footnotes. Would that have been the case in the example of chapter such and such of your justly famed book where the footnotes do not always seem to match the text, having been based on a different translation of Sacred Scripture?' Your father was mildly furious and he shot into the house and upstairs to the library where there was great tossing about of Scriptures. Finally he came downstairs and said: 'What is that man's name?' I tried to sketch a bit of Jim's psychology and procedures and I said that he

was really affectionately well intended. Your father replied: '*That* is not the point. The point is he is quite correct!' We all enjoyed a good laugh.

At Chicago, in 1959, Christopher Dawson gave the annual Thomas More lecture which was attended by an audience of 1,000. He spoke of American Catholicism as 'a sleeping giant – or perhaps rather it is a giant that has not yet learned to speak.' He went on to stress the point that at last the Catholic laity were awakening to the riches of their cultural inheritance and the non-Catholic world were more ready than ever before to listen to what was being said on the subject; it only remained to speak to them in the right language.

But pre-eminently his great scheme for the study of Christian culture in American colleges was put forward at St Mary's College, Notre Dame, Indiana, where he addressed the third annual symposium for Christian Culture under the chairmanship of Prof Bruno Schlesinger. The scheme which linked the studies of history, art, literature, theology and philosophy was unique among other contemporary pro- grammes of General Education, which had been undertaken by such universities as Columbia, Princeton, Harvard and Yale, for it was the only one that attempted to study a civiliza- tion from the Christian standpoint and although St Mary's was a Catholic college the course was devised as being 'undenomi- national'.

All these ideas which he had expounded in countless writings and lectures in America were assembled in two books, *The Historic Reality of Christian Culture* (1960) and *The Crisis of Western Education* (1961), but in fact these books marked the final stage in a process of thought going back over thirty years: both were concerned with the survival of civilization in the West.

As an independent scholar, he had aimed first to write a history of culture and to show how religion formed it and he had begun this with *The Age of the Gods*, which to the his- torian remained his greatest single achievement. But almost at once the crises of the Thirties and the war had directed his energies towards the survival of civilization and more urgent writing. Then the devastation of Europe, the chief centre of Christian culture, its degradation by indifference at home and hostility abroad, the growing ignorance of a sub-religious culture, all drove him to emphasise education as the most necessary of activities, above all for Christians.

It was in fact the indolence and ignorance of Christians themselves about their own culture which most concerned him, especially in English-speaking lands. For culture was essentially social, while the English and North American treatment of religion as a private affair had excluded it from social life. When education was secular, society was secular, and Christians could either abandon their religion or retire into a ghetto. Their one escape from this dilemma was to revive their own culture and to show the society in which they lived that this was the vital element in it, the spirit to challenge their frustration and despair, to become again a new people.

This hope had a clear appeal to the New World, especially to the North American people in the years after the war, from which they had emerged as the champions of Western culture. If in the past century they had received an influx from every land in Europe, more recently they had admitted not only illustrious exiles, an Einstein, a Thomas Mann, but musicians and poets, publicists and professors: representatives of the higher culture either lived in or looked to America, not only as a refuge, but as a foundation where manuscripts would be preserved in the new Dark Ages.

This time and place is the background to *Crisis in Western Education* and its author addressed himself to an American public. In America he found a response for his criticism of education. Classical education had taught what it knew of Greece and Rome but little else. Its replacement by state education based on utility and scientific training highly specialised had branched into confusion:

> The result has been an intellectual anarchy imperfectly controlled by the crude methods of the examination system and of payment by results. The mind of the student is overwhelmed and dazed by the volume of new knowledge which is being accumulated by the labour of specialists, while the necessity for using education as a stepping-stone to a profitable career leaves him little time to stop and think. And the same is true of the teacher, who has become a kind of civil servant tied to a routine over which he can have little control.

Christopher Dawson's answer to the dilemma was his revolutionary idea of a new liberal arts course, based not on world history nor the study of civilization in general but on Christian civilization, which as Toynbee himself had shown was inseparable from Western civilization. On a more practical note the book concluded with an appendix contributed by Mr John J. Mulloy giving specific programmes for the study of Christian culture.

This book came under heavy fire from a Catholic reviewer in *The Harvard Educational Review*, Mr Justus George Lawler from St Xavier College who not only criticised the thesis of the book and the ideas which it embodied but launched into a violent personal attack on the author's historical views and judgements. As Prof Bruno Schlesinger put it in a letter to the editor of the review:

> His (Mr Lawler's) tone is sometimes almost savagely impertinent towards a devoted scholar of international repute and Mr Lawler misrepresents Prof Dawson altogether by associating him with the school of Chesterton and Belloc which Prof Dawson has frequently criticised.
>
> His quoting brief passages out of context misleads the reader. The most disagreeable purpose which seems to be served by this is to make Prof Dawson who is essentially an eirenic figure, appear to be a narrowminded bigoted special pleader, ignorant of American history and unable to learn from his experience here.

Christopher, in his letter of 16th September 1961 thanked Prof Schlesinger for his outspoken reply to *The Harvard Educational Review* and commented:

> Lawler has really surpassed himself in this review. .... I cannot quite account for the element of personal malice in his attack which gives it such an unpleasant flavour. I seem to have annoyed him by saying he was a representative of the *avant-garde* of Catholic educationalists but it is nothing to get so excited about. Unfortunately by and large the Catholic educationalists seem to be the greatest enemies of Catholic culture!

The debate was continued at the invitation of *The Harvard Educational Review* in a competent and learned reply written by Mr John J. Mulloy and in a further postscript by the author of the review.

In *The Historic Reality of Christian Culture* (1960), subtitled *A Way to the Renewal of Human Life*, Christopher again discussed the survival of Western civilization and the problem of secularisation in a technological age. It was a book that carried some terrifying warnings but also a message of hope: the new Babylon of modern materialist civilization had been built on the soil of Christendom and it was threatened by an even more catastrophic and suicidal end than any of the world empires of the past. He compared the situation to that which the early Christians faced during the decline of the ancient world:

> Everything now depends on whether the Christians of the new age are equal to their mission – whether they are able to communicate their hope to a world in which man finds himself alone and helpless before the monstrous forces which have been created by man to serve his own ends but which now have escaped from his control and threaten to destroy him.

Both here and in an earlier book, *The Movement of World Revolution* (1959) he discussed the relationship between Christianity and the Oriental cultures.

But particularly he was concerned with the crisis that had developed through nationalism in the relations between East and West. Further there was the danger that if Christianity failed to fulfill its role as mediator in this revolutionary world then Communism would step into the breach and reap its own harvest of totalitarian terror.

TRAVELS IN AMERICA

On 12th October 1959, a year after his arrival at Harvard, Christopher celebrated his seventieth birthday. A party was given to mark the occasion organised by Fr Sweeney SJ at Boston College. Alec Guinness was among the principal guests.

In his address Christopher said that he never expected to celebrate his seventieth birthday in America. Although all his life his taste and traditions had been bound up with English country life and he had always avoided living in cities, he never felt the slightest doubt or hesitation in accepting the Stillman professorship. He said:

> All my life for fifty years I have been writing on one subject and for one cause – the cause of Christendom and the study of
> Christian culture. When I began it was in the days of Charles

Peguy and Belloc and Chesterton and my eyes were fixed on
Europe and the European tradition. But to-day I have come to feel
that it is in this country that the fate of Christendom will be
decided .... There is a great opportunity in America today that
may never be repeated. That is why I am here.

A week before this event, he had been awarded the Catholic
Action Medal at St Bonaventure University which had been
inaugurated by Pope Pius XI in 1931 'to honour annually a
layman who had contributed notably to Modern Catholic
Apostolates.' The citation mentioned Christopher Dawson's
work as a philosopher of history and culture, his contribution
to the present day knowledge of the past and his call to
Christian educators.

In that same year of 1959 he was also awarded an honorary
degree of Doctor of Humane Letters, at St John's University,
New York. It coincided with the publication of *The Movement of World Revolution*, in which, as was pointed out in the
address, he envisioned 'salvation through Europe, which is and
must remain the centre of world history, and through
Christianity, which is an ecumenical faith and is offered a great
opportunity in the East.'

But his seventy years began to take their toll: having led the
life of a semi-invalid all his life, he had suddenly, at an age when
most people have already retired, plunged headlong into a life
of intense activity and while this stimulated his mind it over-
taxed him physically. As a result, in December 1959, after little
more than a year in America, he suffered a minor stroke,
which, while fortunately it did not incapacitate him seriously
either mentally or physically, nevertheless made him realise
that he must take life at a slower pace. From now on he decided
to cut down on outside activities and concentrate solely on his
work at Harvard.

One of the exceptions to this rule was the Smith History
Lecture, which he delivered at the University of St Thomas,
Houston in March 1960. The subject of this was 'America and
the Secularisation of Modern Culture' and here he demonstrated how the glorification of material values had apparently
left no place for spiritual ones:

The relatively poverty stricken peoples of mediaeval Europe
erected vast cathedrals and abbeys but these were the expression of

their common faith and their hopes for eternity. But to-day we build temples greater than the Egyptian pyramids or the gothic cathedrals and they are dedicated to toothpaste or chewing-gum or anything that anyone wants, so long as enough people want it.

Modern technological society had become so highly organ-ised that it absorbed almost the whole of life and it was be-coming almost impossible for the individual to stand out against the mass pressure which makes for conformity. Examples were drawn from Russia and China but even in the modern democratic state the same forces were at work. He compared modern Western man to Frankenstein 'who created a mechanical monster which he became unable to control so that it came to threaten his life.'

He thought that the pressure of the technological order and the challenge of Communism could only be overcome if Western civilization should recover a sense of spiritual purpose or spiritual order, and it was a question of life or death for modern civilization. It was a fact of history, he concluded, that every civilization had recognised the existence of a higher spiritual order which was above conflicting individual interests or the collective will of the state:

> This great and ancient truth, as Edmund Burke wrote, is the ultimate foundation of human society, and no society which denies it or loses sight of it, can endure.

Although Christopher curtailed his public activities, he and Valery continued to travel and see as much of America as possible in the few years they were to spend there. In every way their life in America was a complete antithesis of the quiet country life they had lived for so many years in England – the tragedy was that the experience came too late.

Air travel held no fears for them although again they took to it late in life and in fact they enjoyed it more than any other means of transport. Apart from the summer of 1960 when they made a journey back to England to see the family, they spent the vacations travelling far and wide to escape from the extremes of climate in Cambridge – the ice and snow in winter and the humid heat of summer. Bermuda, Miami and Santa Fe in New Mexico were among the places they visited. They also made two journeys to Canada to see their daughter, Juliana, who was teaching in a convent at Baie Comeau up the St Lawrence River in Quebec Province.

But it was at Wethersfield, the country house of Mr Chauncey Stillman near Amenia in New York State, that Christopher and Valery spent their happiest days while they were in America and they kept an affectionate memory both of the place and its owner until the end of their lives.

To stay at Wethersfield is to go back in time about 150 years, to the days of carriages and high-stepping horses – one of Mr Stillman's accomplishments is that he can drive a four-in-hand – to a world of complete peace in which the only sounds to be heard are those of bird-song, perhaps the screech of a peacock and the distant lowing of cattle. It is only some 100 miles from New York yet one feels totally remote from the turmoil of 20th century civilization – although Wethersfield represents the height of civilization in the true sense of the word.

Approached first through farmland, then through a wooded park, the brick and pink sandstone house at the top of a hill in the uplands east of the Hudson River is almost concealed until one comes upon it hidden among the trees and yew hedges of its magnificent classical gardens.

From the tall windows of the blue drawing-room, one looks past the lawns and clipped yew hedges, the green of the long walks and the blue of the oval swimming pool towards a Palladian arch and from there towards the distant Catskill Mountains and the Berkshires.

It is a garden full of surprises – the formal Italianate garden is surrounded by pastures and woods and suddenly one is in a wilderness such as might be found in the park of an English country house but here at every turn there is classical statuary by the American sculptor, Joseph Stachura, or in the depths of a wooded hollow one finds an Orpheus and Eurydice by the English sculptor, Peter Watts. It is a perfect alliance of nature and art which has been devised by Mr Stillman over the years since 1937.

Within the house the work of Pietro Annigoni is much in evidence, not only in the pictures (including portraits of Mr Stillman's two daughters) but in the annexe to the house, a building rightly called a 'gloriette'. The painter frescoed its curved ceiling and wall panels in high Renaissance *bravura*

depicting what Mr Stillman has described as 'dream land-
scapes'.

Christopher found Wethersfield an ideal place to relax from
his professorial duties at Harvard. He was able to browse in Mr
Stillman's library and he enjoyed walking in the park or driving
out in a carriage which must have reminded him of his Victorian childhood. Mr Stillman wrote to me:

> This house is the place with which your parents are mostly associ-
> ated in my mind. I can see your father sitting for hours on a bench
> in the garden, talking to Fr John Lafarge, a beloved old Jesuit
> friend whom he found most congenial. Your mother was more
> amused by the lighter-minded inhabitants such as my daughters
> and Harry FitzGibbons (a family friend).

Christopher and Valery spent a week at Wethersfield every
summer that they were in America, that is to say on four
occasions. Mr Stillman enjoyed Christopher's dry humour and
his comments on people and events, for with all his appearance
of scholarly vagueness he was more astute than was generally
realised. There was the story, recounted by his host, of the
time when a 'self-important ornithologist' came to call, who
reminisced interminably about a dinner given at the Royal
Ornithological Society. In the chair was a well-known duke
who, according to the ornithologist, introduced him as the
most brilliant lecturer he had ever heard! Christopher, who
never suffered a bore gladly, appeared to switch off and stared
into space. It was only when the man had left that he remarked
laconically: 'Odd that a bird fancier should set such store on
dukes.'

For Valery, these visits to Wethersfield were just as much a
relaxation as they were for Christopher, but in another way.
She remarked to Mr Stillman that people at Harvard often
seemed to be in awe of her because they thought she must also
be a highbrow: 'But I'm not', she said, 'I just like music and
laughter.' Mr Stillman remembered her enthusiasm and evident enjoyment of all the family activities. But the fact was that
he himself was the perfect host and managed to make them feel
at their ease as no one else could have done so far from home
and from their English roots.

FAREWELL TO HARVARD

The winter of 1962 was a particularly severe one at Cambridge and Christopher's health suffered as a result of it. He and Valery spent Christmas at Miami as guests of the Assumption nuns, but he was ill practically all the time he was there. Soon after his return to Harvard he suffered another stroke, after which he decided regretfully that he would have to resign from his professorship in the summer and return to England, a year before the five year term was up. It was a bitter blow for him for he felt that there was little left for him to do; speech was difficult for him and writing also – the few letters he wrote after this time are in a very shaky hand.

He made this decision in April 1962, and at the end of the term in June he relinquished his appointment. Before they left America, Christopher had the pleasure of seeing his wife awarded an honorary degree at Regis College by Cardinal Cushing. Valery was amazed at the seeming incongruity of herself as Doctor of Laws.

In the citation Cardinal Cushing quoted from the Book of Proverbs:

> A good wife is a rare treasure and none is so honoured as her husband when he sits in council with the elders of the land.

and he went on to add:

> Without the light and sweetness and strength which Valery Mary Dawson brought to the labors of her husband, some of the world's most enlightened scholarship would never have come to exist.

On 2nd June Cardinal Cushing gave a farewell dinner party to honour Christopher Dawson and this according to Prof Stendhal of Harvard's Divinity School was a great and historic occasion. The Cardinal was in exuberant form and spoke for forty minutes. Introducing his testimonial speech he said:

> There are only a very few men in each generation of whom it may be said: 'He changed men's minds.' Tonight we honor just such a person.
>
> Christopher Dawson is one of those rare human spirits who stands back from the world in which he lives and takes the true measure of time and man.

He described him as more than a historian; rather he was a

philosopher of history and a historian of the mind who 'accepts the fact that what men think is more important than what they do.' He then paid tribute to him as the first occupant of the Stillman Chair and to his achievement at Harvard saying:

> I know of no figure in the Catholic world who could have brought that combination of personal reticence and intellectual excellence which has launched the Stillman Chair at Harvard University. Undoubtedly, in the years ahead, many great and impressive figures will be here, but each will look back with admiration and gratitude at the first occupant of this post who in his way, set the direction of its future.

Cardinal Cushing ended by reading a telegram from Pope John XXIII sending his Apostolic blessing on the occasion of Christopher Dawson's retirement. In an aside he said: 'That cost me 500 dollars!'

There were other farewell functions of a less formal nature; the Catholic community at Harvard and Radcliffe College presented Christopher Dawson with a reproduction of a painting of Harvard Yard in the snow by the Chinese artist, Chiang Yee. Christopher kept it in a place of honour above the fireplace in his library in England.

His former assistant, Daniel Callahan, in a tribute in the *Commonweal* wrote of 'the grandly cosmic, historical scope of Catholicism and Christianity' which Christopher Dawson brought to his courses in the Harvard Divinity School, and how he did much to dispel the doubts of those who questioned the idea of such a chair of Roman Catholic Studies in a Protestant Divinity School. He compared Christopher Dawson's achievement at Harvard with that of the Oxford Movement, which had brought about the first genuine bond between Catholics and Protestants in the Anglo-Saxon world. 'After Newman, Manning and W. G. Ward', he wrote, 'Oxford was never quite the same; perhaps in a somewhat similar sense, after Christopher Dawson, Harvard will never be quite the same.'[5]

CHAPTER THIRTEEN

The Last Years

Christopher and Valery left New York in the *Queen Elizabeth* on 18th July 1962, arriving at Southampton on the 23rd. Among the passengers was General Eisenhower. Fr Francis Sweeney, SJ, from Boston College accompanied them on the voyage and he remembered how at the time the ship's doctor predicted that Christopher would have about eight months to live – in fact that eight months proved to be eight years.

It was with the greatest sadness that they left America and the friends they had made there behind them and if it had not been for Christopher's illness, they would probably have settled there even after his Harvard term of office came to an end, for the possibility had been mooted of a centre for the study of Christopher Dawson's ideas at Notre Dame or one of the other Catholic universities where he might have retired in an honorary capacity.

At seventy-two, Christopher seemed prematurely aged and as he came off the ship in a wheel-chair his appearance was in marked contrast to that of the man who had left England only four years before, full of enthusiasm for his new post and with an almost youthful sense of adventure.

They returned to Budleigh Salterton, but not to their former house which had been sold, but to another, named Fountain Hill House, which had had the disadvantage of being half-way up a precipitous hill – an inconvenience even for someone in good health. Christopher was disabled by successive strokes and Valery later developed arthritis, and for them it was an unwise choice to say the least. Had it not been for the devoted service of their former housekeeper, Miss Blake, who stayed with them to the end of their days and later on the care of Sister Mary Long, a nursing sister from the Bon Secours Convent in Liverpool, they would not have been able to stay there. As it was, they were able to spend their last years in comfort and security. A lift was installed to reach the upper floor and adjacent to their bedroom there was a sun-room which commanded a view over the sea. All important to Christopher there was space to house his library; he seldom read any of these books in these last years but it gave him comfort to think they were around him like old friends.

Now Christopher had come to the end of his working life. Mercifully the strokes he had suffered had not affected his brain but both speech and writing became increasingly difficult for him. With the help of Edward Watkin, who often visited him from Torquay, he managed to get the first two volumes of his Harvard lectures into book form, and they were published by Sheed & Ward in America. *The Dividing of Christendom* appeared first in 1965, dedicated to Chauncey Stillman, and this was followed by *The Formation of Christendom* in 1967. Much to Christopher's disappointment there was no simultaneous publication by Sheed & Ward's London office, but the first volume was published after his death by Sidgwick & Jackson in 1971 with an introduction by David Knowles.

Christopher welcomed the Second Vatican Council with all its promise of spiritual and cultural renewal for which he had spent his whole life working. There was nothing in the Documents of that Council to which he would have taken exception, and even the call for more use of the vernacular in the liturgy he would probably have accepted as inevitable in a changing world.

What he could not have foreseen were the post-Conciliar changes of thought and the radical changes in the liturgy brought about by *avant-garde* theologians and liturgists. The immemorial Latin Mass of Gregory the Great, brought to England by Augustine, was abandoned for a vernacular parish Mass, something which Ronald Knox might have described as 'neither wholly Catholic nor wholly Protestant' and which Cardinal Heenan himself declared was never intended by Pope John and the Council bishops.[1]

Although, on account of his illness, Christopher was unable to attend Mass for some years before his death, he was well aware of the changes that were taking place and he deplored them. In a letter to Edward Watkin he wrote: 'I hate the changes in the liturgy and even the translations are so bad.' This letter, written in the 1960s but undated, referred to the earlier changes, the tip of the iceberg, before the present *Novus Ordo* was introduced in 1970. He had always been deeply attached to the Latin liturgy and the old Roman Mass and this letter is evidence that he had not changed his views.

In the early days of the Vernacular Movement in the 1950s, Christopher strongly defended the necessity of a common liturgical language, as a bond of unity within the Church. In 1953 he wrote:

> The existence of a common liturgical language of some kind is a sign of the Church's mission to reverse the curse of Babel and to create a bond of unity between the peoples. The nations that are still divided from one another by the barriers of race and language leave their divisions and antipathies at the door of the Church and worship together in a tongue which belongs to none and yet which is common to all.[2]

And in another letter he quoted the fact that Negro converts to Islam were prepared to learn classical Arabic in order to read the Koran, a language far more remote from their own than Latin from Western Europeans.

An interesting corroboration of the value of the Latin language is attributed to Stravinsky who, when composing the *Oedipus Rex* for a Latin translation rather than French, described Latin as 'a language not dead but turned to stone: and therefore immune from vulgarisation'.

Christopher was devoted wholeheartedly to the cause of Christian unity but he never thought this could be achieved by a change of rite, still less by bringing about a new reformation based on 16th century lines. In one of his last letters to Edward Watkin he wrote: 'It is extraordinary to read the pro-Lutheran utterances in the Catholic press. I can't understand how they reconcile this with their liturgical principles but I don't believe it is a very serious movement.'

While much that was going on in the Church was evidently contrary to his own concepts of renewal, he adhered as strongly as ever to his traditional Catholic faith and it was his great strength and support through the last years of his life.

He had become resigned to the thought of his own death and it is only logical to suppose that he was actually looking forward to it. Many years before, he had written an article on 'the future life' in which he foresaw the life to come as a vast cosmic change which might restore and preserve that which was spiritually valuable in the present world:

> The world to come may be no less different from the world of our sensible experience than is a symphony of Beethoven from the complicated mechanism which has been framed to transmit it.[3]

Christopher lived to share with Valery their golden wedding anniversary on 9th August 1966, which was celebrated with their family and some of the grand-children. Another memorable occasion was his eightieth birthday on 12th October 1969. *The Tablet* published a tribute to him written by Edward Watkin.[4] A telegram unexpectedly arrived from somewhere in Arizona: 'Exegisti monumentum. Affection and admiration from your pupils – Maisie and Frank Sheed.'

In May 1970, Christopher had a sudden heart attack; at first he seemed to recover from it and was soon sitting up in bed asking for champagne and a copy of *The Times*, of which he had been a lifetime reader, but he soon after contracted pneumonia which proved fatal.

Chauncey Stillman, who was on a visit to England, came to see him shortly before he died and Christopher was able to smile at him and say: 'Good-bye, Chauncey.' Edward Watkin also came to see his oldest and greatest friend for the last time. When he had left, Christopher said to his nurse, Sister Mary: 'You know he made me a Catholic.'

On Trinity Sunday he sank into a coma from which he never rallied except for one brief and remarkable moment which Sister Mary has recalled:

> All of a sudden he opened his eyes and staring at the painting of the crucifixion, which was on the wall at the foot of his bed, he had a beautiful smile and his eyes were wide open. He then said: 'This is Trinity Sunday. I see it all and it is beautiful.' He then returned to the coma never to regain consciousness.

No one had told him that it was Trinity Sunday since he had been unconscious all that day.

He died the next day, 25th May, on the feast of St Bede, with his family and also his sister present. At the moment of his death, Fr Michael Ryan, the parish priest, who had already administered the Last Rites of the Catholic Church to him, happened to call in and gave him his blessing.

The funeral took place at Budleigh Salterton and he was buried in Burnsall churchyard in Yorkshire, next to his parents' grave.

Valery survived him for four years and died at Budleigh Salterton on 28th September 1974, after a short illness.

A Summing Up

> He was perhaps fortunate in the moment of his death.
> His age was finished and his work was done.[1]

So Christopher Dawson wrote of Edward Gibbon, and if the summing up was true of Gibbon, it could also be an epitaph for himself. But just as Gibbon's work holds a perennial message so too does Christopher Dawson's.

If in the age of renewal in the Catholic Church, his ideas and values have been disregarded, they cannot, as Edward Watkin has pointed out, be refuted, 'for his interpretations are anchored securely to historical fact.' Already in America there are signs of disillusionment with the new trends of thought and a growing recognition that the pre-conciliar Catholic writers had something to say after all. Michael Novak writing in *Commonweal* looked back on the ten years since the Second Vatican Council with some cynicism quoting a remark made by Gustave Weigel: 'All things human, given enough time, go badly.' Novak called attention to the collapse of morale among many of the clergy; the susceptibility of many liberal Catholics to merely secular attitudes and the direction of their energies into political outlets: 'It is as though all those powerful writings of Dawson, Maritain, Guardini and so many others had never really taken roots. As though people had not been convinced by them, never really changed by them.'[2]

Among Catholic writers, Christopher Dawson's name has often been linked with that of Maritain but in actual fact he had little in common with him. To Christopher, Maritain's medievalism was his great fault for he tended to ignore all that had taken place between the Reformation and the Thomist and Gothic revival. Modern Catholic history in Christopher's view derived from the centuries of humanism however incompletely this was received by the Church. As a Catholic writer and thinker, Christopher Dawson belonged more to an earlier tradition – that of Newman, von Hügel and Acton.

In England the British Academy published a memoir written by Prof David Knowles, the monastic historian, with contributions from Edward Watkin and John J. Mulloy. Assessing Dawson's work, Prof Knowles considered that his strength lay in his vast erudition, the flowing prose style in which he expressed his ideas, and his power in deploying those ideas, which made his work very influential over many years. 'In his field', he wrote, 'he was the most distinguished Catholic thinker of this century.'[3]

Many years before, after the appearance of *Progress and Religion* and *The Making of Europe*, T. S. Eliot, lecturing in the United States, was, according to Maisie Sheed, asked what writer was then the most powerful intellectual influence in England. He answered, 'Christopher Dawson'.

For Christopher's influence extended not only to those who shared his orthodox Catholic beliefs but also to many who were aware of the dark forces of materialism and secularism threatening the very existence of civilization. In his own life, begun in the Victorian age, he had seen two world wars, the rise of the totalitarian powers and of revolutionary nationalism, as well as a return:

> To all the evils which the 19th century thought it had banished for ever – proscription and persecution, torture and slavery, and the fear of sudden death – and with them new terrors which the past did not know.

He recognised, too, the progressive force of evil and the unlimited prospects for its development which the modern world provides and with which Alexander Solzhenitsyn has made us all too uncomfortably familiar. He viewed the disintegration of Western culture as a far worse disaster than that of the fall of Rome. For the one was material; the other would be a spiritual disaster which would strike directly at the moral foundations of our society and destroy not the outward form of civilization but the soul of man, which is the beginning and the end of all human culture.

Christopher Dawson's final message was, however, one of hope. As he wrote in one of his last books:

We today are living in a world that is far less stable than that of the early Roman Empire. There is no doubt that the world is on the move again as never before and that the pace is faster and more furious than anything that man has known before. But there is nothing in this situation which should cause Christians to despair. On the contrary it is the kind of situation for which their faith has always prepared them and which provides the opportunity for the fulfilment of their mission.[4]

Christopher Dawson: The Historian of Ideas

by James Oliver

The surprise in the discovery of a new writer, as in that of a land, lies naturally not only in what distinguishes him from others, but in his resemblance and reference to them. The greater the writer, the wider the field of reference, evidence the endless commentaries on Isaiah, Dante, Shakespeare.

This consideration has a particular bearing on Christopher Dawson because this field of reference was precisely his subject. His first books on which his reputation was based, *The Age of the Gods* and *Progress and Religion*, surprised scholars no less than critics by the number and variety of their references, by the sympathy towards differing points of view, by the serenity with which they were refined or reconciled.

Every historian has to judge and balance references, but the historian of ideas has to be familiar with many periods, to examine them with subtlety and in depth. The history of ideas presents the further difficulty of a new discipline which necessarily intrudes on others, not only ancient, medieval and modern history, but sociology, anthropology, literature, art, comparative religion, philosophy and theology. It demands wide reading, deep learning, discernment and judgement.

That Christopher Dawson had such qualities was hardly disputed by critics, for his books were reviewed by specialists who admitted his scholarship and discernment even when they disagreed with his conclusions. Literary critics were no less impressed by his wit and by the clarity of his style. This gave a wider public access to his work, and those who had once read him remained with him, drawn less by his theme than by enjoyment of his writing.

This appreciation by scholars and serious readers would have been more marked if it had not been partly countered by a natural resistance to his subject in other disciplines. There was a tendency for historians and sociologists, literary critics and students of comparative religion, philosophers and theologians to dismiss his work as really the concern of another department, not their own. So while he was certainly more learned than Spengler and less of a philosophic idealist than Toynbee, he was opposed by much the same barriers as were erected against them. He had the further disadvantage of being labelled 'a Roman Catholic writer', though for most of his life he was more appreciated outside his communion than within it.

For such reasons as these anybody who encounters his work for the first time has to adjust to its scope, to realise that he is foremost a historian of ideas. The best introduction to it is *Progress and Religion*, the examination of an idea, or such a selection as *Religion and World History*, which reflects its unity.

The history of ideas exacts so much knowledge, and so enters into world history, that its exponents, from Burckhardt and Huizinga to Friedrich Heer, are hardly to be confined to their own subject. Christopher Dawson first envisaged his work as a history of culture, but the two volumes of this history which were published already gave in their sub-titles an indication of other developments: *The Age of the Gods* was 'a study in the origins of culture in prehistoric Europe and the ancient East' while *The Making of Europe* was 'an introduction to the history of European unity'. The first in fact showed its mastery most in the balance between different theories of origins, while the second openly disclosed his interest in the European movement and the discussion of ideas to which later works were devoted.

Between these two appeared *Progress and Religion*, the most representative of his works in this context, after them *Enquiries into Religion and Culture* and *Mediaeval Religion*, which assessed ideas from cycles of civilization, Christianity and sex to Church and state and the origins of the Romantic tradition in Moslem Spain.

Significantly, the works written in the critical years before 1939, when public events most aroused political passions, were direct contributions to the history of ideas. While others engaged in furious controversy, he serenely investigated the origins of Fascism and Communism and showed them to be typical aberrations of the modern state. Some even confused this scholarly detachment with sympathy for Fascism, though it was of real interest to the history of ideas that Hitler should so reject the best of his central Europe–Prussian devotion, Austrian Catholicity, South German good-nature – and so unite the worst – Prussian militarism, Austrian Pan-Germanism, South German political romanticism.

In those years when men otherwise rational saw events in black and white, in the gross outlines of cartoons and the features of dictators, Christopher Dawson's influence increased because he was one of the few able to understand the course of events, as Bernard Wall testified in his *Headlong into Change*:

> But Christopher, with his vast knowledge of world culture, his special studies in European history, mediaeval and modern, seemed to me far better equipped to give an all round picture of our condition .... in the general hysteria of the time, he went on calmly disentangling the sociological threads in Europe.

He saw too that the crisis was a symptom of changes in all modern states and realised then, what is generally admitted only today, the intimate union of Capitalism and Parliaments, as he expounded in *Religion and the Modern State*, where he warned Christians against all worldly systems:

> Apparent success often means spiritual failure, and the way of failure and suffering is the royal road of Christian progress.

This hope in the hour of darkness recurs in *Beyond Politics* (1939) and in *Judgement of the Nations*, published during the war, where his anguish issues in an appeal for a united Europe as a necessity imposed by the times. As editor of the *Dublin Review* he gave prominence to the history of ideas and chose articles on this from European and particularly German exiles: in that period of war it became the most international of reviews.

After the war the importance of Europe was emphasised in articles and in such works as *Understanding Europe*, while the history of ideas was the background both to his Gifford lectures on *Religion and Culture* and to his later Harvard lectures on Christendom. But the outstanding theme of this third period was *The Crisis of Western Education*, a title issued in 1961. In a process of thought going back over thirty years he had come to the conclusion that the history of ideas was the remedy to this crisis: Western society was withering because it had lost touch with the roots of its own culture.

In essence this had always been the principle of his thought, that religion was the spirit that informed every culture, which collapsed with the collapse of its belief – or as Balzac had maintained, when an effect is no longer related to its cause, the organism is corrupt. The new emphasis on education came from a recognition that many who accepted and defended civilization were quite unaware of the efforts and qualities still necessary to sustain it, qualities not taught, not even admitted, by secular education. Wellington a century before in a typical aphorism had already condemned an education which produced only 'clever devils'.

While historians of science still recognised ideas received from the Greeks, Western man no longer respected other elements in his culture. The classics of Greece and Rome had enabled him to measure his own politics, ethics, and art against theirs, but the decline of classical education removed this safeguard. Nor was this replaced by study of the creative elements in European history, for which a national course was no substitute. In an unpublished lecture Christopher Dawson pointed out:

> For paradoxical though it may appear, there can be no doubt that the peoples who are most ignorant of history are those who are most dependent on the past .... the more we know of the past, the more free we are to choose the way we will go.

This will not seem exaggerated to those aware of the misunderstandings of today and it is a keynote of his message.

APPENDIX TO THE TRANSACTION EDITION

Neville Braybroke

In 1948 when I was running a magazine called *The Wind and the Rain* I wrote to Christopher Dawson asking him to contribute. I had in view an article that might perhaps analyse the sort of academic mind which is prepared, say, to give full weight to Christianity's role in European culture. In Dawson's last book, *The Gods of Revolution,* published posthumously in 1972, he remarks that the world of the Ancient East has been brought far closer to us than Italy was to Britain a century ago. When Dawson's contribution arrived on my desk in 1948, it was accompanied by a diffident, covering note. In it, he explained that what he was sending represented for him a new departure; it was the first chapter of an autobiography which, regrettably, he never completed. The working title, he said, was *Tradition and Inheritance.*

Early in *Tradition and Inheritance,* Dawson claims that Rousseau was the founder of modern autobiography, adding that the Frenchman cared little for inheritance: "All that mattered were his own feelings and his own experiences". Dawson's one chapter of autobiography is, in contrast, a work of *pietas* — a remembering and recalling of all that had gone to the making of himself, his family and their ancestors. A key word for Dawson is "making".

Applied to tradition, it means something active, which has to be worked at; if it is not worked at, then it dies. *Tradition and Inheritance,* in miniature, is a restatement, in personal terms, of Dawson's general view of history in which he sees culture stemming from religion, and not *vice versa.*

On his father's side, Dawson came from a military, landowning Anglican family in Yorkshire. His father was widely cultured, and equally at home in modern science as in modern history, in ancient philosophy as in mediaevel mysticism. For Dante his admiration knew no bounds, and he rated him above Shakespeare and Milton as the world's one perfect poet. There was a set of the *Summa Theologica* in his library, but he did not assiduously study it as he did Plato, Berkeley and the Roman Stoics. The width of his literary appreciation was to be reflected in his son's writings. Christopher Dawson's mother was a Welshwoman, who was passionately devoted to the Welsh countryside and its people. Her son's earliest memory is of a poem which she used to recite about Bran the Blessed, the mythical ancestor of the Holy Families of Wales. One line from it he never forgot: "He who will be chief, let him be a bridge". Dawson, in his books, was to build many bridges between religion and culture. In his autobiographical "notes", as he calls them, he writes: "Thanks to my parents I learnt the essential connection between *story* and *history,* so that I came to know the past, not so much by the arid path of *The Child's History of England,* as through the enchanted world of myth and legend".

Re-reading his opening chapter some thirty years after I first read it in manuscript, I am struck by its strong sense of place. Dawson had an acute sense of the *genus locii,* and refers to "the latent powers of landscape". He contrasts the north and the south of England; and argues that, in the south, nature has been so completely tamed and made to serve the purpose of society that it no longer exists "except as part of the life of man". But in Yorkshire, in the north, with its dark rocks thrusting out of the rising moorland it is otherwise. Dawson is also concerned with the elemental and the scriptural in nature. In 1896 his father built a house above the river Wharfe at Hartlington, near Skipton. In the years that followed, his son was to get to know the voice of the river — its gentle murmur in summer, its wild roar in winter. Texts from the Old Testament, far more than the pious moralities found in Victorian books for children, took on for him a vivid and literal meaning: "Let the floods clap their hands", or "Deep calleth to deep at the noise of Thy water-spouts". One phrase, which has dropped out of common speech, had a particular relevance for Dawson and his generation, even when that generation ceased to be believers. Here is E. M. Forster using it in a book about the history of his own family (and I put it in italics): "They did not know whether they wished the house to stand, to be sold or to vanish off the *spiritual face of the earth"*.

Living in an age of doubt and the beginning of computer-history, Dawson never sought to bridge the centuries by artificial deductions of cause and effect. History, he maintained, was not an objective science, but the study of men. Always, he gave full value to the mysterious and to the unseen. His view of the world, which he experienced as a child in Yorkshire, left a deep mark, and some of his later observations, about the human condition, may well be traced back to his earlier memories of the wealth and poverty that he saw co-existing in the same moorside towns and valleys. I am thinking in particular of his last book where, in the context of the French Revolution, he writes about the nature of rationalism — although his observation is one that has relevance far beyond the boundaries of France or the limits of the eighteenth century. Rationalism, he declares, flourishes best in a prosperous age and a sheltered society; it finds few adherents among the unfortunate and the defeated". This is the comment of an historian who believes in an hierarchical structure of society in which each man has his appointed place. It goes, too, with his belief in an appointed order — and, in the 1930s, Dawson edited a series of short books under the significant title of *Essays in Order*. For Christopher Dawson, order and hierarchy were interchangeable words for tradition and inheritance.

MEMORIES OF A VICTORIAN CHILDHOOD

CHRISTOPHER DAWSON

I. WALES AND WESSEX

THE changes that have been taking place during the present century are so far-reaching that no one can foresee what their ultimate effect on human life will be. But already they have caused a loss of social tradition and a dislocation of human experience such as no previous generation has known since the beginning of history. The world of my childhood is already as far away from the contemporary world as it was from the world of the middle ages and there is a danger that whole ranges of experience will be so lost that in the future they may be inaccessible even to the historical imagination. Yet we ourselves are not changed in the same way as the world around us. In fact Western man is being submitted to the same process which he inflicted on more primitive peoples in the last century. As the Red Indian and the South Sea Islander saw their world and their way of living destroyed by the rifle and the railway and the trader, and were left culturally naked in an alien world, so we too have seen our world destroyed and our culture liquidated under the pressure of anonymous forces and impersonal techniques, which we created with one side of our minds as the instruments of our limited purposes, but which have become our masters.

The great question of our time is whether we can regain control or whether the change has gone so far that Western man is destined to go the same way as the Red Indian and either disappear or survive for a time in a United Europe Reservation.

But whatever the answer to this question may be, we cannot dismiss the past as dead and unimportant. If it is dead, it deserves to be recorded, no less than any other vanished civilization. If it is not dead, but only in a state of revolutionary change, we must study the past in order to discover what elements in its tradition can be recovered, what is lost beyond recall and what is indispensable to the continuity and the identity of Western culture. This must be done in detail, as well as in general. Indeed, it is the record of individual personal and family tradition which is most needed, because this is the element that is most easily lost and most difficult for the historian to recover or to reconstruct from external evidence. It is impossible to study history without being conscious of the tremendous waste of unrecorded experience in every age and generation which could so easily have been preserved, if only the ordinary man had been aware of its value.

For in the past every individual life represented a synthesis of, or a selection from, a series of living social traditions which reached back endlessly in time into the past, though they were confined in space to a limited number of places or even to a single region. When the whole force of social tradition is concentrated in a single channel, as in a primitive tribal society, there is no room for this selective process, and the pattern of culture is unaffected by the passage of time and the change of generations. On the other hand, where the individual is a unit in a mass society, as in the new urbanized and mechanized type of civilization, the family ceases to be the bearer of social traditions and the tradition of culture is also lost or degraded. But in the traditional form of Western culture, as it existed down to our own time, the family was a true social institution with its own internal structure and there was room for an immense variety of cultural traditions within the same society, so that every individual had his own personal access to the past and his own distinct inheritance of culture.

It is of this I wish to write, taking my own early experience and family traditions as a type or rather a specimen. I cannot hope to do this adequately, because it is a new experiment and the whole tradition of modern autobiographical writing is against it. For though there has never been a culture which has produced a richer harvest of autobiography than our own, it has always been characterized by a spirit of romantic introspection and individualism. Rousseau is the founder of modern autobiography and he knew little and cared less about his cultural inheritance—all that mattered were his own feelings and his own experiences.

It is true that the later romantics, like Wordsworth and Ruskin, had a deep and delicate sense of the significance of place and social environment in the formation of the mind and character. On the other hand it is much rarer to find any profound understanding of family and ancestral inheritance. This is partly due to sheer lack of knowledge, for few English families trouble to preserve their records, and even when they do so they usually concern themselves only with a single line of descent. But in addition to this there is a positive antipathy to the past which makes men assert themselves as free individuals and reject their family tradition as an intolerable burden. Indeed some of the most characteristic modern biographies, such as those of Samuel Butler and Edmund Gosse, have been expressions of the revolt of the individual against the family and the bonds of his social inheritance. It requires some courage to reverse this attitude and to regard Aunt Jemima as a sacred rather than a ridiculous figure. Yet it is just at this point that we transcend the relative values of sociology and history and reach the bed rock of spiritual principles which govern the life of culture. For as St. Thomas shows, *Pietas*, which is the cult of parents and kinsfolk and native place as the principles of our being, by whom and in which we are born and nourished, has an essential relation to Religion which is the cult of God as our first principle. Hence piety in the classical sense of the word is not a matter of sentiment or social tradition, it is a moral principle that lies at the root of every culture and every religion, and the society that loses it has lost its primary moral basis and its hope of survival.

If this is so, it is clear that the cult of the family and the native place is not a form of snobbery or false romanticism but the first debt that we owe to society and to the Christian commonwealth. But it is not so easy to put this into practice, when we turn from the archaic tradition of the sacred hearth and the ancestral cult to the study of our own family traditions and background. Nevertheless this attitude is so natural to man that it is present in some degree in everyone's experience. And when this link with the past has been recovered, we shall also find a new key to the understanding of the past. This at least has been my experience, for I have found that the world revealed by the memory of childhood and family tradition is quite a different world from that which the historians have shown us. Written history inevitably simplifies or abstracts from the complexity of the real world, and the history of the immediate past tends to be even more abstract and superficial than that of the more remote past which demands a greater effort of historical imagination.

In particular, the social structure of the world of my childhood was very different from that described by the historians. Certainly it was representative of a type of Victorian middle class society. But the word 'Victorian' can mean half a dozen different things, and the words 'middle class' are even more deceptive. The English habit of speaking of the 'middle classes' in the plural is indeed much truer than is usually realized, for there are in fact a dozen different middle classes, each of which was a little world of its own, and many of which are almost ignored by the historian.

My own middle class differed from the corresponding class on the continent or the U.S.A. in that it was completely rural, so that it seems ridiculous to call it 'bourgeois' as the Marxians would, since in the literal sense of the word it was just the opposite. Neither my parents nor their parents nor theirs—almost ad infinitum—ever lived in a town, and I find it exceedingly difficult, not merely uncongenial but unnatural, to do so myself.

Yet neither I nor my predecessors have been rooted in one spot or even one part of England. Even from childhood I belonged equally to several different regions, so that I do not feel myself to be a northerner or a southerner or an Englishman or a Welshman, but a Briton.

The three districts to which I belong and which have impressed themselves so deeply on my mind and heart are, firstly, the South Welsh-Hereford border; secondly, the Itchen valley above Winchester, and thirdly, the West Yorkshire Dales, from Bolton Abbey in Wharfedale to Settle in Ribblesdale.

[I]

I was born at Hay in the Wye Valley—'the Welsh Hay' as they used to call it, though it crosses the national frontier. This was my mother's home and it probably influenced me more than any of the others. If anyone wishes to know the environment, they can find it well described in Kilvert's Journals[1]—in fact the people whom Kilvert knew were my mother's family and friends, and though Kilvert strikes the reader as archaic in 1870, things as I remember them in the 'nineties were almost exactly the same. One of the peculiar things about this society which made it unlike either Wales or England was that it was a sort of Anglican theocracy, for the landowners were largely clergymen and the clergy were either landowners or brothers of landowners, so that there was a complete unification of political, religious, economic and social authority and influence.

The house where I was born was a Tudor building constructed in and out of a mediæval castle originally built in the twelfth century by the de Braose. The builder, Maude of St. Valery, of whom Giraldus Cambrensis speaks, remained a great figure in Welsh tradition; in fact she had become fused with some mythical Celtic figure, so that she was supposed to have built the castle in a night, and a megalith which stands in Clyro churchyard across the river was pointed out to us as one of the stones which she dropped from her apron on her way to the castle.

From the windows of the castle one looked down into the street of the little town below and then across the river to the mountains. On market days when the farmers came down from the hills, one heard the Welsh: otherwise it was an entirely English-speaking district. But even the little town itself was quite different from an English one, and as early as I can remember I was conscious of the co-existence of two worlds—the rich Herefordshire countryside and the poor and wild Welsh hills of Radnor Forest to the North and the Black Mountain which rose immediately behind Hay to the South. If I remember aright, the division between these worlds was not a religious one between Anglican and Nonconformist, for in that part of Wales the people were largely Anglican and the Nonconformists were largely middle class, though it was a different middle class to my own—an alien world in fact.

My grandfather was devoted heart and soul to the cause of the established Church of Wales, and during his fifty-six years as Vicar of Hay and twelve as Archdeacon of Brecon he contributed a good deal to the work of reform that went on during Thirlwall and Basil Jones' episcopates. But in spite of this, and although he came of Welsh stock and spent eighty-six out of his eighty-seven years in Wales, he always seemed to me very un-Welsh in temperament— unemotional, cool, critical, dispassionate. My mother on the other hand was thoroughly Welsh by nature, passionately devoted to the Welsh country and country people and the Welsh traditions, above all to the Welsh saints, a subject on which she was an expert. In fact she was an unusually learned woman, rather in the tradition of that curious South Welsh school of antiquaries like Iolo Morganwg

[1]. Edited by William Plomer in 3 Volumes (1938-40).

and W. J. Rees, and at the same time very much attached to the literary traditions of the Marches—Henry Vaughan and Herbert, and in later days, Traherne. I acquired these tastes from her at a very early age, for she had a simple and childlike gift of communication. I think my earliest literary memory—and it is very early—is a poem she used to repeat about Bran the Blessed, the mythical ancestor of the Holy Families of Wales—the story of the Lodestone river and the saying 'He who will be chief, let him be a bridge'. I have never succeeded in rediscovering what this poem was or who was the author, but it shows how children can assimilate or appreciate very remote ideas, however young they may be.

But what I felt most at Hay was the feeling of antiquity—the immense age of everything, and in the house, the continuity of the present with the remote past, and this feeling was reinforced by the fact that nothing had changed since my mother had been a child in the same house and that all the family relations existed in duplicate, so that alongside of my parents, my nurse and my uncles and aunts, I saw my mother's parents and her nurse and her uncles and aunts. I don't think Proust mentions this, but it increases his central idea of Time as a dimension in which past and present coexist and of the human mind as a Titanic power that brings the two together, transcending the process of generation and corruption. And Proust did realize that it was the mind of childhood and the child's memory that are the key to this miracle.

[II]

The other place which influenced my childhood most was my father's mother's house at Easton, near Winchester. This was a very different household and region—a typical English village in the heart of Wessex. An old house at the end of the village looking down on a small Norman church and the water meadows of the Itchen beyond— a more beautiful river to my mind than even the Wye. Beautiful country also where it was always spring, for we used to come there every Easter, year after year, and I never knew it any other season.

My grandmother, who lived at Easton, had been a widow for forty years, even when I first remember her, for my grandfather, an officer in the Carabineers, had died soon after their marriage in 1854 and my grandmother and her two sons had lived with her parents until their death. Thus it was her family rather than the Dawsons who were the predominant influence, and her long widowhood had caused a sort of dislocation of the generation so that she lived in an almost pre-Victorian world.

Her family differed from my mother's in being a family of soldiers rather than clergymen, though it was equally, or even more religious in temperament. Its traditions had been formed or strengthened in the age of the French wars in which it had been involved for two generations. Her grandfather had been killed commanding his regiment in the battle of Castricum—that blind battle of the dunes which ended the disastrous Anglo-Russian invasion of Holland in 1799.

The Duke of York, who was the commander of that unfortunate expedition, offered commissions to the dead man's sons, and my great grandfather who was the eldest accordingly received a commission in his father's regiment, the 20th, in 1800, when he was aged fourteen, though he had begun life in the navy. He had a long career in the army for sixty years and since his brothers and brothers-in-law and sons and sons-in-law were almost all of them soldiers, the family acquired a strong military tradition. It was, however, a pre-Victorian tradition, since as I have said, it took shape in the age of the French war, and though my great grandfather served far into Victorian times, it was his Spanish years which he spent on Wellington's staff that were the decisive ones in his life. It is remarkable that though he left several drafts of his memoirs, they all end as far back as 1812, at the moment when the army ended the retreat from Burgos.

I have the impression not only from my grandmother but also from other old people I knew in childhood that this experience was not uncommon—we see a literary expression of it in Thomas Hardy's books: so that what we call the Victorian tradition, on one side of it at least, originated in these early years and remained fixed throughout the century. It seems strange that the infinitely greater wars of our own age, in which moreover a far larger proportion of the population has taken part, have not made so deep an impression on the social consciousness. No doubt modern war by its nature transcends the experience of the individual. It is more like an earthquake and less like a prize fight. So far as human suffering is concerned, no war has ever made a deeper impression on men's minds than that of 1914-18, but the experience of suffering does not create social traditions; by itself it acts rather as a dissolvent force. And among the things which these two wars destroyed were the old European armies with their intense *esprit de corps* and their highly specialized professional traditions.

Now the old British army was in many respects the most conservative of them all. For it preserved down to the end the voluntary professional character which had been common to all of them at an earlier period. On the other hand, while the great continental armies were the dominant factor in the life of the nation and while their officers procured great social prestige, the British army lived in a world apart, outside the main currents of national life. Wellington, perhaps the most typical product and representative of British military tradition, once wrote: 'It is an exotic in England, unknown to the old constitution of the country ... disliked by the inhabitants, particularly by the higher orders, some of whom never allow one of their family to serve in it.' 'Service in the army is an advantage to none. The officers and soldiers of the army are an object of dislike and suspicion to the inhabitants while serving with their regiments, and of jealousy afterwards, and they are always ill-treated.'[2]

[2]From his very characteristic memorandum on the proposal to introduce the Prussian system of discipline into the army (22nd April, 1829).

I do not think that the nineteenth-century soldier was quite 'as much of a social pariah, as Wellington's words suggest, but it is true that the army was the Cinderella of English society as compared with the more favoured professions of politics, business and law. There were no great prizes to be won and a man was lucky if he did not lose his life or his health in one of the innumerable little wars in unhealthy climates which were little more than police operations. But the absence of social recognition and reward was compensated by an intenser professional pride. If their opposite numbers on the Continent looked on them as amateurs, they in turn regarded the new mass armies of the great powers as a sort of militia: 'Very good militia,' as old Lord Clyde said when he inspected the Prussian infantry somewhere about 1860. I remember that my father always liked the Austrian army best because it had preserved the old spirit of professional integrity and impersonal loyalty and had not sacrificed this tradition to the new idol of chauvinist nationalism.

In many respects this English military tradition was a narrow one which allowed plenty of room for stupidity and conventionalism, but on the other hand it preserved certain elements in English life from being extinguished by the social and economic competitiveness of nineteenth-century society. It was the army above all that kept alive the tradition of disinterested public service and devotion to duty which was in many respects opposed to the spirit of the age as expressed in the utilitarian philosophy and the practice of economic individualism. We see this even in so prosaic and non-religious a man as Wellington himself, but perhaps it is most completely represented by his successor, Fitzroy Somerset, the Lord Raglan of the Crimean War, who was regarded with admiration and devotion by the milieu of which I am speaking. And the fact that he was the target of so much undeserved criticism by the politicians only strengthened this attachment.

I have said that the military tradition was often marked by stupidity and conventionalism, but it is only fair to remember that it also produced no lack of original and even eccentric types—picturesque survivals from the past like Lord Mark Ker, religious enthusiasts like Gordon, and many forgotten champions of lost or unpopular causes. Certainly the soldiers, whom I knew as a child, were on the whole better educated and with wider interests than the civilians. No doubt this was largely due to my father whose tastes were literary and scientific and who chose his friends accordingly. Although he had been a soldier all his life, he had little interest in the social side of regimental life. He cared nothing for sport and devoted himself mainly to the scientific side of his profession. When I was a small child, he was lecturing at Woolwich, but my memories only begin when he was attached to the Southern R.A. Command and we were living at Alverstoke close to Stokes Bay, where the steamers crossed the Solent to Ryde. Here the army and navy dominated the whole life of the place, even the vicar was the uncle of the Secretary of War and the curate a brother of Lord Jellicoe. But though my childhood was also dominated by the same military tradition, I never liked Portsmouth and Alverstoke. Not even the sea and the fascinating Victorian fortifications, which even a child could understand, compensated me for the raw ugliness of Gosport and Southsea and the loss of what I called 'the real country'. I felt no living contact with the place itself; it was merely somewhere we happened to be staying at for a time. Fortunately Easton was not far away and at Easton I found all the elements that were missing at Alverstoke. Every tree and field and stream and even the furniture and books were unchangeable and real and right and lived in my mind as well as outside me. Here no less than in Wales, an old tradition went on undisturbed, ignoring the contemporary world, skipping a generation or two, taking no account of the new economic and political forces which are the only things the historians are concerned with. In contrast to these, the remote past remained alive and strong. The world of Barchester was passing away but in the interstices between that world and the new England one felt the presence of a much older world. Winchester itself contained an immense hoard of memories of the old Christian England, like the bones of the Kings of Wessex, heaped up indiscriminately in the sarcophagi above the choir screen in the Cathedral.

As one came over the shoulder of the down from Easton one saw the vast bulk of the cathedral lying across the valley and dominating the city, and then from the cathedral to Wolvesey Palace and the College and on across the Meads to St. Cross there was an unbroken series of noble buildings continuous in space and time. Here time seemed the preserver, not the destroyer: nothing seemed lost or out of place, and behind it all there stood the power of religion, still deeply rooted in the social life I knew—a massive, objective, unquestioned power that impressed its seal on the outer and the inner world alike and held past and present together as a living whole.

This whole which we call culture, seemed to a child simply the real world. I did not know that the world into which I had been born was dissolving like snow in a thaw, so that in a few years it would have vanished like Alfred's Wessex or even perhaps like the lost world of the forgotten men whose camps and dykes still mark the surface of the southern downlands. But even as a child I was not entirely unaware that the world was threatened. That is why I disliked Alverstoke, since it gave me a sense of insecurity which was not personal or immediately related to family life, but had its source in the social background and the vague sense of the existence of an alien world which was irreconcilable with the world I knew, although it did not seem strong enough to overcome and replace it.

For a time these feelings were pushed into the background when we left Alverstoke and went to live among the Yorkshire dales which were still untouched by change. But even before the end of the Victorian age, I became conscious, in my mind as well as in my feelings, of the power of the new forces and the fact that the world that I had accepted as the solid foundation of my own life and the life of my family and the life of England was not the world of my contemporaries, but a detached fragment of the past which had somehow managed to survive on the margin between the present and the past. And so for me the last year of the century was indeed the end of an age and marked a break in the unity and continuity of my experience.

II. Return to the North

IN 1896 my father left the army and we went to live in Yorkshire where he had built a house on a hill above the river Wharfe at Hartlington, which he had inherited only a few years before from his grandfather who had lived to be nearly ninety-nine. This meant a complete break with our social background and our immediate past, for though my family had kept their land in Yorkshire, they had left Craven for Southern England in the middle of the eighteenth century and had inter-married for two successive generations with wives of French Huguenot families—Regis and Aufrère—both of them women of strong personality who left their mark, both physically and spiritually, on the family. Thus we had not much Yorkshireness left by the time we returned, and my father's choice was due to a conscious desire to recover contact with lost family traditions, for this was the age of Maurice Barrès and the reaction against the rootlessness of nineteenth century culture.

In the eighteenth century, before the industrial revolution had begun, our family had abandoned their home in the remote Yorkshire dales for the urbanized south. They had bought a house in Windsor Forest which Wyatt rebuilt for them in his neo-Gothic fashion. Now at the end of the nineteenth century when the urban revolution was almost completed my father left the South to return to his native country. He loved building, and planting and planning, and the making of Hartlington occupied him for years, so that he did not feel the lack of society. I think my mother felt this social isolation more, and was often homesick for Wales and the closely-integrated family society of Hay and the Welsh border.

For me this return to the North seemed no less of an adventure than if we had gone to a new country. Indeed, Yorkshire was a new world and the whole aspect of the country with the stone walls climbing the hills and the naked rock thrusting itself out in great scars and promontories, like sea cliffs, was entirely unlike anything I had seen before. Even the houses with their grey stone walls and roofs were different, and I could hardly understand the northern speech which was then far more strongly differentiated from southern English than it is to-day. In fact there are few districts in England that preserved their regional individuality more strongly than Craven. In the past it had been a kind of island, separated from both Yorkshire and Lancashire by a ring of forests—the forests of Trawdon and Rossendale to the south, Knaresborough Forest to the east, the Forest of Bowland to the west and Stainmoor Forest to the north.

Even to-day, if one goes north along the line of the Pennines one cannot fail to be struck by the abruptness of the contrast. For forty or fifty miles one sees nothing but the sullen black barren moors that divide the most thickly-peopled regions of England, and suddenly one comes into a new country in which the earth and sky have a different colour: white cliffs after black stones, open pastoral country covered with bright green grass, like that of the downs, after the dark peat mosses and heather. This limestone country goes on for twenty or thirty miles to the head of the dales and the summits of Ingleborough and Pennyghent and then the moors close in again and we come to the desolate highlands of Mallerstang and Stainmoor Forest.

Our house was built where the two countries meet—on one side, the dark fells, on the other the green hills. It stood on a glacial moraine thrust out into the valley of the Wharfe, falling steeply on two sides to the main valley and to a tributary stream which had cut a deep ravine through the limestone rocks. The sound of falling water was always present as a gentle murmur in summer and rising to a thunderous roar in the winter floods when the hill seemed to vibrate like a taut string. There is something about running water that appeals to a child's mind, even when it is no more than the trickle of a brook, and a mountain torrent in full flood gave me a sense of irresistible power like nothing else I ever experienced. I got to know that stream in all its moods. It was as real an influence on mind and heart as any person, and how much more satisfying to the child's view of reality than the artificial and restricted reality of the grown-up world! On summer days the brown waters giggling and chattering among the rocks were a constant companion and friend, but better still were the days of sudden storm, when it was changed into a roaring torrent, rising foot by foot and hour by hour until the whole appearance of the valley was transformed. I think these early impressions of the elemental force of nature have a great importance in one's education, and it seems to me a misfortune for the children of our own time that instead of such psychologically manageable natural forces they have had to face the inhuman elemental force of man's own destructiveness in the force of high explosives and incendiaries.

Moreover this love of the river had a certain literary and religious significance. For it was in the Old Testament, and there only, that I found these things written about, and it seemed clear to me that in those days they felt about these things as I did. 'Deep calleth to deep at the noise of Thy waterspouts', 'Let the floods clap their hands, let the hills be joyful together.' 'The River of Kishon swept them away, that ancient river the river Kishon, O my soul thou hast trodden down strength.' 'The glory of the Gentiles like a flowing stream.' Such things compensated me for the boredom of so much that seemed dull or incomprehensible in the long Anglican office and made me feel that religion was not simply concerned with the pious moralities which held such a prominent place in Victorian books for children, but stood close to that wonderful non-human world of the river and the mountain which I found around me.

Behind the house the stream ran back for miles into the hills, entirely solitary, without road or house, sometimes narrowing to a deep chasm between the rocks and then widening again to a wooded valley. At one point, about a mile upstream where the valley changed its direction and turned north, there was a deserted lead mine with lateral shafts driven into the hillside. Here one could sit on a stone platform high up on the hillside looking down on the treetops two hundred feet below and see the whole extent of the solitary valley, running up on the right to the high moors backed by the heavy mass of Great Whernside where the snow lay far into the spring and sometimes even the early summer. The greater part of Craven is covered with these deserted mines which were still flourishing in mid-Victorian times when England was the chief lead-producing country in the world, but now towards the end of the century they were all abandoned and their remains increased the loneliness of the country. The larger mines on Greenhow Hill and Grassington Moor which had employed hundreds of miners always gave me a sinister feeling of ruin and desolation, but this was not at all the case with the small outlying mines on the limestone hills which had been taken back into the landscape like prehistoric remains of remote antiquity.

These relics of the recent past accentuated the contrast between Craven and the industrial West Riding. A hundred years ago Craven had had its mines and its factories—small cotton and silk mills run by water power in almost every village down the dales. Now all this had gone and the population was much smaller than it had been at the beginning of the nineteenth century. Yet this did not give one any impression of destruction and social decay. On the contrary, Craven seemed a far more thriving and prosperous society than that of Wales or the agricultural south. No doubt this was mainly due to the absence of an agricultural proletariat. There was no class of agricultural labourers. For the farm servant or hind was a part of the household and often himself a farmer's son. I remember one farmer whose cousin would arrive every year on his own horse and work for several months, like James Pigg and his cousin Deavilboger in *Handley Cross*.

The whole social structure of Craven was, in fact, quite different from that of the other three parts of England that I had known. It was more democratic and more archaic. There was no squirearchy, except in the south western parts towards Lancashire which differed in many respects from the dales that were the heart of Craven. Here society still showed traces of its medieval pattern, when there was nothing between the lords of the great feudal and monastic estates and the peasants. In the Middle Ages Craven was divided between the Percys and the Cliffords; and their heirs, Lord Hothfield and the Duke of Devonshire, still hold the remains of their estates at Skipton and Bolton. But apart from these there were never any large unified estates as in the rest of England. The fall of the monasteries was a real social revolution which was bitterly opposed by the dalespeople who took a considerable part in the Pilgrimage of Grace. But it was followed not by the rise of a wealthy class of landowners, as in the rest of England, but by the development of a large yeoman class, like the 'statesmen' of Westmorland and Cumberland where the conditions were closely similar. Some of these yeoman families prospered, some declined, many died out, so that in my time Craven had become mainly a country of tenant farmers, who yet preserved much of the essential character of the old yeoman class.

The history of this development is of far more than local significance, for it throws light on some of the most characteristic features of the English class system, above all its stability and its fluidity, which are the paradoxical key to English history.

On the one hand there are ancient families which remain peasant farmers as they were in the Middle Ages, on the other there are families that rose very fast and very far in the age between the fall of the monasteries and the Civil War. The most remarkable example of this was the family which has taken its name and title from Craven and which derived its origin from the next hamlet to Hartlington. The founder of this family, William Craven, was a parish apprentice who went to London in the days of Queen Elizabeth and eventually became Lord Mayor. But his son, the first Earl, was not content to found a family, like so many 'new men' of his generation. This tradesman's son who was despised by the sophisticated courtiers of the Restoration, maintained almost to the end of the seventeenth century the antiquated ideals of medieval chivalry, devoting his sword and his wealth to the distinterested service of Elizabeth of Bohemia, and at the end of his life as officer in command of the Guards at Whitehall he was one of the few men who stood fast in his loyalty amidst the general tide of treachery and demoralization of 1688.

The same tendency to revert to an archaic social tradition is to be seen at the other end of the social scale in Lady Anne Clifford, the last of her race, who was one of the most remarkable women of the seventeenth century England. In spite of her real intelligence and strength of character, her life was spent in the attempt to preserve the old feudal way of life in the age of Cromwell and Charles II. Her married life had been an unhappy one. 'The marble pillars of Knowle and Wilton', she writes, 'were to me oftentimes but the gay arbours of anguish, insomuch that a wise man who knew the inside of my fortune would often say that I lived in both these my lords great families as the River Roan or Rodanus runs through the Lake of Geneva without mingling any part of its stream with that lake.'

And so, as soon as the Civil War ended, she shook the dust of London and Wiltshire off her feet and went back to her Northern lands which she had not seen for nearly fifty years. While England as a whole was going through the novel experience of a revolutionary dictatorship, Lady Anne Clifford was carrying out a revolution in the opposite direction, re-asserting her feudal rights as Lady of the Honour of Skipton and hereditary High Sheriff of Westmorland, restoring her six castles of Skipton, Appleby, Barden, Brougham, Brough-under-Stainmoor and Pendragon-in-Mallerstang, and going on progress in a horse litter from castle to castle over 'these mountainous and almost impassible ways' that separated Craven from Westmorland.

The strange thing is that there is no evidence of any conflict between her and the other great personality of seventeenth century Craven—General John Lambert, who ruled the North under Cromwell and who lived only a few miles from Skipton Castle which he had besieged and dismantled during the civil war. Nor did her re-assertion of feudal rights bring her into serious conflict with the yeomanry. Indeed there can be little doubt that they admired her as the embodiment of the old way of life which was so profoundly different from that of the new aristocracy. For Lady Anne was a woman of intense piety after the medieval fashion—a restorer of churches as well as castles, averse from personal indulgence, bringing the poor to eat at her own table and often spending her days, as a contemporary records, among her sisters at the almshouses at Bolton and Appleby, 'like an abbess among her nuns'. But though her attempt to restore medieval social order was as hopeless as King Uther's legendary attempt to change the course of the Eden at Pendragon Castle,[1] it was undoubtedly one of the factors which helped to maintain the distinctive social character of the region, for it checked the formation of a squirearchy, though it did little to interfere with the rise of the yeoman class.

The seventeenth century was in fact the great age of the yeomanry in Craven, and all over the country one can still see the homes of the new landowners, solid, well-proportioned farm houses and halls with the initials of their owners over the doors together with the date, which usually belongs to the middle decades of the century. The early history of my own family belongs to this development. In the sixteenth century Christopher Dawson (I) was a tenant of the Cliffords at Halton Gill and Foxup at the very head of Littondale. His grandson Christopher (II) in 1641 built the old Hall which is now the farmhouse at Halton Gill, while another grandson who was also named Christopher (III) built the house at Knight Stainforth in Ribblesdale which bears his initials and the date 1649. The son of Christopher II of Halton Gill, Josias, acquired Langcliffe Hall at Settle and it was his son, Christopher (IV) who first came to Hartlington in consequence of his marriage to Margaret Craven of Apple-

---

[1] This is a local Westmorland legend, recorded by The Revd. W. Nicholls, in his *History of Mallerstang Forest* (1883).
Let Uther Pendragon do all he can
Eden will run where Eden ran.

trewick, whose elder sister Mary was the wife of Sir Edmund Andros, the first governor of New York. Their son, William Dawson, spent his long and prosperous life at Settle and Langcliffe, but his eldest son Christopher (V) inherited the estates of his mother's family, the Pudseys, and became the squire of Bolton by Bowland in the south western corner of Craven, while his son by his second marriage with Elizabeth Marsden of Gisburn, William II, who inherited Hartlington, went south to seek his fortunes and was the ancestor of my own branch of the family.

This genealogical excursion shows how my family was continually moving up and down the dales and eventually outside Craven altogether. Nor was this by any means unusual among the old yeoman families in Craven. It was characteristic of the whole population, from the more important families like the Cravens and the Franklands down to the tenant farmers themselves who were not so closely united to the village community as in the agricultural south. Indeed the real social unit was not the village or manor but the dale or the region, so that Craven as a whole possessed a greater degree of social unity and stability and tradition than any district of England that I have known. This was no doubt largely due to its remoteness which had made it almost inaccessible before the coming of the motor bus. The old vicar of Arncliffe, Archdeacon Boyd, who died just before I first knew the country, has recorded how when he went to York to be instituted, the Archbishop had said 'Arncliffe! Arncliffe! I have no such living in my diocese, Sir'. And when he set out by way of Ripon and asked for a conveyance to drive to his new cure nobody at the inn knew where it was or how it could be reached. Finally he found a man who said he knew 'a famous big rock called Kilnsey Crag' and he fancied 'Arncliffe was near that'; it was only after spending the night at Kilnsey that he finally reached his destination and when he got there he found the vicarage was being used by the farmers as a store house for wool. Thus in Craven, eighteenth century conditions were prolonged far into the Victorian age. Indeed even in our own parish of Burnsall, which was relatively accessible, the old type of yeoman parson which had long disappeared elsewhere survived as late as the 'forties.

In this respect Craven was very different from the other parts of England that I had known where the Anglican Church had held a position of undisputed social and cultural leadership. Yet it had not always been so. The fragments of the Anglian high crosses and the ruins of the great northern abbeys recalled the times when the Church had been more of a power here than in most parts of England. Nowhere was the destruction of the monasteries more bitterly resented than in Craven. Ever since the days of St. Cuthbert and St. Wilfred, save for the period of the Danish conquest, the great abbeys had dominated the spiritual and economic life of Northern England, and when the Commons rose in 1536 in defence of this inheritance of nine hundred years under the banners of St. Cuthbert and the Five

Wounds, it was the most spontaneous popular movement ever known in the north.

The fall of the abbeys left a gap in northern culture which was never filled either by the Church of England or the Nonconformists and the attempt of the new yeoman class to fill it by the foundation of the village grammar schools that are a characteristic feature of Craven[2] was but a superficial solution.

But the ruins of the deserted monasteries remained, and Bolton Priory, which lies a few miles from Hartlington down the Wharfe, always seemed to me the perfect embodiment of this lost element in the northern culture—a spiritual grace which had once been part of our social tradition and which still survived as a ghostly power brooding over the river and the hills. In those days we used to travel to Craven by way of Bolton so that the abbey (as we called it[3]) was the first thing we saw on coming and the last on leaving. When we came to the brow above the river on the north where the Victorian Gothic monument stands to the Cavendish who was assassinated at Dublin in 1882, the carriage used to stop so that we could look down on the abbey lying in the arm of the Wharfe beneath the guarding hills— hills not high enough to dwarf it but which none the less, as Ruskin said, convey an indefinable sense of 'the strength and greatness of this wild northern land'.

This was my earliest impression of Craven and it still remains with me as a true expression of the *genius loci* which has survived the religious revolution of the sixteenth century and the industrial revolution of the nineteenth century. For it is not a mere romantic imagination to believe that a land may possess latent powers which are not always manifested or exhausted by their actual social state. In the south and in many of the lowland areas of the continent, one often feels that nature has been so completely tamed and made to serve the purposes of society that it no longer exists except as a part of the life of man. There are other regions, like those barren moorlands between Lancashire and Yorkshire, which remain untameable and hostile to man, so that man can only assert himself as an alien power, cutting across the grain of the country with his towns and railways and factories. But in regions like Craven nature and man exist as independent but not unfriendly powers, so that there is a vital tension between them out of which something new may be created. I have been told that the same thing is true of the dales country in Sweden—Dalarne—which was the heart of the national tradition. It is certainly true also of the Four Forest Cantons of

---

[2] The grammar school at Burnsall was founded by the first Sir William Craven in 1602, that at Bolton by Robert Boyle, the chemist, in 1700 and that at Theshfield a few miles beyond Burnsall by a seventeenth century rector, Matthew Hewett. These dales schools were probably similar to the one Wordsworth attended at Hawkshead rather than to Mr. Squeers' Academy at Bowes.

[3] It was really a priory of Austen Canons, like Bridlington and Nostell.

Switzerland. But these regions achieved their cultural expressions centuries ago, whereas Craven has been too small and too poor to have a history of its own. To-day it has been taken into the orbit of the great industrial cities as their playground, if not their suburb. But in my childhood it still lived its own life and one felt the presence of the towns chiefly by the darkness that would come when a wind brought up the drifting smoke clouds high above the hills from the south.

Altogether it was a solitary life—rich in mental associations and impressions but poor in social relations. This did not trouble my father who had a natural taste for solitude, and always looked back with pleasure to the years he had spent as British representative of the International Circumpolar expedition of 1882-3 at a post in the far north of Canada. As I said in the first part of these notes he was far from being a typical soldier nor did he share the ordinary tastes of a country gentleman. He never shot or fished or hunted, nor did he suffer fools gladly. He had always been a great reader, and when he retired from the army he was able to indulge his taste for books to the full. I do not think I have ever known anyone who had more catholic tastes, for he was equally interested in modern science and ancient philosophy, medieval mysticism and modern history, Victorian novels and classical poetry. He had left Harrow early for the army crammer and Woolwich so that he was largely self-educated in literary matters, with no German and but little Greek. On the other hand he was devoted to the Italian classics, above all to Machiavelli and Dante, and most of all the last. Even when he was still in the army, he had acquired the great Berlin edition of Botticelli's Dante drawings in three immense volumes which no bookcase could hold, and which impressed my childish imagination as the largest books in the world. His admiration for Dante had no limits, he rated him far above Shakespeare and Milton as the world's one perfect poet. This love of Dante no doubt stimulated his interest in Catholicism and helped to dispel the Protestant prejudices of his upbringing. It was certainly by Dante that he had come to know St. Thomas. But though he had a copy of the *Summa Theologica*, he did not read it in the assiduous way he read Plato and Berkeley and the Roman Stoics. His Catholic sympathies were, however, religious as well as intellectual. He always used Catholic books of devotion—Horstius, the *Spiritual Exercises,* Avrillon, Surin and the like. He abolished the traditional Victorian family prayers in favour of Terce and Compline which were said in Englsh by the whole household at nine in the morning and ten at night.

It is strange that these sympathies never led him to become a Catholic, for he had little of the *via media* Anglicanism of the High Church party. But he had a kind of hereditary 'political' loyalty to the Church of England, and I remember he once said to me that no man has the right to leave the church to which his fathers belonged. In this he was more Roman than Catholic; nor was he consistent in this social traditionalism, for in many ways he was a strong individualist—his return to Craven was in part a deliberate reaction against the Protestant tradition and an attempt to recover lost spiritual roots in a past which he felt to be Catholic.

It is true that there were few remaining traces of Catholic tradition in Victorian Craven. Of the two old Catholic families of the region one—the Inglebys—had conformed to the established Church early in the nineteenth century and there now remained only the Tempests of Broughton. Nor was there any strong Anglo-Catholic tradition, for as I have said the Anglican revival of the nineteenth century was slow to reach the dales. On the other hand with regard to literary culture Craven had never become so barbarous as many of the remoter districts of England. At the beginning of the nineteenth century, Richard Heber of Marton was one of the greatest of English bibliophiles in the great age of English libraries, and in the next generations this tradition was carried on by Miss Frances Currer of Kildwick, who was almost the only woman book collector of early Victorian times. In my own time our local member of Parliament, Walter Morrison, who lived in the middle of the moors at Malham Tarn, was a man of very wide interests and a real patron of culture, who did his best to make the great Victorians visit and appreciate Craven, from John Stuart Mill and Darwin to Ruskin and Tom Hughes and Charles Kingsley.

Thus in spite of the absence of social life, and partly because of it, the life of Craven was not unfavourable to the things of the mind, and though it was above all to my parents that I owed my education, their teaching did not conflict with the spirit of the land, as it had done at Alvestoke, and as it was to do at my private school. I loved the freedom and the absence of social constraint which were due not only to the wild moorland country, but also to the scattered type of settlement which had come down from Scandinavian and Celtic times, and which made almost every farm and household a separate unit. Everything depended on the family, which was still a true economic society as it had been from the beginning of Britain and as it remained until the coming of motor transport. For the family was not simply a man and his wife and children, it included all the working members of the social unit, as the word itself denotes. In the seventeenth century a Craven farmer could still say that he 'had a very great family consisting of 15 or 16 persons for all or most of the year, and 50 or 60 persons at some seasons when his husbandry affairs required many hands'.

In the past, the whole of England had been built of these societies from the noble household, like that of the Cliffords, which formed a little court, down to the peasant household of the yeoman farmer, who as a freeholder—*liber et legalis homo*—was the basic unit of the

---

⁴ Brayshaw and Robinson. *History of the Ancient Parish of Giggleswick* (p. 117).

English commonwealth. This system had for centuries been falling to pieces under the pressure of social centralization and the influence of the capital on the upper classes and the industrial revolution and the new economic forces on the peasant farmers. But in outlying regions like Craven something of the old spirit still survived and though the yeoman economy had passed away about the middle of the nineteenth century, the farmers of the dales still preserved the old yeoman way of life and type of character.

Similarly the country house in the Victorian age still stood for the old tradition of the family society, so long as it was not important enough to be dominated by London society, and at Hartlington the remoteness of the situation and my father's conscious desire to build up a self-sufficient social unit strengthened this tradition. The family was a society that rested on the three essential institutions of the kitchen, the stables and the garden. The coachman, who had been a driver in the artillery and had been with my father long before his marriage, and the cook, who came from Hereford-shire, were both important figures in the family society and hold a leading place in my childhood memories. Although the Victorian repression of children was a thing of the past, the modern emancipation of them was still a long way in the future, and the principle of authority played a large place in our lives. One felt that servants were important people, because they held social office and authority, whereas children were only, so to speak, candidates for office, and had no independent sphere of their own except the schoolroom. But the world of the schoolroom was pale and uninteresting in comparison with the warmth and variety of the kitchen over which the cook ruled like a figure in a fairy story, or compared with the saddle room where everything was in its right place and yet the sense of discipline and order was stimulating and not repressive.

Above all this there was my father's room which was at once a workshop, an office and a library, for when he was not reading he was always at work on some mathematical calculation or on the construction of some gadget. This was no great library after the Heber tradition, but it was a room of books that were continually being used and I realized that this was the true centre of the household and that it was for this that it all existed. I spent much of my time here, for my father enjoyed reading aloud and explaining things, and thus I gradually became initiated into almost all his books except the mathematical ones, though I find it difficult to say in which year I discovered which writer. These last years of the Victorian age were a good time for children intellectually, for the writers of the age— Kipling, Stevenson, Belloc, Wells and Andrew Lang—were all giving their best for children in those days, and there were others who did not write for children like William Morris and W. H. Hudson and W. P. Ker, whose work reached one indirectly at secondhand through my parents or others.

Thus books became a second world to me, not merely a dream

world of fantasy into which one could escape but an extension of the real world which enlarged and enriched it. Thanks to my parents I learnt the essential connection between *story* and *history*, so that I came to know the past not so much by the arid path of the *Child's History of England,* as through the enchanted world of myth and legend. In this way I discovered very early that history was not a flat expanse of time, measured off in dates, but a series of different worlds and that each of them had its own spirit and form and its own riches of poetic imagination. As Craven was different from Wales, so the world of the Sagas was different from the world of the Celtic tradition. And as myth passed into history, so history in its turn left its visible imprint on the world I knew. The scattered farms and hamlets of Craven often preserved the names that one found in the Sagas—Grims and Helgis and Thorlaks—and it was on Stainmoor on the northern frontier of Craven that one of the great figures of Viking saga and poetry met his end.[5]

No doubt this initiation into the past had its disadvantages from the practical utilitarian point of view, but it was education in the true sense of the word. Whatever form of education is inflicted on children, they will always find mythical or heroic figures to satisfy their imagination. If they do not have King Arthur and Peredur or Sigurd and Regin, they will content themselves with Donald Duck and Dick Barton. It may even be argued that the latter are healthier because they are more spontaneous and near to contemporary reality than Branwen the daughter of Llyr or Burnt Njal. But are they more real because they are more at home in our impoverished world? I believe the old myths are better not only intrinsically, but because they lead further and open a door into the mind as well as into the past. This was the old road which carries us back not merely for centuries but for thousands of years; the road by which every people has travelled and from which the beginnings of every literature have come. I mean the road of oral tradition. It may be that the changes of our generation, the increased speed of life and the mechanization of popular culture by the cinema and the radio have closed this road for ever. But if so, those of us who remember the world before the wars have witnessed a change in human consciousness far greater than we have realized, and what we are remembering is not the Victorian age but a whole series of ages—a river of immemorial time which has suddenly dried up and become lost in the seismic cleft that has opened between the present and the past.

---

[5] Eric, the son of Harold Fairhair, whose death is commemorated in the *Eriksmal* and for whom Egil Skallagrimson composed his famous ode of ransom at York in 945.

Notes

CHAPTER ONE *First Beginning*

1. Christopher Dawson, 'Tradition and Inheritance', *The Wind and the Rain* V, 4 and VI, 1 (1949); reprinted, with an introduction by John Mulloy, St Paul, Minnesota, 1970, 11. (This and subsequent page references are to the 1970 edition.)
2. William Plomer (ed.), *Kilvert's Diary*, London 1971.
3. From unpublished notes.
4. 'Tradition', 12.
5. 'Tradition', 12.
6. Vivien Noakes, *Edward Lear*, London 1968, 279–81.
7. *Kilvert's Diary* I, 216.
8. *Kilvert's Diary* I, 226.
9. *Kilvert's Diary* I, 46f.
10. From an unpublished family history by Mrs M. L. Dawson. This legend is also recorded in Agnes Strickland, *The Lives of the Queens of England* II, London 1901, 265.
11. *Kilvert's Diary* I, 220.
12. 'Tradition', 19.
13. 'Tradition', 16.
14. 'Tradition', 13.
15. From the unpublished family history.
16. 'Tradition', 19.
17. From the unpublished family history.
18. From the unpublished family history.
19. 'Tradition', 19.
20. 'Tradition', 20.
21. 'Tradition', 21.
22. From unpublished notes.
23. 'Tradition', 32.
24. 'Tradition', 20.
25. 'Tradition', 26.
26. 'Tradition', 28.
27. 'Tradition', 30.
28. 'Tradition', 32.

CHAPTER TWO *The Alien World*

1. From unpublished notes.
2. Christopher Dawson, *Understanding Europe*, London and New York 1952, 245.
3. From unpublished notes.
4. From an unpublished letter to E. I. Watkin, 1925.
5. From unpublished notes.
6. Christopher Dawson, *Beyond Politics*, London 1939, 29.
7. E. I. Watkin, 'Christopher Dawson (1889–1970)', *Proceedings of the British Academy* LVII.
8. Christopher Dawson, 'Why I am a Catholic', *The Catholic Times*, 21st May 1926.
9. 'Christopher Dawson (1889–1970)'.

CHAPTER THREE *Oxford in the Golden Age*

1. Compton Mackenzie, *Sinister Street* II, London 1914, 507.
2. The obituary by David Knowles, *The Tablet*, 6th June 1970. The quotation on Newman above is from Christopher Dawson, *The Spirit of the Oxford Movement*, New York 1933, 32.
3. Ernest Barker's review of *The Judgement of the Nations* in *The Spectator* CLXX (1943), 152.
4. 'Why I am a Catholic'.
5. Christopher Dawson, 'Dark Mirror', *The Dublin Review* CLXXXVII (1930) (reprinted in James Oliver and Christina Scott [edd.], *Religion and World History*, New York 1975).
6. George Tyrrell, *Autobiography* I, London 1912, 153.
7. 'Why I am a Catholic'.
8. *The Spirit of the Oxford Movement*, 59.
9. Evelyn Waugh, *Ronald Knox*, London 1959, 100.
10. J. H. Newman, *Apologia pro Vita Sua*, London 1864, chap. 3.
11. 'Why I am a Catholic'.
12. From a review of Arnold Toynbee, *The Study of History* in the *Observer*, 17th October 1954.
13. This and subsequent extracts from E. I. Watkin's unpublished diaries are reproduced by kind permission of Mrs Magdalen Goffin.

CHAPTER FOUR *Love and Conversion*

1. John Henry Newman, *Essay on Development of Christian Doctrine*, London 1846 (revised edition 1878), 8, 97.

2. From an interview with Frank Sheed in *The Sign*, December 1958.
3. *The Spirit of the Oxford Movement*, 50.
4. Christopher Dawson, 'Religion and Life', *The Dublin Review* CXLII (1933), 9.
5. 'Why I am a Catholic'.
6. 'Tradition', 28.

CHAPTER FIVE *Early Married Life*

1. Ernst Troeltsch, *Christian Thought, its History and Application*, London 1923, 25.
2. 'Sociology as a Science', *Science for a New World* (ed. Arthur Thomson and J.E. Crowther), London 1939 (reprinted in *Dynamics of World History*).
3. 'Cycles of Civilizations', *The Sociological Review* XIV (1922), reprinted in *Enquiries into Religion and Culture*, London and New York 1933.

CHAPTER SIX *Exeter*

1. F.J. Sheed, *The Church and I*, London and New York 1974.
2. F.J. Sheed, *The Church and I*.

CHAPTER SEVEN *Achievement*

1. Christopher Dawson, 'Religion and the Life of Civilization', *The Quarterly Review* CCXLIV (1925), reprinted in *Dynamics of World History*, 128.
2. Vera Brittain, *Time and Tide*, 17th May 1929.
3. D.H. Lawrence, *A Propos of Lady Chatterly's Lover*.
4. H.A. Fisher, *The English Review* (1932).
5. Aldous Huxley, *The Spectator* CXLIX (1932).

CHAPTER EIGHT *Return to the North*

1. René Hague (ed.), *Dai Great-Coat: Letters of David Jones*, London 1980.
2. George Sampson, *The Concise Cambridge History of English Literature*, 3rd edition (revised by R.C. Churchill) Cambridge 1970, 896, 924.

CHAPTER NINE   *Crisis in Europe*

1. *The Catholic Herald*, 17th August 1935.
2. Bruno Schlesinger, *Christopher Dawson and the Modern Political Crisis*, Notre Dame 1949.
3. From the collection of Douglas Woodruff's papers in the University of Georgetown Library.
4. Christopher Dawson, *The Gods of Revolution*, London 1972 (posthumously published).
5. 'Spain and Europe', *The Catholic Times*, 12th March 1937.
6. V. A. Demant, 'The Importance of Christopher Dawson', *Nineteenth Century* CXXXIX (1951), 66–75.

CHAPTER TEN   *A Writer's War*

1. Editorial in *The Dublin Review* CCXX (1947).
2. *The Dublin Review* CCXX (1947).
3. Robert Speaight, *The Property Basket*, London 1970, 219.
4. René Hague (ed.), *Dai Great-Coat*.
5. F. J. Sheed, *The Church and I*, 340.
6. From a letter of Archbishop Amigo to Bishop Bell of Chichester, 17th August 1942.
7. F. J. Sheed, *The Church and I*, 253.
8. From a letter to Douglas Woodruff, 1943.
9. In a detailed reply to Fr Beck, Dawson made the following comment: 'With regard to Christian Unity, I think you have quite misunderstood my reference to "common beliefs, common sacraments" etc. which I was using primarily in quite an objective sense. That is, the common beliefs are represented by the two great creeds; the sacraments are *all* possessed by a large number of separated bodies, while one of them, Baptism, is common to practically all forms of Christianity except the Quakers. Finally, by "common form of worship" I meant primarily the form of prayer in the name of Christ (according to John 16:24, 26) and secondarily common liturgical forms such as the use of the Psalter, the Lord's Prayer, etc.'
10. From a letter of Bishop Beck to *The Times*, 15th November 1949.
11. Interview by David Wesley Soper.

CHAPTER ELEVEN   *A Wider Public*

1. *The Times Literary Supplement*, 27th December 1957, 781.

2. Louis Bouyer, *The Spirit and Forms of Protestantism*, London 1956.
3. *Pio XII: Pontifex Maximus*, Rome 1956.
4. Bede Griffiths, *The Golden String*, London 1979 (reprint), 169.
5. 'Revolt of the East and the Catholic Tradition', *The Dublin Review* CLXXXIII (1928), reprinted in John J. Mulloy (ed.), *Christianity in East and West*, La Salle, Illinois 1981.
6. 'Study of Christian Culture as a Means of Education', *Lumen Vitae* V (1950), 185.
7. *The Harvard Theological Review*, April 1973, 163.

CHAPTER TWELVE *American Adventure*

1. Ford History Lecture, 1959.
2. Daniel Callahan, 'Christopher Dawson at Harvard', *Commonweal* LXXVI (1962), 294.
3. *The Razor's Edge*, Cambridge Mass. 1958.
4. *The Sign*, 1958.
5. Daniel Callahan, 'Christopher Dawson at Harvard'.

CHAPTER THIRTEEN *The Last Years*

1. John Carmel Heenan, *The Crown of Thorns*, London 1974.
2. From a letter to Col Ross-Duggan, 18th June 1953.
3. 'The Future Life', *The Spectator* CLI (1933), reprinted in *Religion and World History*, 345.
4. E. I. Watkin, 'Tribute to Christopher Dawson, *The Tablet*, 4th October 1969.

A Summing Up

1. 'Edward Gibbon', *Proceedings of the British Academy* XX (1934).
2. Michael Novak, 'The Political Identity of Catholics', *Commonweal*, 16th February 1973.
3. M. D. Knowles, 'Christopher Dawson (1889–1970)', *Proceedings of the British Academy* LVII.
4. *The Historic Reality of Christian Culture*, London and New York 1960, 28 (reprinted in *Religion and World History*, 265f).

A Selected Bibliography

Grateful thanks are due to Dr Claude Locas, who originally compiled this bibliography, and to the *Harvard Theological Review*, in which it was first published with the journal's official 'Minute on the Life and Services of the first Charles Chauncey Stillman Professor of Roman Catholic Theological Studies'.

TABLE OF ABBREVIATIONS

AG   : *The Age of the Gods*
BP   : *Beyond Politics*
CNA : *Christianity and the New Age*
CWE : *The Crisis of Western Education*
DG   : *The Dividing of Christendom*
DWH: *The Dynamics of World History*
ERC : *Enquiries into Religion and Culture*
HR   : *The Historic Reality of Christian Culture*
JN   : *Judgment of the Nations*
MD   : *The Modern Dilemma*
ME   : *Mediaeval Essays*
MR   : *Mediaeval Religion*
MWR: *The Movement of World Revolution*
PR   : *Progress and Religion*
RA   : *The Revolt of Asia*
RC   : *Religion and Culture*
RMS : *Religion and the Modern State*
RWC : *Religion and the Rise of Western Culture*
TM   : *The Making of Europe*
UE   : *Understanding Europe*

I. PUBLICATIONS DURING CHRISTOPHER DAWSON'S
LIFETIME

1920
- 'The Passing of Industrialism'. *The Sociological Review*, XII, 6–17. In ERC.
- 'The Nature and Destiny of Man'. *God and the Supernatural*. Edited by Fr Cuthbert, O.F.S.C. London, Longmans Green & Co.

1921
- 'On the Development of Sociology in Relation to the Theory of Progress'. *The Sociological Review*, XIII, 75–83. In DWH.

1922
- 'Cycles of Civilizations'. *The Sociological Review*, XIV, 51–68. In ERC.
- 'Herr Spengler and the Life of Civilizations'. *The Sociological Review*, XIV, 194–201. In DWH.

1923
- 'The Evolution of the Modern City'. *Town Planning Review*, X, 101–08. In DWH.
- 'Rome: a Historical Survey'. *The Sociological Review*, XV, 132–47; 296–312. (With Alexander Farquharson.)

1924
- 'Progress and Decay in Ancient and Modern Civilizations'. *The Sociological Review*, XVI, 1–11. In DWH.
- 'Scheme of British Culture Periods, and of their Relation to European Culture Development'. *The Sociological Review*, XVI, 117–25.
- 'Catholicism and Economics'. *Blackfriars*, May, June and July.

1925
- 'Religion and the Life of Civilization'. *The Quarterly Review*, CCXLIV, 98–115. In ERC, DWH.
- 'Religion and Primitive Culture'. *The Sociological Review*, XVII, 105–19.
- 'Civilization and Morals'. *The Sociological Review*, XVII, 174–81. In ERC, DWH.

1927
- 'Christianity and the Idea of Progress'. *The Dublin Review*, CLXXX, 19–39.
- 'Crisis of the West'. *The Dublin Review*, CLXXXI, 261–77. In PR.
- 'The Mystery of China'. *The Sociological Review*, XIX, 297–303. In ERC.

1928
- *The Age of the Gods*. A study in the origins of culture in prehistoric Europe and the Ancient East. London, J. Murray. (New York, Sheed & Ward, 1933).
- 'Revolt of the East and the Catholic Tradition'. *The Dublin Review*, CLXXXIII, 1–14.

1929
– *Progress and Religion*. An historical enquiry into the causes and development of the idea of progress and its relationship to religion. London, Sheed & Ward. Paperback. Image Books. (New York, Doubleday and Company Inc., 1960).
– 'The New Leviathan'. *The Dublin Review*, CLXXXV, 88–102. In ERC.

1930
– *Christianity and Sex*. Criterion Miscellany, No. 13. London, Faber and Faber.
– 'Saint Augustine and His Age'. *A Monument to Saint Augustine*. A symposium by Martin C. D'Arcy and others. (New York, Dial Press). In ERC and partially in DWH.
– 'Islamic Mysticism'. *The Dublin Review*, CLXXXVI, 34–61. In ERC.
– 'European Democracy and the New Economic Forces'. *The Sociological Review*, XXII, 32–42.
– 'The Dark Mirror' with postscript on 'Spiritual Intuition in Christian Philosophy'. *The Dublin Review*, CLXXXVII, 177–200. Postscript in ERC.
– 'The End of an Age'. *Criterion*, IX, No. XXXVI.

1931
– *Essays in Order*. Edited by Christopher Dawson and T. F. Burns. London, Sheed & Ward, 1931–34. 14 vols. New series edited by Christopher Dawson and Bernard Wall. 1936. 2 vols.
– General introduction to the series *Essays in Order*. *Religion and Culture* by Jacques Maritain. London, Sheed & Ward.
– *Christianity and the New Age*. Essays in Order, No. 3. (New York, Macmillan. New York, Sheed & Ward, 1940).
– Introduction to *The Necessity of Politics* by Carl Schmitt. Essays in Order, No. 5. London, Sheed & Ward. (New York, Macmillan, 1932).
– 'Classical Tradition and the Origins of Mediaeval Culture'. *Studies*, XX, 209–24. In TM, ch. 3.
– 'Scholasticism and the Origins of the European Scientific Tradition'. *Clergy Review*, II, 108–21.
– 'The Origins of the European Scientific Tradition: St. Thomas and Roger Bacon'. *Clergy Review*, II, 195–203.
– 'New Decline and Fall'. *The English Review*, LII, 413–21.
– 'Problem of Wealth'. *The Spectator*, CXLVII, 485.

1932
– *The Making of Europe.* An introduction to the history of European unity. London, Sheed & Ward. (Paperback, New York, Meridian Books, 1958). Excerpts: 'The Carolingian Empire as an Embodiment of Christian Idealism'. *Critical Issues in History.* Edited by Thomas W. Africa, Richard E. Sullivan, and J. K. Sowards. (Boston, D. C. Heath and Co., 1967).
– *The Modern Dilemma: The Problem of European Unity.* Essays in Order, No. 5. (New York, Sheed & Ward).
– 'The Origins of the Romantic Tradition'. *Criterion*, XI, 222–48. In MR, ME.
– 'Dark Ages and Ireland'. *Studies*, XXI, 259–68. In TM, ch. 9.
– 'New Decline and Fall'. *Commonweal*, XV, 320–22.
– 'Tribute to the Memory of Victor Branford'. *The Sociological Review*, XXIV, 24.
– 'Significance of Bolshevism'. *The English Review*, LV, 239–50. Also in *The American Review*, I (Apr., 1933), 36–49. In ERC, DWH.

1933
– *Enquiries Into Religion and Culture.* (New York, Sheed & Ward. Freeport, N.Y., Books for Library Press, 1968. A reprint.)
– *The Spirit of the Oxford Movement.* London, Sheed & Ward, 1945. (New York, Sheed & Ward).
– 'William Langland: The Vision of Piers Plowman'. *The English Way.* Studies in English sanctity from St Bede to Newman. Edited by Maisie Ward. London, Sheed & Ward. In MR, ME.
– 'Religion and Life'. *The Dublin Review*, CXLII, 1–16. In ERC.
– 'The World Crisis and the English Tradition', *The English Review*, LVI, 248–60. In ERC, DWH.
– 'What the World Needs'. *Catholic World*, CXXXVII, 92–94. Extracts from *The Dublin Review*, CXLII.
– 'Man and Civilization'. *Catholic World*, XXXI, 435–40; 458–60.
– 'Future Life: a Roman Catholic View'. *The Spectator*, CLI, 889–90.
– 'Interracial Cooperation as a Factor of European Culture'. (Reale Accademia D'Italia: *Convegno Volta* 1932).

1934
– *Mediaeval Religion and Other Essays.* The Forwood Lectures, 1934. London, Sheed & Ward.
– 'A Roman Catholic View'. *After Death?* The Spectator Booklets, III. London, Methuen.
– Edward Gibbon. *Proceedings of the British Academy*, XX. Separate publication, London, H. Milford. Also as the preface to the *Decline and Fall of the Roman Empire* by Edward Gibbon.

Everyman Edition, London, J.M.Dent and Sons Ltd. (New York, E.P.Dutton and Co., 1954). In DWH.
- 'Sociology as a Science', *Science for a New World*. Edited by Sir Arthur Thomson and J.G.Crowther. London, Eyre and Spottiswoode. (New York, Harper Bros). In DWH.
- 'Prevision and Religion'. *The Sociological Review*, XXVI, 41–54. In DWH.
- 'Communism, Capitalism and the Catholic Tradition', *Ave Maria*, XXXIX, 695.
- 'Real Issue of the Conflict between Christianity and Marxism'. *Colosseum*, I, 17–31.
- 'Rome, Ireland and the European Tradition'. *G.K.'S Weekly*, XX, 89–90.
- 'Last Words on Mr. DeBlaccam (and His Dislike for Rome)'. *G.K.'S Weekly*, XX, 178–79.

1935
- *Mediaeval Christianity*. Studies in Comparative Religion, No. 25. London, Catholic Truth Society.
- 'Future of National Government'. *The Dublin Review*, CXLVI, 236–51.
- 'Modern Dictatorship'. (A Lingard Society lecture.) *The Tablet*, CLXV, 509.
- 'Catholicism and the Bourgeois Mind'. *Colosseum*, II, 246–56. In DWH.

1936
- *Religion and the Modern State*. London, Sheed & Ward.
- *Twelve Selections from Christopher Dawson*. Sheed & Ward samplers. (New York, Sheed & Ward).
- 'The Re-making of Europe'. *The Tablet*, CLXVII, 428–29.
- 'The Recovery of Spiritual Unity'. *Catholic World*, CXLIII, 349–50.
- 'Religion in the Age of Revolution'. *The Tablet*, CLXVIII, 265–66; 301–02; 336–38; 477–79; 516–17; 549–51.
- 'Religion and Romanticism'. *Christendom*, I, 577–92.

1937
- 'Catholic Attitude to War'. *The Tablet*, CLXIX, 365–68. In *Catholic Digest*, I (June), 15–19.
- 'Not Pacifists but Peacemakers'. *Catholic World*, CVL, 102–04.
- 'Industrialism and Social Order'. *The Tablet*, CLXIX, 625–26.
- 'Church, State and Community'. *The Tablet*, CLXIX, 873–75; 909–10.
- Contribution to 'Symposium on War and Peace'. *Colosseum*, III, No. 13.

1938
- 'The Kingdom of God in History'. *The Kingdom of God in History: A Symposium.* Edited by H. C. Wood et al. London, George Allen. In DWH.
- 'Moral of Austria'. *The Tablet*, CLXXI, 538.
- 'Social Factor in the Problem of Christian Unity'. *Colosseum*, V, 7–15. In *The Tablet*, CLXXI, 529–31.
- 'Frontiers of Necessity; Social Factors in Religious Belief'. *The Tablet*, CLXXI, 697. Following an article in *The Tablet*, CLXXI, 568–69.
- 'Now Is the Acceptable Time'. *Catholic World*, CXLVII, 361–62.
- Letter to the Editor. *Sign*, XVII, 756–57.
- 'Tragedy of Christian Politics'. *Sign*, XVIII, 7–10.

1939
- *Beyond Politics.* London, Sheed & Ward.
- 'New Community'. *The Tablet*, CLXXIII, 5–7.
- 'Toward Christian Unity'. *Sign*, XVIII, 407–09.
- 'Vital Question'. *Catholic World*, CXLVIII, 746–47.
- 'Hitler's *Mein Kampf*'. *The Tablet*, CLXIII, 373.
- 'The Breakdown of the League'. *The Tablet*, CLXXIV, 665–66.
- 'Hour of Darkness'. *The Tablet*, CLXXIV, 625–26. Abridged in *Catholic Digest*, IV (Feb. 1940), 19–21.
- 'The Nation and the European Unity'. *The Tablet*, CLXXIV, 717–18.
- 'European Unity and International Order'. *The Tablet*, CLXXIV, 741–42.
- 'Hungarian Middle Ages'. *The Hungarian Quarterly*, V, No. 4.

1940
- 'Century of Change'. *The Tablet*, CLXXV, 470–71.
- 'Threat to the West'. *Commonweal*, XXI, 317–18. Reply: N. Matson, *op. cit.*, 385.
- 'On Nationalism'. *The Tablet*, CLXXV, 348–49.
- Editorial Note. *The Dublin Review*, CCVII, 1–3; 129–31.
- 'Democracy and Total War'. *The Dublin Review*, CCVII, 4–16. In JN.
- 'Moral Basis of National Unity'. *The Tablet*, CLXXVI, 172.
- 'Propaganda'. *The Tablet*, CLXXVI, 265.
- 'Religious Origins of European Disunity'. *The Dublin Review*, CCVII, 142–59. In *Catholic Digest*, V (Feb. 1941), 7–13. Abridged in *Homiletic and Pastoral Review*, XLI (1941), 528, and in *Theological Studies*, II (1941), 271–72. In JN.

1941
- 'Sword of the Spirit'. *The Dublin Review*, CCVIII, 1–11. Separate publication in the series Sword of the Spirit Pamphlets. London, Sands, 1942. In JN.
- 'Baser Currency'. *Catholic World*, CLII, 489–90.
- 'Christian Freedom'. *The Dublin Review*, CCVIII, 137–49. Abridged in *Catholic Digest*, V (July), 12–18.
- 'Spiritual Foundation of Order'. *Catholic Mind*, XXXIV, 16–18.
- 'Europe and Christendom'. *The Dublin Review*, CCIX, 109–19.
- 'Christianity and Culture'. *The Dublin Review*, CCVIII, 137–49.

1942
- *The Judgment of the Nations*. London, Sheed & Ward.
- *The Sword of the Spirit*. Sword of the Spirit Pamphlets, No. 1. London, Sands.
- 'The Natural Law'. *The Future of Faith: A Diversity of Views*. Edited by Percy Colson with a preface by Lord Vansittart. London, Hurst and Blackett.
- 'Freedom and Vocation'. *The Dublin Review*, CCX, 1–11.
- 'Religion and Politics'. *Catholic Digest*, VI (Feb.), 49–56. Extracts from RMS.
- 'Principle of Vocation'. *Catholic World*, CLIV, 743–44.
- 'What about Heretics'. *Commonweal*, XXXVI, 513–17.
- 'Papacy and the New Order'. *The Dublin Review*, CCXI, 97–104.
- 'The Foundations of Unity'. *The Dublin Review*, CCXI, 97–104.

1943
- *The Renewal of Civilization*. Peace Aims Pamphlets, No. 20. London, National Peace Council.
- *Christian Freedom*. Sword of the Spirit Pamphlets, No. 5. London, Sands.
- *In the Power of the Spirit*. London, Sword of the Spirit.
- 'Democracy and the British Tradition'. *The Dublin Review*, CCXII, 97–103.
- 'Europe and the Smaller Peoples'. *The Dublin Review*, CCXIII, 1–10.
- 'Politics of Hegel'. *The Dublin Review*, CCXIII, 97–107.

1944
- 'Religion and Mass Civilization – the Problem of the Future'. *The Dublin Review*, CCXIV, 1–8.
- 'Peace Aims and Power Politics'. *The Dublin Review*, CCXIV, 97–108.
- 'Foundations of European Order'. *Catholic Mind*, XLII, 313–16.

1945
- 'The Two Currents in the Modern Democratic Tradition'. *Democracy and Peace* in collaboration with Malcolm Spencer. Peace Aims Pamphlets, No. 30. London, National Peace Council.
- 'Democracy and the Party System'. *Month*, CLXXXI, 127–33. In *Catholic Mind*, XLIII, 513–20.
- 'Parties, Politics and Peace'. *Catholic Mind*, XLIII, 372–73.
- 'Europe, a Society of Peoples'. *Month*, CLXXXI, 309–16. Separate publication, London, Catholic Truth Society, 1946.
- 'Yogi and the Commissar'. *Blackfriars*, XXV, 361–65.
- 'Left-Right Fallacy'. *Catholic Herald*, London, Nov. 9. Reprinted 1946 in *Catholic Mind*, XLV, 251–53.

1946
- 'Education and the Crisis of Christian Culture'. *Lumen Vitae*, I, 204--14. In *Catholic Mind*, XLV (1947), 266–77. Separate publication in Human Affairs Pamphlets. London, Henry Regnery and Co., 1949.
- 'Power of Spirit – or Spirit of Power'. *Sword* (Jan.), 1–3.
- 'S.O.S.' *Sword* (Apr.), 1–4.
- 'Italy and the Peace of Europe'. *Month*, CLXXXII, 267–72. In *Catholic World*, CLXVI, 177. (Excerpts under the title 'Margin of Safety.')
- 'Omnicompetent State'. *The Tablet*, CLXXXVIII, 98.

1947
- *It Shall Not Happen Here.* London, Sword of the Spirit.
- 'Religious Liberty and the New Political Forces'. *Month*, CLXXXIII, 40–47.
- 'The Task of Christian Education'. *Catholic World*, CLXV, 463–64.
- 'The Living Tradition of Christianity'. *Catholic Herald*, Oct. 10, 3.

1948
- *Religion and Culture.* London, Sheed & Ward. (Paperback. New York, Meridian Books Inc., 1958).

1949
- 'Ideas and Beliefs of the Victorians'. BBC publication.
- 'Relation between Religion and Culture'. *Commonweal*, XLIX, 488–90.
- 'T. S. Eliot on the Meaning of Culture'. *Month* (n.s.), I, 151–57.
- 'Vital Question'. *Catholic World*, CXLVIII, 746–47.
- 'Tradition and Inheritance'. *The Wind and the Rain*, Vol. V, No. 4, Vol. VI, No. 1.

1950
– *Religion and the Rise of Western Culture*. Gifford Lectures, 1948–1949. London, Sheed & Ward. Paperback. Image Books. (New York, Doubleday and Co. Inc., 1958).
– Preface to *The Limits and Divisions of European History* by Oscar Halecki. (New York, Sheed & Ward).
– 'Study of Christian Culture as a Means of Education'. *Lumen Vitae*, V, 171–86.
– 'European Literature and the Latin Middle Ages'. *The Dublin Review*, CCXIV, 31–36.
– 'Roman Catholics in the Modern World', *Geographical Magazine*, XXII, 471–76. In *The Tablet*, CXCV, 419–21 and abridged in *Catholic Digest*, XIV (Sept.), 59–63.
– 'Christian Culture in Eastern Europe'. *The Dublin Review*, CCXXIV, 17–35.
– 'Victorian Background: the Vanishing Protection of the Last Hundred Years'. *The Tablet*, CXCVI, 245–46.
– Review of *The English Catholics*, 1850–1950. Edited by Bishop Beck. *The Dublin Review*, CCXXIV, 1–12.

1951
– *Situatión Actual de la Cultura Europa*. Trans. by E. Pujals. Madrid.
– 'Religious Enthusiasm'. A discussion of *Enthusiasm* by R. A. Knox. *Month* (N. S.), V, 7–14.
– 'Byzantium and the Christian East'. Review of *Orient et Byzance: Le Trefonds Oriental De L'Hagiographie Byzantine* by R. P. Paul Peeters, S.J. *The Dublin Review*, CCXXV, 23–30.
– 'The Problem of Metahistory: the Nature and Meaning of History and the Cause and Significance of Historical Change'. *History Today*, I, 9–12. In DWH.
– 'The Christian View of History'. *Blackfriars*, XXXII, 312–27. In DWH. Also in *Modern Catholic Thinkers*. Edited by A. Robert Caponigri with an Introduction by Martin C. D'Arcy. London, Burns and Oates. (New York, Harper & Row Publ., 1960).
– 'La tradición de la cultura occidental: sus siete fases'. *Arbor*, XX, 327–47.
– 'H. G. Wells and *The Outline of History*'. *History Today*, I, 28–32. In DWH.
– 'Sanctions of Mass Democracy'. *The Tablet*, CXCVIII, 285–86.

1952
– *Understanding Europe*. London, Sheed & Ward. (New York, Sheed & Ward, 1953). Paperback. Image Books. (New York,

Doubleday and Co. Inc., 1960). Excerpts: 'A New Christian Society'. *Commonweal*, LVI, 431–33.
- 'La expansión de Europa. La colonización occidental del imperio Britanico'. *Estudios Americanos*, IV, 27–51.
- 'La tradición Norteamenicana'. *Estudios Americanos*, IV, 349–73.
- 'The Problem of Christ and Culture'. A review of *Christ and Culture* by H. Richard Niebuhr. *The Dublin Review*, CCXXVI, 64–68.
- 'Christianity and the Humanist tradition'. *The Dublin Review*, CCXXVI, 1–11. Also in *A Christian Approach to Eastern Literature: An Anthology*. Edited by A. A. Norton and Joan Thelluson Nourse. The College Reading Series. Westminster, Md.; The Newman Press, 1961.

1953
- 'Education and Christian Culture'. *Commonweal*, LIX, 216–20.
- 'Education and the Study of Christian Culture'. *Studies*, XLII, 293–302.

1954
- *Mediaeval Essays*. A study of Christian culture. London. (New York, Sheed & Ward). Paperback. Image Books. (New York, Doubleday and Co. Inc., 1959).
- 'Education and Christian Culture'. *Commonweal*, LIX, 526–27; LX, 138–39. In *Catholic Mind*, LII, 193–203.
- 'Future of Christian Culture'. *Commonweal*, LIX, 595–98. In *Catholic Mind*, LIII, 104–12.
- 'Art and Society'. *Four Quarters*, III (Apr.), 1–4. In DWH.
- 'European Revolution'. *Catholic World*, CLXXIX, 86–95.
- 'Dealing with the Enlightenment and the Liberal Ideology'. *Commonweal*, LX, 138–39.
- 'Ages of Change'. *The Tablet*, CCIII, 489–90.
- 'St. Boniface and His Age'. *Month*, XI, 325–32. Also in *Saints and Ourselves*. Edited by Philip Caraman, S.J. London, Burns Oates and Doubleday (Image Books) New York (1958).
- 'Historiç Origins of Liberalism'. *Review of Politics*, XVI, 267–82.
- 'Today's Challenge to U.S. Colleges'. *America*, XCIX, 537–38.
- 'Hope and Culture: Christian Culture as a Culture of Hope'. *Lumen Vitae*, IX, 425–30.
- 'Toynbee's Odyssey of the West'. *Commonweal*, LXI, 62.
- 'Europe in Eclipse'. *Criterio*, (Buenos Aires) (Dec.); *Catholic International Outlook*, XV June, 1955), 5–11. In DWH.

1955
- Introduction to *The Mongol Mission*. Narratives and letters of the

Franciscan missionaries in Mongolia and China in the XIIIth and XIVth centuries. Translated by a nun of Stanbrooke Abbey. London. (New York, Sheed & Ward).
- 'Toynbee's *Study of History*. The Place of Civilization in History'. *International Affairs*, XXI, 149–58. In DWH.
- 'Education and Christian Culture'. *Commonweal*, LXI, 678.
- 'Outlook for Christian Culture Today'. *Cross Currents*, V, 127–36.
- 'Rights of Man'. *South Atlantic Quarterly*, LIV, 194–36.
- 'Problems of Christian Culture'. *Commonweal*, LXII, 34–36.
- 'Christian Culture in General Education'. *America*, XCIII, 63–65.
- 'Institutional Forms of Christian Culture'. *Religion in Life*, XXIV, 373–80.

1956
- 'Civilization in Crisis'. *Catholic World*, CLXXXII, 246–52.
- 'Challenge of Secularism'. *Catholic World*, CLXXXII, 326–30.
- 'Christian Culture, Its Meaning and Its Value'. *Jubilee*, IV (May), 37–40.
- 'Christianity and Ideologies'. *Commonweal*, LXIV, 139–43.
- 'Study of Christian Culture in the American College'. *Catholic World*, CLXXXIII, 197–201.
- 'Christianity and the Orient'. *The Tablet*, CCVIII, 192–73; 196–98.
- 'Christianity and the Oriental Cultures'. *The Tablet*, CCVIII, 222–24; 245, 247.
- 'Fall of the Mountain'. *Four Quarters*, VI (Nov.), 1–10.
- 'Relevance of European History'. *History Today*, VI, 606–15. In MWR.
- 'Mr. Dawson Replies to Fr. Musurillo'. *Thought*, XXXI, 159–60.
- 'Pius XII: Teacher of the Nations'. Contribution to Commemorative Volume for Pius XII's 80th Year.

1957
- *Dynamics of World History*. Edited by John J. Mulloy. London. (New York, Sheed & Ward). Paperback. Mentor Books. (New York, New American Library).
- *The Revolt of Asia*. London. (New York, Sheed & Ward). In MWR, ch. 6, 9, 10.
- 'Birth of Democracy'. *Review of Politics*, XIX, 48–61.
- 'Impact of Religion and the Modern State'. *Commonweal*, LXV, 412–13.
- 'Education and the State'. *Commonweal*, LXV, 427–29.
- 'Dr. Toynbee's Turning away'. *The Tablet*, CCIX, 268–69.
- Review of *Documents of American Church History* by John Tracy Ellis. *America*, XCVII (1957), 126.

– 'The Tradition and Destiny of American Literature'. *Critic*, XVI
  (Nov.), 78f.
– 'Manalive'. *The Spectator*, XCI (1957), 398. (Letter to the Editor.)
– 'Christianity and Oriental Cultures'. *Commonweal*, LXVII, 226.
– 'Universities, Ancient and Modern'. *Catholic Educational
  Review*, LVI, 27–31.

1958
– 'Western Culture and the Mystical Body'. *Catholic World*,
  CLXXXVII, 134–35.
– 'American Education and Christian Culture'. *American Benedic-
  tine Review*, IX, 7–16.

1959
– *The Movement of World Revolution*. London, Sheed & Ward.
– *Espana Y Europa*. Madrid, Punta Europa.
– 'Expansion of Christianity'. *Commonweal*, LXIX, 378–80.
– 'Catholic Culture in America'. *Critic*, XVII (July), 7–9.
– 'Study of Christian Culture'. *Commonweal*, LXXI, 153–54.

1960
– *The Historic Reality of Christian Culture*. A way to the renewal of
  human life. Religious Perspectives, No. 1. London, Routledge and
  Keegan Paul Ltd. (New York, Harper & Row Publ.). Paperback.
  Harper Torchbooks. The Cathedral Library. (New York, Harper
  & Row Publ., 1965).
– *America and the Secularization of Modern Culture*. The Smith
  History Lecture, 1960. Houston, University of St Thomas.
– 'Catholic Imprint on America'. *Catholic Digest*, XXIV (Feb.),
  53–56.
– 'Catholicism, Secularism and the Modern World'. *Current*
  (Harvard Catholic Club publication) (Feb.-Mar.). Also in
  Catholic Mind, LIX, 261–68.
– 'The Study of Christian Culture'. *Thought*, XXXV, 485–93.

1961
– *The Crisis of Western Education*. With a specific program for the
  study of Christian culture by John J. Mulloy and John P. Gleason.
  London. (New York, Sheed & Ward). Paperback. Image Books.
  (New York, Doubleday and Co. Inc., 1965).
– 'Ploughing a Lone Furrow'. *Christianity and Culture*. Edited by J.
  Stanley Murphy, C.S.B., with an introduction by Donald
  McDonald. Montreal. Palm Publ. (Baltimore, Helicon Press).
– Review of *English Influence in Early American Catholicism* by

Mother Mary Peter McCarthy, O.S.U. *Catholic Historical Review*, XLVI, 461–62.
- 'Interview on Church, State and Religious Education in America'. *Jubilee*, VIII, 27.
- 'New Apostolate of the Intellect'. (Grailville Community College speech. Excerpts.) *Catholic Messenger*, LXXIX (June), 8.

1965
- *The Dividing of Christendom*. Foreword by Douglas Horton. (New York, Sheed & Ward). Paperback. Image Books. (New York, Doubleday and Co. Inc., 1967).
- 'Catholic Culture in America'. *Through Other Eyes*. Some impressions of American Catholicism from 1777 to the Present. Edited by Dan Herr and Joel Wells. Westminster, Md., The Newman Press.

1966
- *Mission to Asia*. (New York, Harper & Row Publ.)
- 'Ideas and Beliefs of the Victorians'. (New York, Dutton paperback [reprint]).

1967
- *The Formation of Christendom*. (New York, Sheed & Ward).
- 'Fifty Years of Liberal-Ultramontane Conflict'. *Triumph*, II (Aug.). 21–24.
- 'On Jewish History'. *Orbis*, X, No. 4.

II. POSTHUMOUS PUBLICATIONS

1970
- *Tradition and Inheritance*. (Reprint from *The Wind and the Rain*, 1949, with an introduction by John Mulloy). (St Paul, Minnesota, The Wanderer Press).

1971
- *The Dividing of Christendom*. (English edition with an introduction by David Knowles). London, Sidgwick & Jackson.

1972
- *The Gods of Revolution*. Introduction by Arnold Toynbee. London, Sidgwick & Jackson.

1975
- *Religion and World History*. A Selection from the Works of Christopher Dawson. (Ed. James Oliver and Christina Scott). Image Books. (New York, Doubleday).

Index

University, 198; suffers stroke, 198; Smith History Lecture, 198; travels in USA, 199; and Canada, 199f; at Wethersfield, 200f; resignation from Harvard, 202; farewell dinner, 202f; return to England, 204; last years, 204–08; attitude to Vatican II, 205; and postconciliar changes, 205f; death, 207; burial at Burnsall, 208; summary of work and influence, 209–15

— (published works): *Age of the Gods, The*, 74, 76, 82–5, 194, 212f; *Beyond Politics*, 131f, 214; *Christianity and Sex*, 93; *Crisis of Western Education, The*, 194–6, 215; *Dividing of Christendom, The*, 191f, 205; *Dynamics of World History, The*, 167–71; *Enquiries into Religion and Culture*, 72, 116, 167, 213; *Essays in Order* series, 96, 100; *Formation of Christendom, The*, 191, 205; *Gods of Revolution, The*, 83; *Historic Reality of Christian Culture, The*, 194, 196f, 210f; *Judgement of the Nations, The*, 147–51, 214; *Makers of Christendom* series, 164f; *Making of Europe, The*, 76, 83, 90, 98, 100, 102–04, 157, 191, 210, 213; *Mediaeval Essays*, 120f; *Mediaeval Religion*, 83, 120f, 157, 213; *Modern Dilemma, The*, 100–02; *Mongol Mission, The*, (introduction), 165; *Movement of World Revolution, The*, 197; *Progress and Religion*, 76f, 82f, 87, 89–91, 210, 212f; *Religion and Culture*, 155–7, 214; *Religion and the Modern State*, 124–8; *Religion and the Rise of Western Culture*, 155, 157–9; *Religion and World History*, 213; *Spirit of the Oxford Movement, The*, 115–19, 174; *Tradition and Inheritance*, 9, 160, 174; *Understanding Europe*, 165–7, 214

Dawson, Juliana, 70, 79f, 81, 135, 172, 199f
Dawson (Bevan), Mary Louisa, 13, 15–17, 19, 56f, 60, 79f, 108
Dawson (Regis), Sarah, 24
Dawson (Aufrère), Sophia, 25, 35, 110
Dawson (Mills), Valery, 50f, 59–62, 65–70, 79–82, 97, 105–07, 109, 112, 128, 134, 164, 172, 181, 187, 190, 199–202, 204, 207f
Dawson, William (1676–1722), 24
Dawson, William (1723–1803), 24
Dawson, William (1755–1829), 24
Dawson, Rev William, 13, 34f, 42, 57, 61f, 113
Demant, Canon V.A., 11, 131, 178
Derrick, Thomas, 100
Dru, Alec, 95
Dublin Review, The, 12, 92, 116, 133–7, 140, 214

EDINBURGH, University of, 152–4
Einzig, Paul, 105, 123
Eliot, T.S., 12, 38, 91–3, 116, 133, 192, 210
English Review, The, 116
Evans-Pritchard, Prof E.E., 162
Every, George, 78, 82, 110, 116, 123, 125, 128, 133
Exeter, University (College) of, 75–8, 109

FABER & Faber Ltd, 93
Faber, Geoffrey, 117
Farquarson, Alexander, 72, 75
Fisher, H.A.L., 104, 109
Forwood Lectures, The, 120
Froude, Hurrell, 9, 63, 80, 116f

GEDDES, Sir Patrick, 72
Geidt (Houghton), Mrs Margaret, 11, 80f, 174
George III, King, 24f, 35
Gibbon, Edward, 44, 49, 78, 103, 122, 168f, 209
Gifford Lectures, The, 152–9, 191, 214